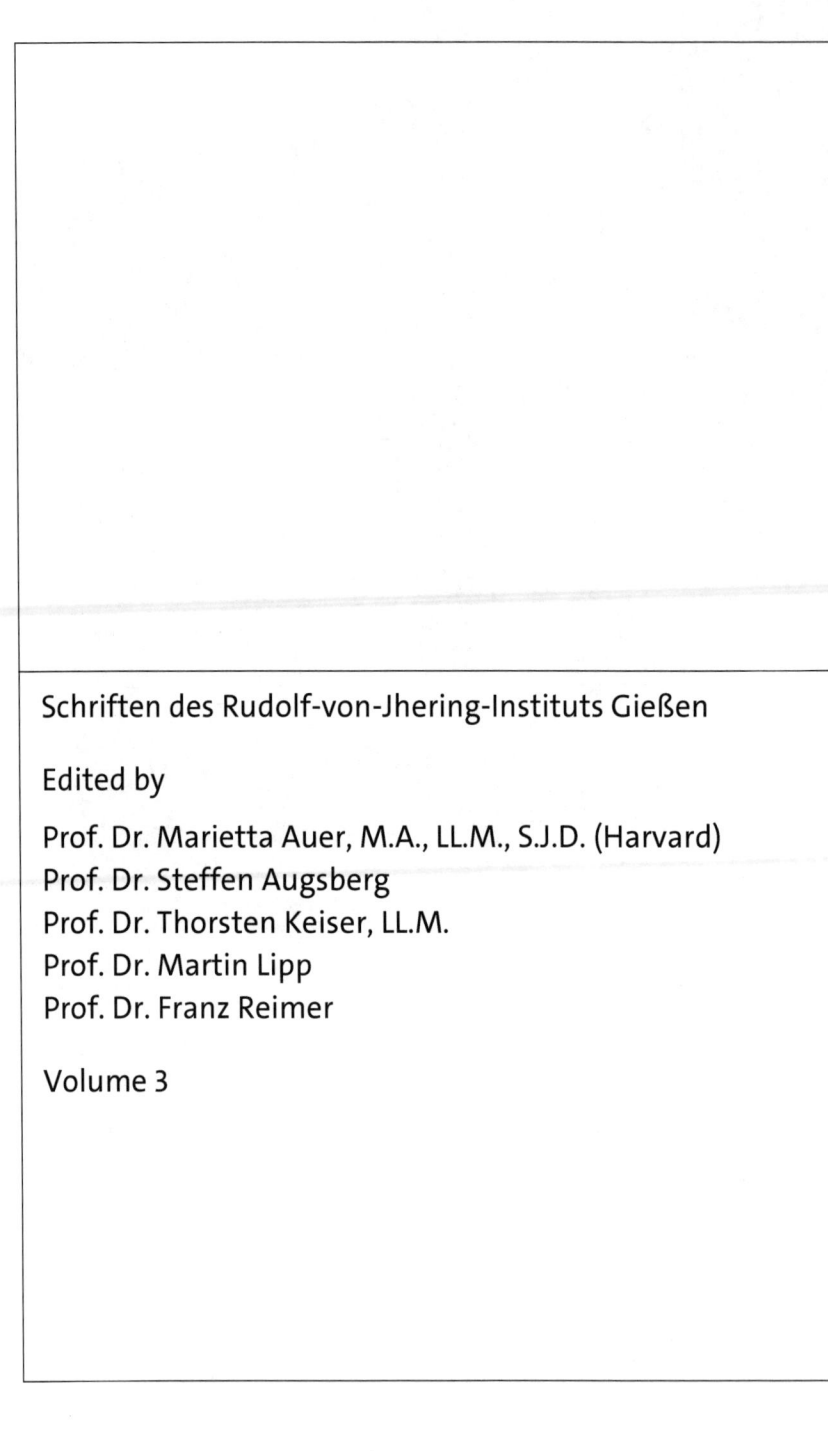

Schriften des Rudolf-von-Jhering-Instituts Gießen

Edited by

Prof. Dr. Marietta Auer, M.A., LL.M., S.J.D. (Harvard)
Prof. Dr. Steffen Augsberg
Prof. Dr. Thorsten Keiser, LL.M.
Prof. Dr. Martin Lipp
Prof. Dr. Franz Reimer

Volume 3

Thorsten Keiser | Greta Olson | Franz Reimer (Eds.)

Feelings about Law/Justice

Rechtsgefühle

The Relevance of Affect to the Development of Law
in Pluralistic Legal Cultures

Die Relevanz des Affektiven für die Rechtsentwicklung
in pluralen Rechtskulturen

 Nomos

Gedruckt mit Unterstützung der Fritz Thyssen Stiftung.

Die Deutsche Nationalbibliothek verzeichnet diese Publikation in
der Deutschen Nationalbibliografie; detaillierte bibliografische
Daten sind im Internet über http://dnb.d-nb.de abrufbar.

The Deutsche Nationalbibliothek lists this publication in the
Deutsche Nationalbibliografie; detailed bibliographic data
are available on the Internet at http://dnb.d-nb.de

ISBN   978-3-7560-0629-8 (Print)
         978-3-7489-4260-3 (ePDF)

British Library Cataloguing-in-Publication Data
A catalogue record for this book is available from the British Library.

ISBN   978-3-7560-0629-8 (Print)
         978-3-7489-4260-3 (ePDF)

Library of Congress Cataloging-in-Publication Data
Keiser, Thorsten | Olson, Greta | Reimer, Franz
Feelings about Law/Justice | Rechtsgefühle
The Relevance of Affect to the Development of Law in Pluralistic Legal Cultures
Die Relevanz des Affektiven für die Rechtsentwicklung in pluralen Rechtskulturen
Thorsten Keiser | Greta Olson | Franz Reimer (Eds.)
217 pp.

ISBN   978-3-7560-0629-8 (Print)
         978-3-7489-4260-3 (ePDF)

1st Edition 2023

© The Authors

Published by
Nomos Verlagsgesellschaft mbH & Co. KG
Waldseestraße 3–5 | 76530 Baden-Baden
www.nomos.de

Production of the printed version:
Nomos Verlagsgesellschaft mbH & Co. KG
Waldseestraße 3–5 | 76530 Baden-Baden

ISBN   978-3-7560-0629-8 (Print)
ISBN   978-3-7489-4260-3 (ePDF)
DOI   https://doi.org/10.5771/9783748942603

Onlineversion
Nomos eLibrary

Foreword / Vorwort

„Rechtsgefühl" kann das Gerechtigkeitsempfinden des Individuums „vor dem Gesetz", das Judiz der Richterin im Prozess der Entscheidungsfindung, das emotionale Aufbäumen der unterlegenen Partei nach der Entscheidung, die Rechtsüberzeugung eines Kollektivs bezeichnen. Trotz der verbreiteten Vorstellung, Recht rechtfertige sich durch seine Distanz zu Emotionen,[1] wird der Verweis auf das „Rechtsgefühl" dazu genutzt, Rechtssysteme, Rechtsgebiete oder einzelne Rechtsakte – Rechtsnormen oder Gerichtsentscheidungen – von innen oder von außen zu legitimieren oder zu delegitimieren. Diese Strategie ist umso wirkmächtiger, je monolithischer ein Akteur „das Rechtsgefühl" präsentiert, je bruchloser es sich in kollektive Überzeugungen oder Anschauungen einfügt. Als sozialer Kompass und normative Rechtfertigung muss „Rechtsgefühl" dagegen versagen, wenn es mit zahlreichen gegenläufigen Rechtsgefühlen konkurriert.

Die Frage nach der Fühlbarkeit des Rechts und nach dem Rechtsgefühl (fast durchgängig im Singular) wird aus zahlreichen, insgesamt aber additiv erscheinenden Blickwinkeln bearbeitet. Im Bereich der Rechtswissenschaft hat sie weniger die Methodenlehre – wo das Rechtsgefühl eher kursorisch,[2] zum Teil als Frage nach der Bedeutung von Gerechtigkeit als methodologischem Argument[3] behandelt wird – als die Rechtstheorie[4] und

---

1 Paradigmatisch wohl *Angela Merkel*: „Es gelten bei uns Regeln. Und diese Regeln können nicht durch Emotionen ersetzt werden. Das ist das Wesen des Rechtsstaates" (47. Sitzung des *19. Deutschen Bundestages, 11.9.2018, zit. n.: Das Parlament Nr. 38-39 v. 17.9.2018, Debattendokumentation, S. 10).

2 Etwa: *Karl Larenz / Claus-Wilhelm Canaris*. Methodenlehre der Rechtswissenschaft, 3. Aufl. Berlin u.a. 1995, S. 168 f.; *Dirk Looschelders / Wolfgang Roth*. Juristische Methodik im Prozeß der Rechtsanwendung. Berlin 1996, S. 78 f.; *Franz Reimer*. Juristische Methodenlehre. Baden-Baden 2016, Rn. 60 f., 372, 415; *Thomas M.J. Möllers*. Juristische Methodenlehre. München 2017, § 1 Rn. 25; *Hans-Joachim Strauch*. Methodenlehre des gerichtlichen Erkenntnisverfahrens. Freiburg 2017, S. 41, 542.

3 *Friedrich Müller*. Gerechtigkeit als die „Unruh im Uhrwerk". 2009; *Reimer*. Methodenlehre (Fn. 2), Rn. 531 ff.; *ders.*, Gerechtigkeit als Methodenfrage (Referat im Gesprächskreis „Grundlagen" in der Vereinigung der Deutschen Staatsrechtslehrer, Marburg, 9. Oktober 2019). Tübingen 2020.

4 Zuletzt etwa *Julia Hänni*. Gefühle als Basis juristischer Richtigkeitsentscheidungen. In: Thomas Hilgers u.a. (Hrsg.). Affekt und Urteil. Paderborn 2015, S. 133-142; *Sabine Müller-Mall*. Zwischen Fall und Urteil. Zur Verortung des Rechtsgefühls. Ebenda, S. 117 ff. Zu Vermittlungszusammenhängen durch situative Kontexte, per-

die Rechtsgeschichte aufgegriffen. Fast immer wurde das „Rechtsgefühl" in interdisziplinärer Perspektive thematisiert.[5] Im geisteswissenschaftlichen Bereich ist ein gestiegenes Interesse der Geschichtswissenschaft zu konstatieren.[6] Die kulturwissenschaftliche Behandlung des Rechts (*Law as Culture, cultural legal studies*) wendet sich in jüngerer Zeit vermehrt der Bedeutung von Gefühlen, Leidenschaften und Affektivem im Recht zu.[7] Auffällig ist, dass bei allen interdisziplinären Zugängen die Kategorie „Emotion" oft einen weiten Assoziationsrahmen zur Rechtsordnung eröffnet, bei dem die Relevanz von Gefühlen in verschiedensten Zusammenhängen thematisiert wird.[8] Eine juristische Aufarbeitung des Themas kann nicht von allgemein psychologischen oder soziologischen Emotionskategorien ausgehen, sondern muss die konkrete Bedeutung der Verweise auf Gefühle dort erfassen, wo ihre jeweiligen normativen Implikationen innerhalb des Rechtssystems deutlich werden. Dazu ist gerade das Problem der Widersprüchlichkeit von Rechtsgefühlen in pluralistischen Gesellschaften und Rechtsordnungen zu analysieren. Dieser Aufgabenstellung widmete sich eine interdisziplinäre Tagung aus Rechts- und Kulturwissenschaften, die vom 13.-14. Juni 2019 an der Justus-Liebig-Universität Gießen stattgefunden hatte. Organisiert wurde die Tagung vom Institut für Anglistik und vom Rudolf-von-Jhering-Institut für rechtswissenschaftliche Grundlagenforschung. Der vorliegende Band versammelt einige der Beiträge. Dem Konzept der Tagung entsprechend betreffen diese historische, kulturwissenschaftlich-vergleichende, politische und rechtspraktische Ebenen des Themas Rechtsgefühl.

Die Rechtsgeschichte kann den Erfahrungsschatz des Rechts in affektiver Hinsicht deutlich machen, um Orientierungswissen für die gegenwär-

---

formative Vollzüge und phänomenales Erscheinen vgl. *Eva Schürmann / Levno von Plato* (Hrsg.). Rechtsästhetik in rechtsphilosophischer Absicht: Untersuchungen zu Formen und Wahrnehmungen des Rechts. Baden-Baden 2020.

5 Nicht selten mit Verbindungen zu Literaturwissenschaft, siehe etwa *Sigrid G. Köhler / Sabine Müller-Mall / Florian Schmidt / Sandra Schnädelbach* (Hrsg.). Recht fühlen. Paderborn 2017; *Hilge Landweer / Dirk Koppelberg* (Hrsg.). Recht und Emotion (2 Bde.). Freiburg 2016.

6 *Dagmar Ellerbrock / Sylvia Kesper-Biermann*. Between Passions and Senses? Perspectives on Law and Emotions. In: InterDisciplines (6.2). 2015; siehe auch *Jan Plamper*. The History of Emotions. An Introduction. Oxford 2015, S. 284.

7 *Greta Olson*. The Turn to Passion: Has Law and Literature become Law and Affect? In: Law and Literature (28.3). 2016, S. 335 ff.; *dies*. From Law and Literature to Legality and Affect, Oxford 2022; *Julia J.A. Shaw*. Law and the Passions: Why Emotion Matters for Justice. Abingdon und New York 2020.

8 Vgl. etwa *Susan A. Bandes*. The Passions of Law. New York und London 1999.

tigen Debatten zu erarbeiten. Gerade die als sehr aktuell empfundene Pluralität der Rechtsquellen (und daher womöglich auch ihrer gefühlsmäßigen Grundierung oder Rezeption) war daher in historischer Hinsicht zu kontextualisieren, wobei deutlich wurde, dass Rechtspluralismus auf lange Sicht gesehen der Regelfall und nicht die Ausnahme war. Diesen Themen widmeten sich die Beiträge von Sylvia Kesper-Biermann und Thorsten Keiser.

In rechtstheoretischer Sicht spielten stets die Betrachtungen Rudolf von Jherings eine besondere Rolle. Für Jhering ist das Rechtsgefühl einer Person nicht rational; wie er im *Kampf um's Recht* schreibt: „Die Kraft des Rechts ruht im Gefühl, ganz so wie in der Liebe; der Verstand kann das mangelnde Gefühl nicht ersetzen."[9] Gabriele Britz widmet sich vor diesem Hintergrund den aktuellen juristischen Implikationen affektiver Elemente. Deutlich wird dabei, dass Gefühle[10] auch heute die Rechtsfindung bzw. Rechtserzeugung im Einzelfall prägen; sie sind subjektive Faktoren der Mobilisierung von Recht.[11] Sie können Triebfeder für eine vertiefte und verbesserte Rechtsfindung sein und in diesem Sinne durch die methodischen Standards mediatisiert werden, sie können aber auch als inhaltlich anleitendes „Rechtsgefühl" oder „Judiz" professionalisiert, rationalisiert und in ihrer Emotionalität invisibilisiert werden. Aus der Perspektive der Praxis juristischer Entscheidungsfindung analysiert Jeanne Gaakeer Chancen und Risiken einer individuellen Befragung des Rechtsgefühls. Franz Reimer lenkt im gleichen Kontext den Blick auf die Rechtsentstehung.

Als emotionale Gesamteinschätzung der Gerechtigkeit oder Ungerechtigkeit einer Situation nimmt „das Rechtsgefühl", auch wenn es von einem Individuum stammt, Repräsentativität und gesellschaftliche Relevanz in Anspruch, sobald es mit normativer Absicht geäußert wird. Das ist in einer homogen gedachten Rechtsgemeinschaft mit Blick auf Minderheiten problematisch; in einer sich als plural wahrnehmenden Gesellschaft erhalten derartige nichtkognitive Entscheidungsfaktoren offene Brisanz. Frans-Willem Korsten untersucht die politischen Auswirkungen einer Mobilisierung des Rechtsgefühls für populistische Bewegungen.

Der Begriff des Rechtsgefühls nimmt vorweg, was die rechtskritische US-amerikanische *legal consciousness*-Bewegung seit den 1990er Jahren be-

---

9 *Rudolf von Jhering.* Der Kampf um's Recht (1872). Wien 1894, S. 41 f.
10 Pointiert *Wolfgang Gast.* Juristische Rhetorik, 5. Aufl. Heidelberg 2015, Rn. 477: „Affekte sind, obwohl Affektkontrolle zur professionellen Sachlichkeit gehört, nicht ausgeschlossen: Betroffenheit darf sich in den gehörigen Formeln äußern („Besonders verwerflich ist das Verhalten des Angeklagten deshalb, weil...")."
11 Näher *Susanne Baer.* Rechtssoziologie, 3. Aufl. 2017, § 7 Rn. 3 ff.

schreibt: Der erlebte Umgang mit Rechtsinstitutionen und -prozessen ist von der jeweiligen Stellung einer Gruppe in Hinsicht auf ihre gesellschaftliche Privilegiertheit abhängig und wird durch Narrative über diesen situativen Umgang vermittelt.[12] Jherings „Rechtsgefühl" spielt darüber hinaus im Zuge des Interesses am Affektiven in den *critical legal studies* eine Rolle.[13] Diese Forschung unterscheidet sich von der Orientierung an rationaler Erkenntnis, wie sie seit den 1990er Jahren auf dem Feld von *law and emotion(s)* betrieben wurde. Im Rahmen von *Law and Emotion* sind empirische Untersuchungen mit dem Ziel durchgeführt worden, die Bedeutung von Gefühlen bei Urteilen, Jury-Entscheidungen und im Vorfeld von Hassverbrechen zu bestimmen.[14] Demgegenüber behandelt der *Law and Affect*-Ansatz das Recht als nicht ausschließlich durch rationale und lineare Mittel und Wege juristischer Interpretation prozedierend. Dieser Forschungsstrang fügt sich in einen größeren „affective turn in legal studies" ein.[15] Jhering betont, dass das Recht – fern davon, nur die schlimmsten Leidenschaften des Menschen zu besänftigen und affekthaft aufgeladene Konflikte zu entschärfen – ein Instrument des Leidens sei.[16] Affekttheoretiker behandeln Recht als a-rational, um im Wege einer radikalen Rechtskritik menschliche Materialität und Partikularität einzubeziehen.[17] Daher ist zu fragen, warum, mit welchem Erkenntnisinteresse und mit welchen Erträgen es in den kritischen Rechtsstudien zur Ausrichtung auf Affektivität kam. Greta Olson geht der Frage nach, wie die Kategorie des Affektiven dazu beitragen kann, juristische Abläufe und individuelle Sichtweisen zur jeweiligen Rechtsumgebung neu und besser zu verstehen.

---

12 *Patricia Ewick / Susan S. Silbey*. The Common Place of Law: Stories from Everyday Life. Chicago und London 1998; *Susan S. Silbey*. After Legal Consciousness. In: Annual Review of Law and Social Science (1). 2005, S. 323-368.

13 *Cassandra Sharp / Marett Leiboff*. Cultural Legal Studies: Law's Popular Cultures and the Metamorphosis of Law. Abingdon 2015, S. 304 ff.

14 *Richard A. Posner*. "Emotion versus Emotionalism in Law". In: Susan A. Brandes (Hrsg.). The Passions of Law. New York 1999, S. 309-329, 327; *Terry A. Maroney*. "Law and Emotion: A Proposed Taxonomy of an Emerging Field". In: Law and Human Behavior (30). 2006, S. 119-142; *Martha Nussbaum*. From Disgust to Humanity. Oxford 2010; *dies*. Hiding from Humanity: Disgust, Shame, and the Law. 2006; *Jeanne Gaakeer*. "The Legal Hermeneutics of Suffering". In: Law and Humanities (3.2). 2009.

15 *Olson* (Fn. 7); *Scott Veitch*. Law and Irresponsibility. On the Legitimation of Human Suffering. London 2007.

16 *Jhering* (Fn. 9). S. 12-13.

17 *Andreas Fischer-Lescano*. Radikale Rechtskritik. In: Kritische Justiz (47.2). 2014, S. 171-183, 177.

Die Beiträge dieses Bandes gehen der Frage nach, ob und in welchem Sinne Rechtsgefühl in der gegenwärtigen Situation das Verständnis und die Anwendung des Rechts in einer pluralen Gesellschaft fördern und eine positive Relevanz für Rechtspraxis (Gaakeer, Reimer, Britz) nicht nur im Sinne der Rechtsanwendung, sondern auch der Rechtsentwicklung (Keiser, Kesper-Biermann) und Rechtstheorie (Gaakeer) wie auch im politischen Umgang mit Rechtsphänomenen (Olson, Korsten) haben kann. Daher soll nach Pluralisierungsprozessen sowie den möglichen Folgen für die Relevanz der Kategorie des „Rechtsgefühls" und benachbarter Konzepte wie Emotionen und Affekte in Bezug auf rechtliche Phänomene gefragt werden. Insgesamt zeigt der Blick auf die Rechtsgeschichte, dass Rechtsgefühl individuell, aber auch kollektiv, theoretisch, praktisch oder politisch, nicht zuletzt auch christlich-religiös formuliert sein kann.[18] Im NS-Staat war darüber hinaus die Verwendung als propagandistisches Drohmittel („gesundes Volksempfinden") zu beobachten.[19] In jedem der Bereiche transportiert es eine spezifische Normativität und kann gleichzeitig Indikator für ein bestimmtes Verständnis juristischer Rationalität sein, die eventuell als Gegenbild zu einer gefühlsmäßigen Normativität Konturen gewinnt. Gleichzeitig versuchten manche Rechtslehren, den Gegensatz zwischen Rationalität und Gefühl aufzuheben. Rechtsgefühl als juristische Erkenntniskategorie war damit emotional und wissenschaftlich zugleich.[20]

Um die Heterogenität des Begriffes der „Rechtsgefühle" herauszustellen, ebenso wie die Unterschiedlichkeit von Rechtsgefühlen zu unterstreichen, die sich nach den rechtssystemischen und gesellschaftlichen Kontexten richtet, in denen diese Gefühle auftreten, ist hier die Rede von Rechtsgefühlen und nicht von singulärem Rechtsgefühl. Wie die folgenden Beiträge zeigen, können Rechtsgefühle als historische Erklärung für

---

18 Zu letzterem Aspekt *Hans-Peter Haferkamp*. Christentum und Privatrecht im Vormärz. In: Nils Jansen, Peter Oestmann (Hrsg.). Rechtsgeschichte heute. Religion und Politik in der Geschichte des Rechts. Schlaglichter einer Ringvorlesung. Tübingen 2014, S. 181-191 (185 ff.).

19 Hierzu insbes. *Joachim Rückert*, bspw. zum „gesunden Volksempfinden", vgl. *Joachim Rückert*. Das „gesunde Volksempfinden" – eine Erbschaft Savignys? In: ZS Germ (103). 1986, S. 199-247; auch in: *Rückert*. Ausgewählte Aufsätze, Bd. 1. Grundlagen, Geschichte, Bewältigungen. 2012, S. 577 ff.; *Angelika Kleinz*. Individuum und Gemeinschaft in der juristischen Germanistik. Die Geschworenengerichte und das »gesunde Volksempfinden«. In: Frankfurter Beiträge zur Germanistik (36). Heidelberg 2001; *Jan Thiessen*. Gute Sitten und „gesundes Volksempfinden". Vor-, Miss- und Nachklänge in und um RGZ 150, 1. In: FS Jan Schröder. Tübingen 2013, S. 187 ff.

20 *Haferkamp*. Christentum und Privatrecht. S. 187 ff.

die Entwicklung des Rechts, als ein Argument für ein Recht, das sich an höheren Werten wie Gerechtigkeit orientiert, als eine Form von Rechtskritik und als ein Synonym für den politischen Umgang mit imaginiertem und gefühltem Recht verstanden werden. Daher ist eine interdisziplinäre Fragestellung nach der Bedeutung von Rechtsgefühlen relevant.

Thorsten Keiser, Greta Olson und Franz Reimer

Table of Contents/Inhalt

13

I: From *Rechtsgefühl* to *Rechtsgefühle*?

I: Von „Rechtsgefühl" zu „Rechtsgefühlen"?

Why *Rechtsgefühle*? The Turn to Emotion and Affect in Legal Studies
(What are impassioned feelings about law and justice, and why are they pertinent?)

Greta Olson

1. On the Pertinence of Understanding Rechtsgefühle (Passionate Feelings about Law)

Two recent events speak for the relevance of addressing *Rechtsgefühle* at this particular historical juncture: the near break-in in the German Reichstag in August 2020 and the storming of the United States Capitol on 6 January 2021. For the time being, I will translate *Rechtsgefühle* as impassioned feelings about law and justice, but will come back to the variability in possible translations of the term.

In Germany, where I have lived for over thirty years, Corona-restriction protesters attempted to break into the historic Reichstag in Berlin (the parliament building) in August 2020, surprising officials who had grown accustomed to anti-restriction protests happening regularly and demonstrating to them that they were entirely unprepared for a break-in into the fortress-like building.[1] Many protesters displayed quite disturbing allegiances to far-right groups by, for instance, carrying flags from the German Reich and the National Socialist period. Others avowed the validity of their protests by displaying posters and signs that listed their fundamental rights according to the Basic Law (the German constitution that has been in place since 1949).[2] See, for instance, the demonstrator in Figure 1. With

---

1 "Entsetzen über Eskalation am Reichstagsgebäude," *Berliner Tageszeitung,* last modified 30 August 2020, last accessed 21 July 2022, https://www.berlinertageszeitung .de/politik/72769-entsetzen-in-der-politik-nach-rechtsextremer-eskalation-am-reichs tagsgebaeude.html.

2 The German constitution is called the Basic Law (*Grundgesetz*), because it was intended to be provisional for as long as Germany remained divided after World War II. In fact, the Basic Law remained the constitution after reunification in 1989. See "Grundgesetz – Warum heißt es nicht Verfassung?" *Süddeutsche Zeitung,* last modified 23 May 2019, last accessed 21 July 2022, https://www.sueddeutsche.de/wi

mottos such as "For the Good of the German People for Freedom and Democracy" and "End the Corona Panic and Give Back Basic Rights," protesters vehemently insisted that their constitutional rights were being infringed on by the then Angela Merkel-led government. In the most extreme and historically problematic cases, the so-called Corona dictatorship was compared by protesters to fascism and to Hitler's totalitarian regime.

Figure 1: A Demonstrator Protesting Corona-Related Restrictions Holds Up a Copy of the German Basic Law. (©dpa)[3]

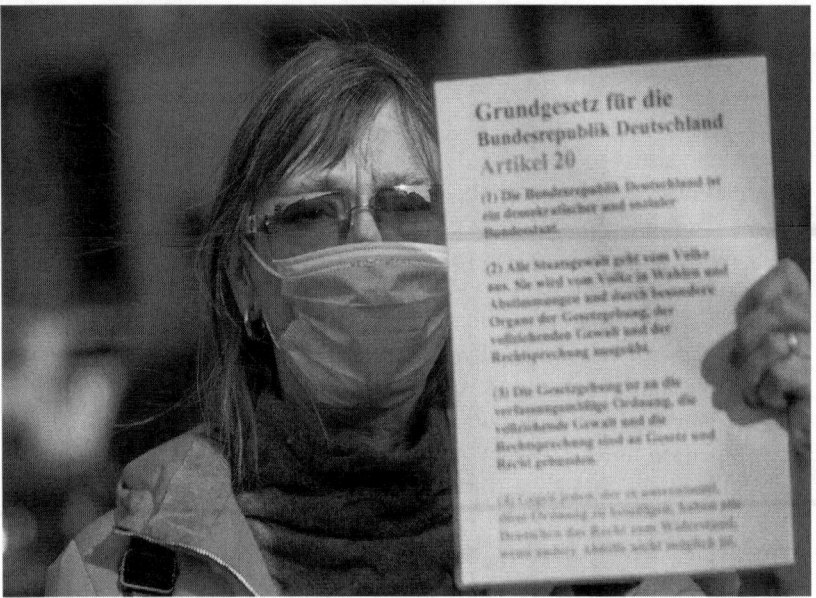

A passionate appeal to law and the *felt* rights it guarantees and protects was made by these Corona-restriction protesters. The protesters' invocation of German constitutional law at the would-be Reichstag break-in and at other demonstrations was based on the argument that the pandemic regulations did not constitute protective measures. Rather, the hygiene restrictions

---

ssen/geschichte-grundgesetz-warum-heisst-es-nicht-verfassung-dpa.urn-newsml-dpa -com-20090101-190523-99-342782.

3 "Polizei nimmt nach Demonstration in Mitte Personalien auf," *Berliner Morgenpost*, last modified 28 March 2020, last accessed 21 July 2022, https://www.morgenpost.d e/berlin/article228797933/Polizei-nimmt-nach-Demonstration-in-Mitte-Personalien -auf.html.

were manifest attacks on the protesters' personal and constitutionally protected liberties. Guaranteed fundamental rights were *felt* by the protesters to have been violated by those in power.

In opposition to this position, any number of constitutional laws were cited as concrete grounds for arresting the anti-restriction protesters, including statutes about endangering others through violating restrictions pertaining to the spread of the COVID-19 virus, such as the mandate to wear masks and maintain social distancing, and the prohibition against violence to the police. Subsequent to August 2020, weekly occurring anti-restriction demonstrations frequently turned violent, with protesters throwing firecrackers at the police. Again a frequent motto in these demonstrations is: "No Corona Dictatorship."[4] In discussions of vetoes of further anti-Corona protests, politicians cited the comparative merits of the right to gather and protest in a pluralistic society versus the prohibition against harming others while doing so.[5]

I now turn to events in the United States, my country of origin, where on 6 January 2021, a mob of would-be insurrectionists laid siege to the Congress building where the Electoral College votes from the presidential election in November 2020 were being certified by Congress members. This violent insurrection was aimed at overthrowing actual election results, which the protesters – reacting to Trump's fallacious narrative – insisted were invalid, calling them the "Big Lie." Violations included forceful and unlawful entry into the Capitol building, violence towards police officers, destruction and theft of property as well as threats to do bodily harm, also sexual violence, to Representatives Alexandria Ocasio-Cortez and House speaker Nancy Pelosi and to hang then Vice President Mike Pence, who was viewed by the mob as a traitor.

Individuals committing these illegal acts insisted that they were entirely justified in fighting against the illegal 'steal' of the election. Flags displayed

---

4 Henry Bernhard, "Anti-Corona-Proteste im Osten / Disparate Angriffe auf 'das System'," *Deutschlandfunk*, last modified 15 February 2022, last accessed 21 July 2022, https://www.deutschlandfunk.de/anti-corona-proteste-osten-rechtsextremismus-100.html.

5 In this context, the German *IfSG* ("infection protection law") states in § 28a sec. 1 and 2 that several fundamental rights are restricted for the sake of preventing Covid-19 outbreaks. Most importantly, the freedom of assembly anchored in Art. 8 GG ("Basic Law for the Federal Republic of Germany") is considered less important than the "right to life and physical integrity" as stated by Art. 2 sec. 2 GG. See also "Corona und Grundrechte: Fragen und Antworten," *GFF Team*, last modified 11 February 2021, last accessed 21 July 2022, https://freiheitsrechte.org/corona-und-grundrechte/#grundrechte.

by mob members recurred to flags and symbols familiar from the Revolutionary War period, which were then meant to protest English tyranny in the U.S. American colonies and have now been repurposed to far-right anti-government aims. Note the South Carolina Moultrie flag in the back of Figure 2, with its crescent moon and liberty inscription, which was used during the Revolutionary War era. All of these symbols bespoke the mob's insistence that it was passionately defending the 'correct' ideals of the Declaration of Independence and the Constitution rather than breaking the law by committing acts of terrorism. One notes the sign quoting the first words of the Constitution in Figure 2. As has been multiply commented on, one of the alarming things about the would-be insurrection was how proudly the mob members documented the break-in, thereby attesting to their impassioned certainty of the validity of their actions. They filmed themselves, produced endless numbers of selfies, and posted their actions incessantly on social media platforms, even as they were damaging property and stealing, fully convinced, as it would seem, of the legitimacy of their actions and their immunity to being sanctioned for these actions afterwards.[6]

Other flags and symbols recurred to the American Civil War (1861-65). One Confederate battle flag-bearer entered the Capitol, and other mob members wore pre-printed shirts commemorating January 6, 2021 as the beginning of a new civil war.[7] The comparison between Confederate flag-bearers in the Capitol attack in January 2021 and would-be Imperial Citizens in the 2020 Reichstag break-in is an obvious one, as both actions were based on the blatant denial of historical facts.

---

6 Seamus Hughes and Jon Lewis, "The Capitol Mob's Gleeful Selfies Are Easy to Mock. They're Also a Warning Sign," *Washington Post*, last modified 19 January 2021, last accessed 21 July 2022, https://www.washingtonpost.com/outlook/2021/01/19/rioters-incompetent-fbi-arrests/.

7 Simon Mallory and Sara Sidner, "Decoding the extremist symbols and groups at the Capitol Hill insurrection," *CNN*, last modified 11 January 2021, last accessed 21 July 2022, https://edition.cnn.com/2021/01/09/us/capitol-hill-insurrection-extremist-flags-soh/index.html.

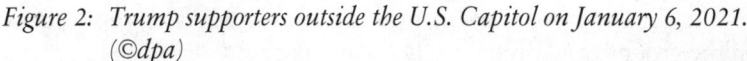

*Figure 2: Trump supporters outside the U.S. Capitol on January 6, 2021.
(©dpa)*

In the former case, secessionist Southerners did not represent a noble 'lost cause' in what supporters continue to refer to as the 'War between the States' rather than the Civil War, thus belying the realities of slavery and its legacy in Jim Crow laws, systemic racism, regularized violence against Black life, and continuous microaggressions against Blacks and persons of color in the U.S. today. In the latter case, so-called Reich citizens believe that Germany was never defeated in WW II; thus, Germany's borders from 1937 remain in place, and the 'grand' empire was never lost. According to this narrative, Germany is still occupied by foreign Allied forces, and therefore the current government has no legitimacy. Far-right German Corona protesters and the violent insurrectionists from January 2021 expressed racist, anti-immigrant, anti-feminist and anti-Semitic views. Members of both groups were inspired by the rhetoric of former president Donald Trump to commit illegal actions.[8] For example, the Camp-Auschwitz

---

8 Katrin Bennhold, "Trump Emerges as Inspiration for Germany's Far Right," *The New York Times*, last modified 5 March 2021, last accessed 21 July 2022, https://www.nytimes.com/2020/09/07/world/europe/germany-trump-far-right.html.

sweatshirt, sported by one Capitol insurrectionist, speaks to connections between the groups in Washington, D.C., and Berlin.

Yet beyond the deniers of historical realities, individuals in both insurrections claimed that their actions were entirely lawful, as they understand 'their' laws to be constituted. They insisted that they were in fact exercising rights to defend democratic processes, and were anything but lawless in their actions.[9] In the U.S. American case, this was a "Rally to Save America," and those who broke into Congress yelled enthusiastic phrases such as: "Keep moving forward! Fight for Trump, fight for Trump!" and "Military Tribunals! Hang them!" and "Arrest Congress!"[10]

Let me be absolutely clear. I am sickened by the events of 6 January 2021 in Washington, D.C., and the deeply felt divisions in my country of origin they have exposed, including the very real threat of a governmental coup to overturn election results and keep Donald Trump in power, and still now, by the threat of an impending civil war between increasingly polarized segments of the U.S. American population. I vividly feel the threat to a peaceful transfer of power that the mob's violent attack represented. I also fear a return to violence by Trump supporters in a Republican Party that has made loyalty to Trump's election-steal lie a "litmus test" for supporters.[11] In February 2022, the Republican Party determined that the riot represented "legitimate political discourse" and it voted to rebuke those Republicans who have condemned it.[12] Here in Germany, arguments with those who continue to deny the reality and dangers of COVID-19 have led to a number of personal falling-outs, as I know those who have died from the virus or who suffer from its long-term effects. Yet I recognize in both of these groups of would-be infiltrators an impassioned, visceral belief in

---

9 In the German case, it may be important to note that Coronavirus denier groups were also composed of vaccine skeptics who adhere to alternative medicine philosophies such as homeopathy.

10 Dan Barry, Mike McIntire, and Matthew Rosenberg, "'Our President Wants Us Here:' The Mob That Stormed the Capitol," *The New York Times*, last modified 10 November 2021, last accessed 21 July 2022, https://www.nytimes.com/2021/01/09/us/capitol-rioters.html.

11 Steve Benen, "The 'Unofficial Litmus Test' in Today's GOP: Embracing the Big Lie," *MSNBC*, last modified 3 May 2021, last accessed 21 July 2022, https://www.msnbc.com/rachel-maddow-show/unofficial-litmus-test-today-s-gop-embracing-big-lie-n1266142.

12 Jonathan Weisman and Reid J. Epstein, "G.O.P. Declares Jan. 6 Attack 'Legitimate Political Discourse,'" *The New York Times*, last modified 4 February 2022, last accessed 21 July 2022, https://www.nytimes.com/2022/02/04/us/politics/republicans-jan-6-cheney-censure.html.

what group members regarded as the correct interpretations of 'their' laws, and a readiness to commit violence – to act illegally according to actual prevailing laws – on the basis of a conviction about the rightness of their interpretations. So convinced are they of the correctness of their felt legal orders that they attempted to overturn the prescriptions of the prevailing system. The insurrectionists understood their actions to be revolutionary, even if for the majority they were committing acts of terrorism.[13]

Here, we find ourselves in the middle of what Rudolf von Jhering entitled *Rechtsgefühl*. In its most straightforward translation, *Rechtsgefühl* can be translated as a feeling for law and justice. The word *"Recht"* in German signifies both "law" and "justice," in the sense of "rightness." In previous work on Law and Affect, I have translated the plural term *Rechtsgefühle* as "legal affects" or as "impassioned feelings about law." Yet any number of translations are viable. In this text I highlight this variability by using the abbreviation of "RG" in parentheses after each one of them. Historically, *Rechtsgefühl* has been used almost exclusively in the singular. Yet for programmatic reasons that will be explained further in the overview of the contributions, the editors of this volume examine *Rechtsgefühle* in the plural to denote the heterogeneity of interpretations of the original term.

Because we live in what has been described by Chantal Mouffe as a period in which agonistic or antagonistic affectively-driven politics alternate with one another, people's individual and group allegiances to what they view as 'their' legitimate and passionately defended laws and legal orders take on a particular salience.[14] These evident passions for law (RG) – or what is perceived or imagined to be law – suggest that the notion of law as the repository of the rational and the rule-driven, and as a complex system for resolving social conflicts is in the best case fragile. The enforcement of law during our present quite affectively charged political era can only transpire successfully if people agree upon the legitimacy of the laws that regulate their behavior. This brings me back to Jhering.

---

13 Ibram X. Kendi contends that the violent insurrection was not met by an adequate police presence because of the whiteness of the mob and the assumption that they would not be violent: "By contrast, the greatest domestic terrorist threat of our time is white supremacists. From my understanding, the local Capitol Police assumed that this demonstration wouldn't turn into an insurrection and wouldn't turn violent. To me, it just flies in the face of all evidence," see Fabiola Cineas, "Ibram X. Kendi on Why White America is Still Shocked by White Supremacy," *VOX*, last modified 12 January 2021, last accessed 21 July 2022, https://www.vox.com/22227102/anti-racism-ibram-kendi.

14 Chantal Mouffe, *Agonistics: Thinking the World Politically* (London and New York: Verso, 2013), 3, 6.

Jhering is remembered in histories of legal interpretation – if he is remembered at all, which is regretfully very little in the Anglophone world – as having ushered in a movement away from an adherence to so-called Roman-law-based forms of legal reasoning and their application in Germany's science of law to a so-called *Interessenjurisprudenz*, based on individual interests. As a law professor, Jhering first published widely on the interpretation of Roman-based law. Yet during his tenure at the University of Giessen between 1852 and 1868, his views changed radically. He began to argue for the credence of an individual and group interest-based interpretation of the law. In his lecture and short volume *Der Kampf ums Recht* from 1872, which I translate as "the fight" or "the battle for law," Jhering describes how law develops out of an impassioned feeling that arises in an individual when – importantly – her or his sense of justice has been profoundly violated. In other words, the intrinsic feeling for law (RG) first becomes appreciable when it has been hurt. Again and again in the 1872 text, Jhering uses images of physical discomfort, including examples of a mother's intimate connection to her child after the pain of childbirth or the relief of pain to an injured limb, to describe an individual's impassioned attachment to law and what is just (RG).[15]

2. Another Understanding of Rechtsgefühl

Before explicating Jhering's seminal work on the impassioned feeling for law and justice (RG) in greater depth, I need to mention two caveats to what has been stated thus far. The first is that the examples of violent actions based on impassioned multiple *Rechtsgefühle* mentioned above were carried out by far-right groups and constitute measures that most readers, as I assume, will condemn. My citing these examples might inadvertently lead to the concept of *Rechtsgefühl* being cast in a highly negative right-populistic light. In my book on affect and the law, I offer counterexamples to the ones described above such as the arts of Black Lives Matter as instances of legal pluralistic interventions into the prevailing U.S. American legal order and its history of perpetrating systemic violence against Black life.[16] Artistic protests, sometimes also illegal ones, are positive examples

---

15 Rudolf von Jhering, *The Struggle for Law*, trans. John J. Lalor (Chicago: Callaghan and Company, 1915) (orig. *Der Kampf ums Recht*, 1992 [1872]).
16 See Chapter 5 of Greta Olson, *From Law and Literature to Legality and Affect* (Oxford: Oxford University Press, 2022).

of efforts to change the dominant legal order that are also based in impassioned feelings about law and justice (RG).

A second point is that there is another tradition of conceptualizing *Rechtsgefühl* than the one based in laypersons' political conflicts with their legal orders, that is, as I am interpreting Jhering's work in *Der Kampf ums Recht* and explicating in the examples above. This tradition is discussed in the essays by Justice and Professor of Legal Theory Jeanne Gaakeer and by the legal historian Thorsten Keiser in this volume. Briefly, the feeling for law and justice (RG) can also be understood as, on the one hand, *Judiz* or a *sensus juridicus* – a jurist's intuitive sense of a right and just legal decision and the jurist's efforts to apply legal norms in a way that will lead to the outcome their sense of law (RG) dictates. Note that discussions of a judge's legal sensibility are based in Roman-law contexts in which the judge or judges determine how legal norms should be applied to the case at hand because there are no juries.

On the other hand, *Rechtsgefühl*, as Jhering used it in the singular, can be understood as a catalyst for legal reform when it functions to disturb and challenge existing legal norms. Jhering's move away from the conceptual jurisprudence in which he had been trained to one based on particularized interests and the feeling for law (RG) was caused by the difficulties he had with the inconsistencies involved in an 1858 case concerning which party should have to pay for a ship's cargo that had been sold twice and was subsequently lost at sea. According to Roman law, both parties would have to pay. This struck him as incorrect and led him to conceive a philosophy of law based on historically contingent particular interests rather than universal principles.[17] In an early manuscript version of his later *Zweck im Recht* (The Purpose in Law), dated from roughly 1865, Jhering writes that

> the human (Mensch) brings nothing into the world other than itself, its desire for self-preservation, its egoism – its spirit, heart, and feeling are nothing more than an unwritten slate in which History has to first inscribe its experiential sentences. Law, customs, and conscience are

---

17 Thorsten Keiser points to an understanding of RG as an inner-juristic process involved in improving or developing current legal standards: "Emotion als innerer Kompass für juristische Entscheidungen: Das Rechtsgefühl bei Rudolf Jhering," Introductory Lecture to the University of Giessen by Thorsten Keiser (2020), unpublished manuscript.

nothing other than historically contingent and well-tested politics of a clear egoism.[18]

Continuing the tradition of understanding *Rechtsgefühl* as a catalyst for legal reforms, Erwin Riezler insisted in a psychological study of law from 1921 that *Rechtsgefühl* can never exist independently of law but rather develops in relation to the existent legal order. Quoting Jhering's published version of *Zweck im Recht* (1883), he insists that "It is not legal feeling [*Rechtsgefühl*] that produces law, but rather law produces *Rechtsgefühl*."[19]

In both cases, the concept of *Rechtsgefühl*, widely associated with Jhering, is understood within inner-juristic discourse rather than in terms of individuals' and groups' affective reactions to their normative orders, based on their felt sense of what is just. "*Rechtsgefühl* is then much more than an instinct or an affect," Keiser writes in this volume to describe Jhering's 1872 formulation[20] and discusses various sources of conceptualizations of *Rechtsgefühl* that preceded and followed it.[21] Gaakeer, in turn, explicates Dutch and German legal theoretical histories of jurists, like

---

18 Michael Kunze, '*Lieber in Gießen als irgendwo anders...*': *Rudolf von Jherings Gieße-ner Jahre* (Baden-Baden: Nomos, 2018), 11-40. Jhering's quote from: Rudolf von Jhering, *Der Zweck im Recht* Bd. 1, early manuscript. The original reads: "der Mensch bringt nichts mit zur Welt als sich selbst, seinen Selbsterhaltungstrieb, seinen Egoismus – sein Geist, Herz, Gefühl ist nichts als eine unbeschriebene Tafel, in die erst die Geschichte ihre Erfahrungssätze einträgt, Recht, Sitte, Gewissen ist nichts als die historisch gefundene u(nd) erprobte Politik des geklärten, einsichtigen Egoismus." (Unless otherwise noted, all translations from German to English are by the author.)

19 Erwin Riezler, *Das Rechtsgefühl: Rechtspsychologische Betrachtungen* (München, Berlin und Leipzig: J. Schweizer Verlag, 1921), 39-40. Jhering's quote from: Rudolf von Jhering, *Der Zweck im Recht*, Bd. 1, (Leipzig: Breitkopf & Härtel 1883), XIII in first edition, XIV in second edition. The original reads: "Einleuchtender erscheint auf den ersten Blick das rein logische Argument, daß das Rechtsgefühl nicht vor dem Gegenstande da sein kann, auf den es sich bezieht, also nicht vor dem Recht, daß mithin auch beim primitiven Menschen das Rechtsgefühl nichts Ursprüngliches, sondern etwas durch das Vorhandensein einer schon bestehenden Rechtsordnung bedingtes sei. Diesen Gedanken formuliert Jherings bekannter Ausspruch: 'Nicht das Rechtsgefühl hat das Recht gezeugt, sondern das Recht das Rechtsgefühl'."

20 The original reads: "Rechtsgefühl sei dabei ebenfalls viel mehr als bloß Trieb oder Affekt."

21 On the contextualization of the history of *Rechtsgefühle* as based also on changing understandings of feeling, see Bertram Lomfeld, "Emotio Iuris: Skizzen zu einer psychologisch aufgeklärten Methodenlehre des Rechts," in *Recht fühlen*, eds. Sigrid G. Köhler, Sabine Müller-Mall, Florian Schmidt and Sandra Schnädelbach (München: Brill | Fink 2017), 9-32.

herself, struggling with "legal consciousness" and a *sensus juridicus* to rec-
oncile the claims of sometimes inconsistent legal norms with the jurist's
knowledge of a just and judicious application of law.

Beyond this, Jhering's other texts, including "Über die Entstehung des
Rechtsgefühles" (On the Development of the Feeling for Law and Justice),
a lecture from 1884, suggest that the feeling for law and the right (RG)
is not universal or homogenous. Rather, prevailing legal feeling (RG)
develops in relation to the constitutive legal order in which it arises and is
therefore highly contingent and legally-historically determined. According
to Jhering, how advanced a society's legal feeling (RG) is depends on the
degree to which that society has developed the ability to abstract legal
feeling in contradistinction to legal rules.[22] Accordingly, legal feeling (RG)
arises out of people's socialization in existing legal norms. Through forms
of strife, the resultant legal feeling leads to the further development of
those norms.

Whether legal feeling (RG) concerns an individual jurist's ability to
apply legal norms to individual cases in just and juristically well-honed
intuitive ways or pertains to the role of discordant legal feeling in the
internal development of laws and jurisprudence, these definitions differ
from the more pluralistic understanding of legal feelings (RG) that I take
in this essay.

3. *Jhering and the Context of His Discussion of the Battle for Law/Justice (RG)*

I leave it to legal historians to delineate in full how a move to an awareness
of a passion for law and rightness (RG) and away from explications of the
spirit of Roman law occurred within Jhering's life work. Instead, I want
now to mention that Jhering described himself as a "man of powerful

---

22 The original reads: "Eine zweifellose Thatsache ist es, dass unser Rechtsgefühl
sich oft den Rechtseinrichtungen widersetzt, dass wir uns im Widerspruch mit
diesen Einrichtungen fühlen. Woher kommt dieser Widerspruch, wenn unser
Rechtsgefühle nichts ist als das Product der Rechtsordnung, die uns umgibt? Und
darauf antworte ich, das beruht auf jenem Abstraktionsvermögen des menschlichen Geistes, ohne das wir uns den Menschen gar nicht denken können, das
bei jedem einzelnen Vorfalle etwas abstrahiert." Rudolph von Jhering, "Über die
Entstehung des Rechtsgefühles" (1984), *Jubiläumsschrift 125 Jahre Wiener Juristische
Gesellschaft. Zeitloses aus 125 Jahren*, ed. Walter Barfuß (Wien: Manz'sche Verlags-
und Universitätsbuchhandlung, 1992), 31-47.

feeling for law/rightness" (RG).[23] His recognition of this feeling, its vehement violence, and its role in the development of law and law's role in mediating conflicts, resulted in part out of a legal battle with a former woman servant who had wanted to leave his family's employment and went to court to get her missing wages. For Jhering, his loss to the former servant in court, despite his knowledge of law and social standing, led to his having a "felt sense of the sting of a suffered injustice, when one knows that one has a legitimate right and the institutions of the state are such that despite one's best intentions one cannot make one's rights be validated, cannot get them carried through."[24] Importantly, as is stressed again and again in *The Struggle for Law*, as *Der Kampf ums Recht* has been previously translated, the fight for law occurs on the basis of a sense of "subjective injustice."[25] As Jhering explicates, the "feeling of legal right [*Rechtsgefühl*] will be excited by an injustice done him [sic], a feeling which does not pulsate in accordance with the abstract notions of the system."[26]

For the moment, I want to point out that Jhering's move away from a legal methodology based on a highly formalistic method of interpreting Roman-law-based legal texts and applying abstract legal norms that were derived from them towards one based on practice, personal interests, and conflict was paradigmatic. It was part of an alteration of German legal sciences, *Rechtswissenschaften*, as the study of law is termed in Germany. Yet, in the context of this volume, what is more central is that it anticipated what I view as the turn to affect in Anglophone legal theory by more than a hundred years.[27] Jhering's concern with the violation of *Rechtsgefühl* bespeaks a critical attitude towards law as causing pain rather than (solely)

---

23 Inge Hanewinkel and Nikolaus Linder, "Ein Mann von kräftigem Rechtsgefühle: Rudolf von Jherings Prozess gegen seine Hausangestellte und der Kampf um's Recht," *Zeitschrift für Neuere Rechtsgeschichte* 42 (1-2) (2020), 61-77. The original reads: "Und diesen Vorwurf mache ich den heutigen Rechtssätzen, sie sind darauf berechnet, daß ein Mann von kräftigem Rechtgefühle heutzutage geradezu gezwungen ist, jenen Akt der Feigheit vorzunehmen, von dem ich vorhin sprach, sein gutes Recht im Stiche zu lassen."

24 Hanewinkel and Lindner, *supra* note 23, at 62. The original reads: "Da habe ich aber, kann ich sagen, gefühlt den Stachel des erlittenen Unrechts, wenn man sein gutes Recht hat und die Einrichtungen des Staates derartige sind ('Bravo!'), daß man mit dem besten Willen sein Recht nicht geltend machen, nicht durchsetzen kann."

25 Jhering, *supra* note 15, at 39.

26 Jhering, *supra* note 15, at 39.

27 Greta Olson, "The Turn to Passion: Has Law and Literature become Law and Affect?" *Law & Literature* 28 (3) (2016), 335-53.

resolving conflicts, as well as a focus on how law obviates its interests and feelings in the name of legal reasoning. In accordance with Jhering's central analogy about the pains of childbirth and a mother's resultant love for and attachment to her baby, the violation of an intrinsic sense or feeling for law (RG) is followed by a personalized sense of having an affective connection to law. Indeed, Jhering frequently refers to "love" in his text on *Rechtsgefühl*:

> The power of law lies in feeling, just as does the power of love; and the intellect cannot supply that feeling when it is wanting. But as love frequently does not know itself, and as a single instant suffices to bring it to a full consciousness of itself, so the feeling of legal right uniformly knows not what it is.[28]

Rechtsgefühle, which I believe have to be understood in the plural, are experienced unconsciously until they become newly tangible to those who harbor them, just as, according to Jhering, the lover becomes aware of her or his sentiment in a kind of a sudden awakening to something that has been present but unconscious over a longer period of time. As a form of unconscious and unrecognized love, or as an experience of acute pain, as in the breakdown of vital bodily organs and the cessation of health, a *Rechtsgefühl* does not arise easily. Rather, it is transformative and violent and is experienced painfully. The collocation of injured legal feelings (RG) and physical pain shows an interesting overlap with the sensory aspects that are highlighted in affective theories of law.

In this essay, I am quoting from the 1915 translation *The Struggle for Law* of Jhering's text published 1879. I ask the reader to mentally amend the references to "the man" to "the person" to cohere with the less gendered language usage of the present:

> The man who has not experienced this pain himself, or observed it in others, knows nothing of what law is, even if he has committed the whole corpus juris to memory. Not the intellect, but the feeling, is able to answer this question, and hence language has rightly designated the psychological source of all law as the *feeling of legal right* (*Rechtsgefühl*).[29]

Once again, Jhering compares the violation of the "feeling of legal right," as the translator renders *Rechtsgefühl*, to a bodily wounding or simply to

---

28 Jhering, *supra* note 15, at 61.
29 Jhering, *supra* note 15, at 61 (emphasis in the original).

pain.[30] If this wounding is not actively fought against, Jhering insists, the individual who has received the wound will ultimately be destroyed. Therefore, a robust and passionately defended *Rechtsgefühl* appears to be necessary not only for the individual's existence but also for the evolution of law in general, something that Jhering expanded on at length in his subsequent *Der Zweck im Recht* (The Purpose in Law, 1877–1883). In the author's own words: "The man who does not feel that when his rights are despised and trampled under foot, not only the object of those rights, but his own person, is at stake."[31] A personally experienced legal pain, or a sense of violated justice (RG), is transferred onto the collective to which the individual belongs.

Another way that Jhering anticipates the Law and Affect research that became prominent at the end of the twentieth century is in his notion of different groups' having quite varying *Rechtsgefühl* or a discrete sense of the law and justice, depending on their cohort's placement within the given social hierarchy. Jhering differentiates between officers, merchants, and servants in his *The Struggle for Law* to point out, for example, that servants have no choice but to have a different and less developed sense of legal right (RG) than officers do, given the circumstances of their class conditions.[32] This point strikes me as highly ironic, given that Jhering's proud and from the current perspective quite unjust refusal to pay his former servant woman the wages she had earned in his family's service was an affective stimulus to his beginning to investigate impassioned legal feeling (RG). From our present purview, we can assume that both his class and his sense of masculine privilege had been injured by the outcome of the case.[33]

At any rate, Jhering's acknowledgement that the feeling about justice and the law (RG) inevitably depends on the social position of the group of people experiencing them anticipates recent work on legal consciousness. According to legal-consciousness theorists, people's subjective relations to

---

30 Jhering, *supra* note 15, at 62, 64.
31 Jhering, *supra* note 15, at xlvi-xlvii.
32 Jhering, *supra* note 15, at 49.
33 Sandra Schnädelbach points to the gendered aspects of *Rechtsgefühl* in the context of "bourgeois masculinity" in her history of the development of the concept in Germany, a point that Thorsten Keiser also discusses in his contribution to this volume. See Sandra Schnädelbach, "The Jurist as Manager of Emotions: German Debates on 'Rechtsgefühl' in the Late 19th and Early 20th Century as Sites of Negotiating the Juristic Treatment of Emotions," *InterDisciplines* 6 (2) (2015), 47-73.

their legal environments depend entirely on their relative social positions within that environment, as individuals and as members of social groups. Members of a given legal order cannot in fact experience their legal environments equally, because depending on their cohort's experiences and histories, they will find themselves to "stand before the law" or to "play with the law" or to be "up against the law," as Patricia Ewick and Susan Silbey point out in a foundational U.S. American text on legal consciousness.[34] The first position channels Kafka's dark short story "Vor dem Gesetz" ("Before the Law," 1915), which relates the story of a man who is condemned to wait before the doors of law into perpetuity without ever having a hearing. For Silbey and Ewick, as for other legal-consciousness scholars, law is made comprehensible and people find strategies for dealing with legal authorities through the stories they tell about these experiences, stories that cohere with how their respective group has been treated previously. In other words, the experiences of tenured professors in dealing with law, like the three individuals who have edited this volume, will differ in kind from those of asylum seekers in Germany, as will the stories we tell about German citizenship and German legal culture.

A consciousness of law and whatever people think of as being normatively binding is highly subjective. I call this experience "legality" elsewhere, expanding on Silbey and Ewick's use of the term in their 1998 volume and in other publications. The expansion of the term functions to include unconscious attitudes and feelings about law (RG) that are only partially based on shared stories.[35] This demonstrates overlaps between Law and Narrative work and the turn to affect in critical legal studies.

4. Genealogies of Law and Affect Research

When describing the interest in affect in recent critical legal studies written in English, one often looks to research in law and emotion that took place during the 1990s and which focused on cognition. In its U.S. American iteration, Law and Emotion research emphasized victim rights and the role of emotion in processes of adjudication, for the judge and the

---

34 Patricia Ewick and Susan S. Silbey, *The Common Place of Law: Stories from Everyday Life* (Chicago and London: University of Chicago Press, 1998). For an overview of work in legal consciousness, see Susan S. Silbey, "Studying Legal Consciousness: Building Institutional Theory from Micro Data," *Droit et Société* 100 (3) (2018), 685-731.

35 Olson, *supra* note 16.

jury, for instance.[36] More recently, and most palpably in the work of the moral philosopher Martha Nussbaum, legal education and constitutional activism have been related to augmenting positively evaluated emotions, such as empathy – as a "capacity for imaginative and emotional participation."[37] For Nussbaum, a narratively constructed sense of empathy stands in contradistinction to the feelings of disgust that lead people to marginalize others.[38] There is an obvious element of normativity about which emotions are acceptable and which ones are not in Nussbaum's work, as Thorsten Keiser and others have pointed out.[39] The binary distinction that is drawn between visceral disgust and narratively-derived empathy renders Nussbaum's considerable body of work on emotion and the law less useful for the less normative investigation of *Rechtsgefühle* that we endeavor to undertake in this volume.

Regretfully, "emotion" and "affect" are often used synonymously in discussions of law, and this leads to several points of confusion. As Simon Stern writes: "Much of the work in law either takes affect and emotion to be synonyms, or else focuses on the performance of emotion in order to document its importance in various legal contexts (criminal trials, divorce litigation, etc.)."[40] Yet Law and Emotion research needs to be differentiated from work on Law and Affect. In its most common application, affect theory differentiates bodily sensations from emotions that are translated into language through a variety of representational practices. Affect theories often reference Baruch Spinoza's *Ethics* (1677) as an early source, with its postulations that body and mind are aspects of the same substance, that human is indivisible from nature. Affect theories feature embodiment and sensation, rather than cognition or objects of consciousness. Further, affect theories – for there are more than one – review insights from the history

---

36 Richard A. Posner, "Emotion versus Emotionalism in Law," in *The Passions of Law*, ed. Susan Bandes (New York: New York University Press, 1999), 309-29, 327. For an overview of traditionalist scholarship on emotion see Terry A. Maroney, "Law and Emotion: A Proposed Taxonomy of an Emerging Field," *Law and Human Behavior* 30 (2) (2006), 119-42.

37 Martha Nussbaum, *From Disgust to Humanity* (Oxford: Oxford University Press, 2010), xix; and on legal education and narrative imagination, Martha Nussbaum, "Cultivating Humanity in Legal Education," *University of Chicago Law Review* 70 (2003), 265-80, xix.

38 Nussbaum, *supra* note 37, "Cultivating," at 270-1.

39 Thorsten Keiser, "Gnade und Rechtsgefühl – Beobachtungen aus juristischer Perspektive" (unpublished manuscript).

40 Simon Stern, "Email on Chapter 3" of *From Law and Literature to Legality and Affect*, 10 June 2019.

of emotions, including that normative emotions represent social practices that are subject to change and are not immutable states. Hence, at the end of the eighteenth century, during what is called the Age of Sensibility in English literary history, a normative person, in other words, a Gentleman was expected to display melancholic emotions much more overtly than a man of the same status group would have been encouraged to do during other historical periods. This is marvelously illustrated in novels such as *The Vicar of Wakefield* (1766), in which the idealized protagonist Dr. Primrose is so paralyzed by feeling that he cannot move to save his daughter Sophia from nearly drowning. As changing reactions to the novel and its sentimental protagonist render clear, notions of appropriate emotional responses are contingent on a variety of socio-cultural factors and are tied up with mutable attitudes concerning appropriate masculine behavior and class membership.[41]

Various histories of emotion have demonstrated how practices of physical punishment, incarceration, and execution alter over time, with a move to a preference for private and invisibilized forms of punishment during the nineteenth century that was, however, anticipated by eighteenth-century literature.[42] It has been postulated that the discovery of human rights was only made possible due to a change in what one might call a culture of emotion, with the new ethical humanitarianism of the novel instigating a normative insistence on intrinsic and universal rights, and with the *Bildungsroman* providing a template for human rights discourse.[43]

An intersectional perspective needs to be taken to histories of normative sentiments and emotions, as they are class, and gender, and ethnicity dependent. Evaluations of what are regarded as appropriate and non-excessive types of emotions take place in the intersections of "gendered, class-based, and racialized hierarchies."[44] This has become evident, for instance, in a new awareness of white fragility as an effective strategy whereby white

---

41 Vera Nünning, "Unreliable Narration and the Historical Variability of Values and Norms: The Vicar of Wakefield as a Test Case of a Cultural-Historical Narratology," *Style German Narratology* I 38 (2) (2004), 236-52.

42 As a particularly prominent example of this type of research, see Jonathan Bender, *Imagining the Penitentiary: Fiction and the Architecture of Mind in Eighteenth-Century England* (Chicago: University of Chicago Press, 1989).

43 Lynn Hunt, *Inventing Human Rights: A History* (London: W.W. Norton & Company, 2007); Joseph R. Slaughter, *Human Rights, Inc.: The World Novel, Narrative Form, and International Law* (New York: Fordham University Press, 2007).

44 Kiran Mirchandani, "Challenging Racial Silences in Studies of Emotion Work: Contributions from Anti-Racist Feminist Theory," *Organization Studies* 24 (5) (2003), 721-42, 722; quoted in Eduardo Bonilla-Silva, "Feeling Race: Theorizing

people can refuse to face their imbrication in upholding systemic as well as personal forms of racism.[45] As Sara Ahmed writes, emotions "should not be regarded as psychological states [feelings], but as social and cultural practices."[46]

Affects are then more primary than are emotions; affects describe the relations between things and bodies and the sensations they produce, at least according to philosopher Brian Massumi.[47] This leads to a differentiation between affect, as preverbal and embodied, and emotion, as a verbalized, cognitive, socially constructed, and historically variable set of practices. Witness discussions of appropriate sentiment in the Age of Sensibility or the increasing number of prohibitions against enjoying displays of violence, whether in executions or in animal blood sports during the eighteenth and nineteenth centuries. Note that, in contrast to Massumi, scholars such as Ahmed stress the collective nature of socially mediated cultural emotions in creating a sense of community or nation.[48]

Rather than Law and Emotion research with its more cognitive emphasis, I wish to highlight a different set of developments in the interest in Affect and Law, which was anticipated by Jhering as well as some of his contemporaries who were also interested in *Rechtsgefühl*. I want to postulate that Law and Narrative research has accompanied interest in Law and Affect as alternate but related avenues for critically investigating legal phenomena. Robert Cover's seminal essays from 1986 on law's inherent violence and the comprehension of law that derives from the embedding of legal concepts, processes, and institutions in a particular narrative universe provided a major impulse in common-law legal theory. Cover calls

the Racial Economy of Emotions," *American Sociological Review* 84 (1) (2019), 1-25.

45 Robin DiAngelo, *White Fragility* (Boston: Beacon Press, 2018), 131-38.

46 Sarah Ahmed, *The Cultural Politics of Emotion* (Edinburgh: Edinburgh University Press, 2004).

47 Brian Massumi, "The Autonomy of Affect," *Cultural Critique* 31 (1995), 83-109.

48 A more complete history of competing theories of affect would include psychologist Silvan Tomkins's model of universal emotions shared through bodily mimicry as a kind of contagion and the adoption of Tomkins's work in queer theory. See Silvan S. Tomkins, *Affect Imagery Consciousness: The Complete Edition. Volume I and Volume II* (New York: Springer, 2008); and Eve Kosofsky Sedgwick and Adam Frank (eds.), *Shame and Its Sisters: A Silvan Tomkins Reader* (Durham and London: Duke University Press, 1995).

this universe the *nomos* of law.[49] According to Cover, law can only be made sense of through the epic narratives a society tells about itself and its origins and the beliefs that lend this society's law its validity. The basis of law's authority suggested in Cover's and other Law and Narrative researchers' work posits that law is constructed and materially bound by the culture out of which it emerges and in which it is applied to particular cases. One founder of the Law and Literature movement, J. B. White, argues that legal rhetoric and reasoning represent a form of narrating "'what happened'" in a plausible way.[50] Law's inherently narrational character allows legal practitioners to practice a poetics of law or legal creation in the positive sense. Understanding the courtroom as a forum for competing narratives became one of the bases for what Peter Brooks has repeatedly called "legal narratology," and was documented in Brooks's co-edited and tellingly named *Law's Stories* from 1996.[51]

Law and Narrative research has progressed since the second half of the 1980s in two competing directions, with some more linguistic and narratologically-oriented work pointing to form-function arguments in legal reasoning and applications. This includes research on how anchored narratives operate in legal proceedings or on how prototypical narrative schemas in trials and other types of law and narrative work point to much larger philosophical questions about how law functions in cultural terms. More linguistically-oriented analysis focusses on minimal units of testimony and on how these recognized units, or what are called prototypical narratives, operate within and without the courtroom and then influence legal procedural outcomes.[52] Other law and narrative work demonstrates, in turn, how personal testimony can function to alter existing legal regimes by leading to the recognition of communal rights that have heretofore been neglected or through bringing an awareness to forms of rights' violations that legal orders had not previously recognized. A case in point

---

49 Robert M. Cover, "The Supreme Court, 1982 Term – Foreword: Nomos and Narrative," *Harvard Law Review* 97 (1) (1983), 4-68; and Robert M. Cover, "Violence and the Word," *Yale Law Journal* 95 (8) (1986), 1601-29.

50 J. B. White, "Rhetoric and Law," in *The Rhetoric of the Human Sciences: Language and Argument in Scholarship and Public Affairs*, eds. John S. Nelson, Allan Megill and Donald N. McCloskey (Madison: University of Wisconsin Press, 1987), 298-318, 305.

51 Peter Brooks and Paul Gewirtz (eds.), *Law's Stories: Narrative and Rhetoric in the Law* (New Haven: Yale University Press, 1996).

52 Bernard S. Jackson, *Law, Fact, and Narrative Coherence* (Liverpool: Deborah Charles Publications, 1988); Joachim Knape, "Narratio," in *Historisches Wörterbuch der Rhetorik* 6, ed. Gert Ueding (Tübingen: Max Niemeyer Verlag, 2003), 98-106.

would be the recent recognition of domestic abuse as extending beyond physical violence to other forms of mental and emotional coercion, for instance.[53] Such work focusses on inequities as well as on what elements of narrative must be present and consistently related for an asylum seeker, for instance, to have her claim to protection be recognized and validated. In Law and Literature, the focus is on how narratives, and in particular fictional prose narratives, function to counter legalistic interpretations of law with stories of contingency and context.

Following out of Robert Cover's work but also Wilhelm Schapp's *In Geschichten verstrickt: Zum Sein von Mensch und Ding* (1953) (Ensnared in Stories: On the Being of Human and Thing) in the German context, has been the increasing recognition that law functions narratively but is also only sensible in terms of how it is imbedded in the various narratives that a culture or a society or a nation tells about itself and its application of legal rules. Simplistically stated, where there is a high degree of narrativity in law and legal processes an enlarged capacity for heightened affective expression and engagement will follow. Thus, higher degrees of narrativehood (whether or not something is a narrative) occur in preambles to constitutions and, occasionally, also to laws, to signal how they speak to larger cultural narratives. Distinct narrative forms underlie not only constitutions, with their identity-coalescing elements, for national collectives. They are also intrinsic to the histories of statutes, ordinances, and cases; and story-telling aspects are part of abstract legal norms and hypotheticals, which are also interpreted using narrative means. Law's narrativity bespeaks its positively connoted capacity to create new truths, to be jurisgenerative – to use one of Cover's terms – that is, to write and to juridicate the new and the potentially better than the status quo. Indeed, Jhering's discussion of personal and group attachments to law intersects with his interest in the evolution of law more widely.

This discussion points to the constructedness and rhetoriticity of law rather than the rational explication of legal norms according to those norms and the methods for applying them. This is the space in which the

---

53 For the discussion in the US., see Melena Ryzik and Katie Benner, "What Defines Domestic Abuse? Survivors Say It's More Than Assault," *The New York Times*, last modified 4 August 2021, last accessed 21 July 2022, https://www.nytimes.com/2021/01/22/us/cori-bush-fka-twigs-coercive-control.html. For the UK context, see Dominic Casciani, "Domestic Abuse: Non-Physical and Economic Abuse Included in Law," *The BBC*, last modified 21 January 2019, last accessed 21 July 2022, https://www.bbc.com/news/uk-46939735?fbclid=IwAR0UkIhgFIvjD-gRQ7F5y-jiFq_2_d0FF70I3UCGAibW9i_X4wUMEJUG87cM.

subjectivity of law opens up and where work in Law and Affect coincides with that of Law and Narrative. Recent foci on metaphor and the unconscious in French and Anglophone legal theory and the renewed interest in Law and Emotion and Law and Affect in Germany are part of this overlap. Law and Narrative research conjoins with legal-sociological work about how law functions in context. Researchers look to Lawrence Friedman's work on legal cultures and to the work of legal sociologists such as Eugen Ehrlich on *living law* before him.[54]

I have argued that the move to affect in feminist and queer studies, in narratology, in political theory, and to a lesser but increasing degree in critical legal studies, represents a major theoretical turn that has large consequences for interpretive methods.[55] This turn moves away from a linguistic and semiotic model of analysis, that is, an analysis of articulations and encodings and representations and their various facets and functions – a methodology most strongly associated with Foucauldian discourse analysis – to considering things in terms of how they matter to one another. This can be in systems theory, in field theory, in actor-network theory, or through an interest in care and affect or what has been called the Material Turn in Law. I note the results of this theoretical turn in work on the metaphoricity, visuality, and unconscious of law and legal practices as well in an interest in law and fictionality.[56]

Affect theory allows one to understand individuals' subjective relations to law – also based on narratively-generated attachments to what is thought of as law – in a way that differs from sociological accounts, which tend to deny the role of the fictive in subjective perceptions of law. This research dovetails with that on legal mentalities[57] and on legal subjectivity, which have occurred more in French scholarship, such as in Pierre Legen-

---

54 Eugen Ehrlich, *Gesetz und lebendes Recht: Vermischte kleinere Schriften*, ed. Manfred Rehbinder (Berlin: Duncker & Humblot, 1986); Eugen Ehrlich, *Fundamental Principles of the Sociology of Law*, trans. Walter L. Moll (Cambridge: Harvard University Press, 1936); Eugen Ehrlich, *Freie Rechtsfindung und freie Rechtswissenschaft: Vortrag, gehalten in der juristischen Gesellschaft in Wien am 4. März* 1903 (Leipzig: C. L. Hirschfeld, 1903).

55 Olson, *supra* note 27.

56 See in particular Maksymilian del Mar, *Artefacts of Legal Inquiry: The Value of Imagination in Adjudication* (London: Hart Publishing, 2020), which charts overlaps between discussions of fictionality in literary theory and the narrative and metaphoric analysis of law; and in Hans J. Lind (ed.), *Fictional Discourse and the Law* (Abingdon et al.: Routledge, 2020).

57 Pierre Legrand, "European Legal Systems Are Not Converging," *The International and Comparative Law Quarterly* 45 (1) (1996), 52-81.

dre's oeuvre. Law and Affect also overlaps with Andreas Fischer-Lescano's legal critique, which suggests that law has to return to upholding a culture of *Rechtsgefühl* if it is to move away from being simply a tool of capitalist interests.[58] Discussions of Law and Affect are more often than not critical, pointing out, in the spirit of Cover or Fischer-Lescano or Scott Vietch, that law is inherently violent and masks its violence in appeals to the rules of legal process.[59]

The recent interest in *Rechtsgefühl* in work originating in Germany references this concept's history in Romanticism and Friedrich Carl von Savigny's insistence on a so-called spirit of the German people that had to be the basis for a unified German law.[60] It also recalls the ugly history of attributing a particular affinity to 'correct' legal feeling (RG) to the German people under Nazi law.[61] Yet it also references the subsequent citation of a higher concept of justice as in Gustav Radbruch's post-war postulation of a "*Rechtssinn*" – a sense of law and justice based on inherent values that overrides positive law[62] – as well as in calls on a universal *Rechtsgefühl* as a reason for considering crimes committed during the Holocaust period to be forever punishable. As then Chancellor Helmut Schmidt insisted in 1979, "It would be an unbearable burden for the *Rechtsgefühl* of our people and the *Rechtsgefühl* of the world, if a perpetrator who had not been

---

58 Andreas Fischer-Lescano, "Radikale Rechtskritik," *Kritische Justiz* 47 (2) (2014), 171-83, 171; and on *Rechtsgefühlkultur*, see Andreas Fischer-Lescano, *Rechtskraft* (Berlin: August Verlag, 2013), 118.

59 Scott Vietch, *Law and Irresponsibility: On the Legitimation of Human Suffering* (Abingdon et al.: Routledge-Cavendish, 2007).

60 "In the earliest times to which authentic history extends the law will be found to have already attained a fixed character, peculiar to the people, like their language, manners, and constitution," Friedrich Carl von Savigny, *Of the Vocation of Our Age for Legislation and Jurisprudence*, trans. Abraham Hayward (Clark: The Lawbook Exchange, 2011 [1831]), 24.

61 Gesetz zur Änderung des Strafgesetzbuchs vom 28. Juni 1935 § 2: "Bestraft wird, wer eine Tat begeht, die das Gesetz für strafbar erklärt oder die nach dem Grundgedanken eines Strafgesetzes und nach gesundem Volksempfinden Bestrafung verdient. Findet auf die Tat kein bestimmtes Strafgesetz unmittelbar Anwendung, so wird die Tat nach dem Gesetz bestraft, dessen Grundgedanke auf sie am besten zutrifft," in "Gesetz zur Änderung des Strafgesetzbuchs," *Reichsgesetzblatt* 1935 (1) (1935), 839.

62 Gustav Radbruch, "Gesetzliches Unrecht und übergesetzliches Recht," *Süddeutsche Juristen-Zeitung* 1 (5) (1946), 105-8, 106; Gustav Radbruch, "Statutory Lawlessness and Supra-Statutory Law (1946)," *Oxford Journal of Legal Studies* 26 (1) (2006), 1-11; see also Gustav Radbruch, "Der Mensch im Recht," *Der Mensch im Recht*, (Göttingen: Vandenhoeck & Ruprecht, 1957), 9-22.

previously recognized came and boasted about his actions after the time limit on legal sanctions had been exhausted."[63] More recently, discussions of legal feeling (RG) have dovetailed with research projects on the history of emotion such as the ongoing one in Berlin.[64]

My recent work attempts to think forward forms of normativity that individuals and groups have impassioned feelings about, and to consider these feelings as objects of competing and violent *Rechtsgefühle*. My understanding of *Rechtsgefühle* is based on Jhering, Ehrlich, and the insights of the legal-consciousness movement in the United States. Legal feelings now frequently arise out of social-media-disseminated exchanges about law and justice. For example, the social-media-infused #FreeBritney movement led in no small part to the critical reexamination of legal conservatorship in the United States in 2021.[65] Note, once again, that this conceptualization of felt law's (RG) relation to society differs from the inner juristic discourse on the need for a *Rechtsgefühl* to counterbalance legal rationality.

I understand the "Law" part of Law and Affect research to encompass everything that people think of and imagine law to be, whether this notion of law or "legality," as I call it, is created through fictional representations of law, discussions of legal events in social media or in more traditional news accounts, or in the experiences of one's cohorts with legal institu-

---

63 Helmut Schmidt, "Deutscher Bundestag. Stenographischer Bericht, 145. Sitzung," (1979), 11579-81, 11580. The original reads: "Wäre es nicht – anders als ein Vorredner heute morgen gemeint hat – eine geradezu unerträgliche Belastung für das Rechtsgefühl unseres Volkes und das Rechtsgefühl der Welt, wenn ein bislang noch nicht bekannter Täter nach Ablauf der Verjährung käme und sich seiner Taten rühmte?"

64 Research Group "History of Emotions," *Max-Planck-Institut für Bildungsforschung*, last modified 2021, last accessed 21 July 2022, https://www.mpib-berlin.mpg.de/research/research-centers.

65 Under California law, the singer was placed under what was intended to be a temporary form of legal guardianship in 2008 during a time in which she was experiencing widely publicized psychological struggles. Against Spears's express wishes, the conservatorship became permanent for a period of more than thirteen years with her father acting as the unwanted and, according to Spears, abusive conservator. The #FreeBritney movement was a social media fan movement that began in 2009. It contested the terms of the conservatorship and galvanized public support in favor of an end of the conservatorship in 2021, and a critical investigation of legal guardianship within the frame of Disability Rights. Laura Newberry, "Britney Spears hasn't fully controlled her life for years. Fans insist it's time to #FreeBritney," *Los Angeles Times*, last modified 18 September 2019, last accessed 21 July 2022, https://www.latimes.com/california/story/2019-09-17/britney-spears-conservatorship-free-britney.

tions and legal proceedings. Feelings about what is perceived to be law – for instance, sentiments about the withdrawal of the U.K. from the European Union – inform affective attachments to law. Considers Brexiteers' passionate avowal of the need to preserve the rule of 'their' English law. A sense of subjective identity is created within people's imagined relation to their legal collective, or what one might call their legal imaginary. An individual's and her cohort's relational attitudes to law is based, in part, on how privileged or disadvantaged a position she and her group has within an existing legal order. These relationships are for most people negotiated in their felt relationships to law (RG), which are widely influenced by narratives and images of law that are transported through reporting on law and through fictional media vehicles.

This is a movement away from understanding medial representations of law as simply distortive and disruptive of legal proceedings, as terms such as "lexitainment" or "law gone pop" make clear.[66] From the point of many legal practitioners, media-based misinterpretations of legal procedures are destructive to legal proceedings. Be this as it may, legal language and legal procedures are so professionalized and rarefied, also in terms of their vocabulary and procedural rules, that what people actually think about as law belongs to a much larger field of expressions and representations than that afforded by legal institutions. As the examples from Germany and the United States in this Introduction show, felt law (RG) is what people perceive it to be.

5. This Volume

Why is the discussion of *Rechtsgefühle* in this volume so important now? The premise of this collection of essays and the 2019 conference at the University of Giessen out of which it emerged is that Jhering's initial impulse to describe the passions inherent to law (RG) has a particularly vivid acuteness at our current historical juncture. First, the present is marked by people's demonstrations of a high level of affectivity regarding what they view 'their' laws to be. If anything, the powerful and conflicting social emotions that have been released in the Corona-pandemic era demonstrate

---

66 Lawrence M. Friedman, "Lexitainment: Legal Process as Theater," *DePaul Law Review* 50 (2) (2000), 539-58; Richard K. Sherwin, *When Law Goes Pop: The Vanishing Line Between Law and Popular Culture* (Chicago and London: The University of Chicago Press, 2000).

an even more urgent need to re-evaluate the place and function of legal passions (RG).

The discussions in these pages concern law, affect, and affect in judicial practice, as in Justice Gabriele Britz's discussion of the role of emotions in legal decisions and in Franz Reimer's powerful defense of emotion in law making and in rendering judgement. Britz also discusses people's emotive responses to law as a justification for calling for political changes, a point that Frans-Willem Korsten will make as well, if in the far more negative context of right-wing political populism. Justice Gaakeer highlights the role of affect in legal consciousness and in a *sensus juridicus*, that is, in the judge's painstaking effort to make the legal norm fit the case and facts at hand while also making the antagonists in a given case, and in some cases the wider public, feel recognized. Legal affects – another translation of *Rechtsgefühle* – are also present in increasingly pluralistic legal environments, such as the EU, or in diverse societies such as Germany's in which arguably a number of *lived* legal orders or competing normative realms exist concurrently.

The pluralization of normative orders includes what has been called the horizontalization of EU legal practices. German federal and constituent state (*Länder*) laws react to the increasing recognition of cultural or religious norms in some family law disputes.[67] Where there is less homogeneity, one might hypothesize, there will be more powerful and conflicting legal affects (RG) regarding law. Alternatively, one might argue that in more pluralistic legal environments, law has to take on the role of a civil religion in order to even out individual differences of belief and value.

The case for law as a civil religion has been argued in response to the United States' demographic plurality[68] and to describe Europe's understanding of itself as identified around a common commitment to human rights.[69] For law to continue doing the business of regulating conflicts and providing the abstract rules and procedures to do so, or for law to continue to legitimize its violence – depending on how critically the reader views law – law has to address legal actors' and laypersons' feelings about what they consider to be law-full and to successfully evoke legal feelings, or *Rechtsgefühle*, in response to laws and court decisions.

---

67 See Franz Reimer on this point in this volume.
68 Robert N. Bellah, "Civil Religion in America," *Dædalus* 96 (1) (1967), 1-21.
69 Helle Porsdam, "Human Rights: A Possible Civil Religion?" in *Civil Religion, Human Rights and International Relations: Connecting People and Traditions*, ed. Helle Porsdam (Cheltenham and Northampton: Edward Elgar Publishing, 2012), 21-41.

The collection of essays presented here addresses this task by taking historical, legal-methodological, and theoretical perspectives to *Rechtsgefühle* into consideration as well as by providing case studies regarding the role of legal affects (RG) in courts in the Netherlands and in Germany in the history of torture. The authors argue for a plurality of *Rechtsgefühle* – feelings for law and justice – rather than any single one, as in Jhering's initial formulation. In the following overview, I describe the contributions in some detail in the assumption that many Anglophone readers will not be able to engage with the German texts.

Part I) Historical Developments of Rechtsgefühl in the German Context

The Role and Function of Rechtsgefühl and the Need to Include the
Contextualization of Emotion in Legal History

Following the preface in German and this introductory essay in English, the volume continues with an overview and a case study regarding the history of *Rechtsgefühl* in the German context. Thorsten Keiser charts developments in understandings of *Rechtsgefühl* in the form of a *longue durée* to demonstrate how law has consistently recurred to a higher power in order to legitimate itself. This legitimation process has alternated between making claims to a higher form of rationality or to God. As Keiser summarizes his projective history of *Rechtsgefühl*, every period's differing understanding of *Rechtsgefühl* and of the emotions implicit in these legal feelings (RG) discloses an individual form of normativity and a differing account of rationality. Both play into the understanding of law and legal processes at any given time. Further, an objective history of *Rechtsgefühl* in German jurisprudence has gone lacking up until the present due to the concept having been associated with legal naturalism and the mysticism of Nazi-era ideology and has led to legal feelings (RG) to be vilified.

In Keiser's historical overview, Jhering's works on *Rechtsgefühl* play only a comparatively minor role. Keiser's assemblage of sources for *Rechtsgefühl* includes Feuerbach's 1795 delineation of a feeling for law/justice (RG) that occurs outside of legal texts and which serves as the legitimating basis for claims to human rights. Given that recent neuro-cognitive work has located a sense of justice within the brain, Keiser anticipates that the study of *Rechtsgefühl* will eventually lose its heretofore esoteric associations and become a matter of the hard science of law.

Following the legal pluralistic aim of this volume, Keiser traces a move from an appeal to a singular *Rechtsgefühl* to multiple ones. He notes the formulation of a typology of various *Rechtsgefühle* in a text in the already cited Erwin Riezler (1923), namely as, one, a feeling for good legal practices with which to achieve case resolution that can be learnt; two, the felt need to apply existing laws properly; and, three, as a desire to achieve a higher ideal of justice and law, given the double meaning *"Recht"* as justice and law in German.

Further, Keiser's essay outlines how an emerging history of *Rechtsgefühl* functions analogously to the periodization of affect and emotion that has occurred in historical studies more widely. For Keiser, insight into the history of emotions needs to inform legal studies more widely. Further, an awareness of the connections between language, sensibility, and jurisprudence has to play a part in neuroscientific work. Keiser's historical work on *Rechtsgefühl*, also in his already cited essay on *Rechtsgefühl* and mercy ("Gnade und Rechtsgefühl"), provides the basis for a new theory for and method of approaching legal history.

The History of Rechtsgefühle in the Context of German Language Discussions of Human Rights

Following Keiser's more general and programmatic overview, Sylvia Kesper-Biermann's essay on the "Role of *Rechtsgefühl(e)* in Human Rights" provides a more specific case history, while also bringing up some general methodological issues such as the role of emotions in human rights discourse. Like Keiser's, her essay highlights the fundamental changes to historical sciences that have been wrought by the generally accepted insight that emotions are at least in part socially constructed and therefore also experienced and represented variously throughout history and across geographies as well as amongst different population groups. Kesper-Biermann calls for histories of emotion to focus on the development of human rights, and to move beyond their previous more or less exclusive attention to the role of empathy. She also points out the importance of differentiating between the development of human rights and the history of humanitarianism, the latter constituting a discourse about the necessity of ending human suffering.

Kesper-Biermann focuses her attention on debates about torture in the nineteenth century in the German context, arguing that a history of the prohibition against torture and the emotions surrounding it stand in archetypically for the development of human rights in general. She points out that torture had already been forbidden in Prussia by the mid-eighteenth century. Explicitly forbidding torture was not necessary

43

in later criminal law discourse, because it could be assumed that it was never practiced. The author highlights how *Rechtsgefühl* was used in German-speaking areas in connection with nascent discourse about human rights through the long nineteenth century (roughly 1789 through 1914), demonstrating in an analysis of law professor Eduard Osenbrüggen's 1854 text that *Rechtsgefühl* came to be understood as an intuitive and naturalized sense of what law could and should be. With recourse to Jhering's 1867 text on guilt in private law, she traces how *Rechtsgefühl* came to be seen as part of the legal-social development of a collective legal culture. An increasing sense of disgust at the use of torture was part of a sense of legal collectivity and was accompanied by a sense of empathy as well as *Rechtsgefühl*, as an implicit sense of justice. This moralized sense of disgust at torture, as a collectively experienced social emotion, was instrumental to an understanding of human rights as moral rights.

Whereas German-speaking jurists no longer needed to discuss torture in the nineteenth century, popular discourse, as the author demonstrates, certainly did. Kesper-Biermann cites numerous novels and offers a close reading of an 1868 print in which a jealous husband, a criminal lawyer, is shown torturing his innocent wife. The young wife's extreme suffering is shown using highly evocative visual means that might arouse lust in some viewers. The popularity of this type of representation demonstrates the ambivalence of disgust as an affective state and the fascination and vicarious pleasure that some people will and do take in depictions of pain and other violations of moral (and legal) norms. The potential for a "pornography of pain" has been pointed out by the historian Karen Halttunen, amongst others.[70] And scenes of torture regretfully are still used in order to arouse audience sensation.

A collective consensus about the inadmissibility and immorality of torture became an essential part of German legal culture and an important vehicle for differentiating German legal culture from supposedly less advanced ones. *Rechtsgefühl* was then entwined with a sense of nation. As an illustration of this, Kesper-Biermann quotes Jhering on the implicit superiority of (German) criminal law:

> But criminal law is the nodal point where the finest and most delicate nerves and arteries come together. Every sensation makes itself sensible and outwardly visible. The face of law, on which the entire individuality of a people, its thinking and feeling, its temperament and

---

70 Karen Halttunen, "Humanitarianism and the Pornography of Pain in Anglo-American Culture," *The American Historical Review* 100 (2) (1995), 303-34.

its passions, its morals and its rawness makes itself known, and are reflected on its soul – criminal law is the people itself.[71]

The prohibition against torture as constituted by a combined sense of empathy, disgust and an intuitive *Rechtsgefühl* enabled nineteenth-century Germans to have a sense of a community within a civilized legal culture.

Part II) Rechtsgefühle in Legal Theory and Practice

The Historicization of Legal Consciousness and Rechtsgefühle Demonstrates Law's Grounding in the Humanities

In a legal theoretical tour de force, Justice and Professor of Legal Theory Jeanne Gaakeer examines varying approaches to *Rechtsbewusstsein* (legal consciousness), to *Rechtsgefühl*, and to a *sensus juridicus*. She unpacks competing notions of legal consciousness and *Rechtsgefühle* in order to elucidate and validate a philosophy of jurisprudence that is grounded in the Humanities. This includes an understanding of law as indivisible from other meaningful forms of human activity. Gaakeer's historical overview extends back to the Roman Jurist Ulpian (died AD 228), who defined law as "derived from justice" and as the "art of knowing what is good and equitable," thereby anticipating concepts of intuitive understandings of law. Her point is to demonstrate that the still pertinent question of whether a sense of justice is inherent to law, or not, extends back to the beginnings of legal theory and is hardly a new consideration. Because "law" is notoriously difficult to define, feelings for law/justice (RG) and the consciousness of law/justice will inevitably remain highly contested concepts. Gaakeer also highlights the need to distinguish between individual and societal understandings of "'*Rechtsbewusstsein*', as a consciousness of (the) law, versus '*Rechtsgefühl*', as an individual's innermost feelings."[72]

---

71 Rudolf von Jhering, *Das Schuldmoment im römischen Privatrecht: Eine Festschrift* (Gießen: Verlag von Emil Roth, 1867), 2-3. The original reads: "Aber das Strafrecht ist der Knotenpunkt, wo die feinsten und zartesten Nerven und Adern zusammenlaufen, und wo jeder Eindruck, jede Empfindung sich fühlbar macht und äusserlich sichtbar wird, das Antlitz des Rechts, auf dem die ganze Individualität des Volks, sein Denken und Fühlen, sein Gemüth und seine Leidenschaft, seine Gesittung und seine Rohheit sich kund gibt, kurz auf dem seine Seele sich wiederspiegelt – das Strafrecht ist das Volk selbst."

72 All quotes are from Jeanne Gaakeer's essay in this volume.

Gaakeer brings the Dutch legal philosopher Johan Jozef Boasson's (1919) investigation of *rechtsbewustzijn* (consciousness of law/justice) into the wider discussion of *Rechtsgefühle* in this volume and notes the distinction that Boasson makes between consulting one's individual consciousness and considering the overall well-being of society when exercising this form of consciousness. It is ultimately the judge who must balance out resultant frequently conflicting interests. Gaakeer uses recent Dutch cases in which affected citizens had radically different notions of what the role of law should be to demonstrate the judge's role in negotiating between public opinion and the application of legal norms. Gaakeer looks to Max Rümelin's study of *Rechtsgefühl und Rechtsbewusstsein* and his thesis that judges need to develop a "legal intuition." (Note that this was the second generation of Rümelins to work on the topic.) Moving through discussions of James Boyd White and Paul Ricœur, Gaakeer attests that a legal intuition provides the basis for the "professional empathy" which is necessary in judging and that differs from an individual sense of sympathy.

Rechtsgefühle have to be considered in terms of the emotions of those whom the application of the law will affect – a point that Gabriele Britz and Franz Reimer highlight as well. Like Keiser, Gaakeer discusses how recent neuroscientific research on the embodied quality of emotions demonstrates that earlier postulations of an innate sense of justice are not in any way romanticized or naive. Gaakeer posits that a feeling for law/justice (RG) combines what Ernst Weigelin called "a sense of what the law requires" with "a feeling for what law ought to be." Thereby "a humanistic, intermediate position [is created] between the value-absolutism of natural law and the value-relativism of legal positivism." This enables the judge to exercise a form of "judicial daring" at times when she must do so. In order to arrive at this point, judges must enact practical wisdom or "phronetic intelligence," as envisioned in Aristotles's *Nicomachean Ethics.*

Gaakeer's larger argument is that legal methodology as well as individual acts of rendering judgement must include insights from the Humanities. Making court decisions adequately requires narrative and metaphoric insight, the latter understood as a capacity to discern patterns of similarity and dissimilarity. Gaakeer advocates for an understanding of *Rechtsgefühl* as a *sensus juridicus*, an ability to apply the general legal norm to the particular case and to withhold judgement when necessary. In the words of twentieth-century legal theorist Paul Scholten, one has to be a "judge, who intuitively 'sees' the decision immediately after the case is presented to him [sic]."[73] To illustrate the necessity of the judge's developing a juridical conscience, Gaakeer cites examples in which the judge's decision required a willingness to render difficult judgements using her "guts" and sense of judicial daring.

The Myriad Ways in which Legal Feelings (RG) Inform Legal Processes

We are happy to offer German Constitutional Justice and constitutional law professor Gabriele Britz's keynote in its original version as well as in an English translation by Laura Borchert with annotations in this volume. The lecture speaks to Gaakeer's empirical and theoretical piece about the act of judging consciously as well as to Justice Britz's own experience of serving as a constitutional justice in post-reunification Germany. Britz offers a masterful overview of five distinct ways in which legal feelings (*Rechtsgefühle*) influence legal processes. This influence transpires, first, in the ways in which both new laws and court judgements can incite emotions amongst the public whose lives these laws and decisions regulate. These feelings include negative and positive ones. For instance, when a third gender was recognized by the German Constitutional Court in 2017, the lived experience of non-binary persons was lent legitimacy. Feelings are also evoked when new laws are descriptively and therefore also affectively named, such as in the "Gute-Kita-Gesetz" (The Good Day Care Center Law) from 2018, which was intended to improve the conditions in and the quality of day care centers.[74] Britz's text also echoes Gaakeer's essay in that it notes the effects of emotional and social contexts on legal decision-making.

Second, laws and judgements reflect on public legal feelings (RG) in terms of how they, for instance, can protect citizens from the unpleasant sensation of being permanently surveilled by the state, as is dictated by the

---

73 Paul Scholten, "General Method of Private Law: Mr. C. Asser's Manual for the Practice of Dutch Civil Law," *Digital Paul Scholten Project, Vol. 1, Chapter 1, Section 28, 'The decision'* (Amsterdam: 2014 [1931]), available at https://paulscholten.eu/research/article/general-method-of-private-law/#title30, last accessed 21 July 2022.

74 On the affective naming of laws and the cultural-political work this does, see Greta Olson and Laura Borchert, "Transing / Narrative Authority, Affective Unreliability, and Transing Law," in *Research Handbook in Law and Literature*, eds. Peter Goodrich, Daniela Gandorfer and Cecilia Gebruers (Cheltenham: Edward Elgar Publishing, 2022).

relatively restrictive German data protection law, or the damages awarded to plaintiffs on the basis of their imagined emotional suffering. Third, a form of legal "intuition" is required when judges apply the law, for example, when they have to determine if a person's treatment by the state has violated their human dignity, the most important value and right according to German Basic Law. The acknowledgment of the intuitive aspect of legal decision-making demonstrates an important overlap between Britz's and Gaakeer's explorations of *Rechtsgefühle*. Yet, as Britz points out in the fourth meaning of *Rechtsgefühle* she enumerates, "disruptive ... gut feelings" are simply a part of the make-up of every professional jurist. These personal emotions have to be rationally questioned and sometimes also dismissed altogether. In the fifth and final meaning of *Rechtsgefühle*, according to Britz, laypersons develop powerful feelings in connection with wished for legal developments, and Jhering named this phenomenon with saliency.

Britz ends her lecture by charting the three parts in Jhering's concept of *Rechtsgefühl* in relation to legal developments and reform. Importantly, Britz uncovers a strategic move that was made by Jhering in response to the authoritarian state in which he lived and in which democratic legislation was not yet in place as a tool for reforming and correcting existing laws. Accordingly, appeals to *Rechtsgefühl* were made to stand in for democratic processes. According to Jhering, *Rechtsgefühl* originates in an individual's private sense of affront, in particular, and are then transferred from the individual's feeling for law and justice (RG) to a sense of the community's suffering when its *Rechtsgefühl* is not appropriately met. Recognizing this pattern led Jhering to postulate that a state can only flourish when its citizens express their healthy *Rechtsgefühl*. Finally, Britz questions the relevance of Jhering's legal reformist strategy based on legal feeling (RG) for legal debates transpiring now. She points out that it is important to not incorrectly label a desire for political change as a legal feeling (RG) to uphold the separation of the judiciary from the legislature and to preserve the independence of the former. This is the case even if legal feelings (RG) will and should always remain present in legal reformist efforts.

Human Emotionality Constitutes Law's Biggest Asset

As the final contribution to the topic of how *Rechtsgefühle* inform legal practices in this volume, Franz Reimer's "'The Empire of Laws and Not of Men': Rule by Law as the Avoidance of Feeling" focusses on the persistent juxtaposition of the rule of law with that of the 'rule by men' (aka humans) as a point from which to question a general understanding of law as being free of emotion. Quoting political philosopher James Harrington's *The Commonwealth of Oceana* (1656) in his title, Reimer focusses on the supposed binary opposition that is perpetually made between an abstract rule of law and a human-based one in the context of the German constitutional state. He demonstrates that law and human actors can never be represented as polar opposites.

His contribution outlines a compelling argument for understanding human actors to be assets in lawmaking and legal decision-making rather than impediments to law's rationality and objectivity. Rather than relegating the role of *Rechtsgefühle* to a negatively connoted form of human capriciousness, Reimer posits that emotions provide an avenue for addressing individual court decisions on the background of increasing social diversity, and can also be vehicles for ensuring that the process of reflecting on norms and laws continues in a period that is increasingly dominated by algorithms and what has been called Legal Tech.

Reimer traces the origins of the juxtaposition of the "law of men" and the letter of law, beginning with the Socratic dialogues and moving up through the twentieth century. The concepts of law as decision-making body and of law as a surrogate for the ruler are introduced in addition to the ideal of law as a form of protection against human arbitrariness. Law's role in providing prototypes for how to deal with conflicts leads to the claim that law should be free of subjective sentiments. Yet rationality is not a necessary criterion for the development of new laws. In fact, an emphasis on rationality would negatively impact on lawmakers' ability to create laws that make emotional appeals. These include the already mentioned "Gute-Kita-Gesetz" (The Good Day Care Center Law, 2018) and the "Starke-Familien-Gesetz" (The Strong Family Law, 2019) and includes the use of preambles in laws to convey their appellative function.

The third section of the essay argues for an understanding of the rule of law and 'the rule of men' as complementary. Laws require people to enforce them. In enforcing legal norms, people learn to empathize with those affected by them. Importantly, Reimer does not posit empathy as an emotion but as a form of introspection that demands a person's abandoning their subjective standpoint. The German legal system demands a disciplining of emotions, which precludes any form of affective sensation with the notable exception of empathy. This disciplining follows out of the institutionalization process and the attendant cementing of the difference between persons and their office. While in office, the office holder has to withdraw subjective views so that law can rule objectively.

The final section argues that the 'rule of algorithms' cannot replace the 'rule of men' in the future. Judicial power has to be entrusted to human actors for some legal cases like those involved in parental custody decisions. *Rechtsgefühle* play a decisive role in how such cases are decided, since the emotional effects of these decisions have to be accounted for by judges – a point that Britz and Gaakeer make as well. Further, emotions may prompt renewed reflections on the applicability of legal norms, on possible gaps in existing laws, and on their constitutionality. Such reflections lead to corrections of legal processes, something that algorithms, as seeming instances of the pure 'rule of law,' cannot accomplish. Reimer concludes that human emotionality, including perceptive, empathetic, and evaluative decision-making capabilities, do not constitute a deficient mode of realizing law but are rather law's greatest assets.

Part III) The Impact of Rechtsgefühle on Political Developments

Jhering's Struggle for Law (Der Kampf ums Recht, 1872) in the Context of Right-Wing Extremist Gamesmanship in Legal Processes

As previously mentioned, Britz's lecture contains a significant political-historical insight. Where legal reforms cannot be achieved through democratic means, they will be sought after in other ways, for instance, through appeals to intrinsic (and implicitly valid) feelings for law and justice (RG). Frans-Willem Korsten's essay on the trials relating to a charge of defamation against the right-wing populist Dutch politician Geert Wilders between 2014 and 2020 renders the political aspect of Jhering's work on *Rechtsgefühl* even more explicit. *Rechtsgefühl* belongs to what Jhering sees as an inevitable and ongoing "struggle for law," and Korsten opens up Jhering's 1872 text to political philosophy as well as to a materialist reading of law.

In 2014, Wilders was charged with group defamation for having made incendiary remarks about Dutch Moroccans at a victory party following elections. While the court found him to be guilty in 2016, it imposed no fine or sentence and this judgement was repeated by the higher Court of Justice (The Hague) after Wilders appealed. In a series of affectively loaded legal moves, Wilders and his defense insisted that presiding judges in both courts had been biased and that the case should never have been brought to court. Wilders publicly contended that the judiciary did not wield authority over him and would fail to represent the Dutch people if it decided against him.

Korsten reads Wilders's and his defense's legal and medial moves as an illustration of the "battle for" and the "game of" law as a struggle for authority that Jhering described as being inherent to legal developments. In this context, Korsten highlights what I also believe would be a better translation of the original text in which Jhering thematized *Rechtsgefühl*, noting that it should be entitled "The Battle" rather than "The Struggle for Law." He points out that *"Kampf"* denotes both "battle" and "competitive contest" in German to demonstrate how Wilders utilized strategies of competitive gamesmanship within law to undermine its authority.

Reading law as a 'cultural technique,' in the sense that German media theorist Bernhard Siegert uses the term,[75] Korsten submits that law can only function by virtue of its collectively agreed upon authority. Law's force is derived through material means, for instance, the authority that is suggested by pronouncing judgements "in the name of the King" in Dutch courtrooms. Law's materiality also extends to the repository of its seemingly timeless authority in court records or files. According to Korsten, these forms of materially manifested authority have now been challenged by the dominance of online social media platforms in the creation of legal feelings (RG). These platforms speak to like-minded groups, reinforcing their beliefs and discrediting traditional sources of fact and authority through disinformation, thus leading to a collapse of a sense of collectively granted belief in law.

Korsten discovers efforts to dismantle the collectivity in the attack on the U.S. Capitol in January 2021, which I mentioned at the beginning of this Introduction, as well as in Wilders's September 2020 insistence that "the Dutch *Rechtsstaat* is 'broken and corrupt,'"[76] because it had found him guilty of group defamation. Korsten expresses that "people's affective attachment to law" has to be constantly fostered through material means and that *Rechtsgefühle* have now become "material for populists to play with," thereby threatening the rule of law and democracy more widely.

---

75 Bernhard Siegert, "Cultural Techniques: Or the End of the Intellectual Postwar Era in German Media Theory," *Theory, Culture & Society* 30 (6) (2013), 48-65.

76 PVVpers, "Geert Wilders: 'De rechtsstaat is failliet en corrupt premier Rutte'," *YouTube*, last modified 17 September 2020, last accessed 21 July 2022, https://www.youtube.com/watch?v=mauSy2PPO2U.

6. Outlook: Theses and Open Questions

The editors of this volume understand this collection of essays to be part of a general interest in thematizing emotion and affect in critical legal studies, on the one hand, and a delayed assessment of the role of *Rechtsgefühl* in German legal history and current legal practices, on the other. The volume can therefore be seen as a complement to *Recht fühlen* (feeling law, 2017) as well as *Rechtsästhetik in rechtsphilosophischer Absicht* (Legal aesthetics in legal philosophical context, 2020), which deals with the role of affect in aesthetic approaches to law.[77]

The themes that come up repeatedly in the essays collected here also point the way towards future research on the centrality and importance of *Rechtsgefühle*. To summarize these themes and the theses they entail in brief:

1) The history of law and of human rights discourse has to now attend to the role of *Rechtsgefühl* (Keiser, Kesper-Biermann).
2) The assertion of *Rechtsgefühle* that are adjudged to be culturally appropriate belongs to the discursive process of nation-building and the creation of nationalistic emotional communities. The assertion of *Rechtsgefühle* therefore also contributes to exclusionary practices (Kesper-Biermann, Olson).
3) *Rechtsgefühle* are intrinsic and necessary aspects of current legal practices and the process of judging (Gaakeer, Britz, Reimer).
4) A reassertion of the centrality of *Rechtsgefühl* can be found in new neuroscientific approaches to law (Keiser, Gaakeer).
5) *Rechtsgefühle* need to be defended given the current calls for automated legal processes. They belong to the humanness of law (Reimer) and to law's indivisibility from the Humanities (Gaakeer).
6) The assertion of what are adjudged to be intrinsically correct *Rechtsgefühle* plays a central role in political developments (Olson, Britz, Korsten). The new importance of articulations of *Rechtsgefühle* also has to be seen in the context of populist calls for new forms of *lived law* (Olson, Korsten).
7) The need to further differentiate the roots and various divergent interpretations of Jhering's and other thinkers' understandings of *Rechtsge-*

---

77 Sigrid G. Köhler, Sabine Müller-Mall, Florian Schmidt and Sandra Schnädelbach (eds.), *Recht fühlen* (München: Brill | Fink, 2017); Eva Schürmann and Levno von Plato (eds.), *Rechtsästhetik in rechtsphilosophischer Absicht: Untersuchungen zu Formen und Wahrnehmungen des Rechts* (Baden-Baden: Nomos, 2020).

fühle. First, how one defines the affect and/or emotion that underlines a *Rechtsgefühl* or multiple *Rechtsgefühle* determines the resultant understanding of the legal feeling (RG). Second, how narrow or wide the definition of law is will determine whether one considers legal affects (RG) to be an intrinsic part of legal history and theory or to belong to a wider conversation about normative orders and ideology.

These theses raise a number of questions, for instance, about the historical role of *Rechtsgefühle* in political processes, and the degree to which these impassioned feelings about law and justice are democratic or not. Further, the question remains open of whether *Rechtsgefühle* will be acknowledged as legitimate aspects of legal processes, since as the legal practitioners and the legal theorists in this volume all agree, they play an inevitable part in them. Third, a historicization of changes in dominant legal emotions (RG) may alter our understanding of normative orders and the ways in which they legitimate themselves.

We leave it to future researchers to continue to assess the importance of impassioned feelings about law and justice (RG) in social developments more widely.

II: Historical Developments of *Rechtsgefühle* in the German Context

II: Historische Entwicklungen von Rechtsgefühlen im deutschen Kontext

Von der Vernunft zum Rechtsgefühl?
Zu den Wechselwirkungen von Emotionalitätsforschung und historischer Rechtswissenschaft

Thorsten Keiser

I. *Einleitung: Emotionalität und rationales Recht*

Ergebnisse juristischer Entscheidungsfindung wie Rechtsnormen werden in der Regel als transparente, nachvollziehbare Verstandesleistungen und Ergebnisse logischer Denkprozesse dargestellt. Daraus resultiert ein nicht geringer Teil ihrer Legitimität, den sie brauchen, um ihre Ordnungsfunktion für menschliches Zusammenleben erfüllen zu können. Moderne Rechtsordnungen sind von dem Anspruch geprägt, allgemein einsichtigen Mustern zu folgen. Notwendigerweise sind solche die Domäne des Rechts, das sich als Inbegriff von Rationalität präsentiert[1] und teilweise sogar durch die Herausbildung einer eigenen Dogmatik seine Geltungsmit Wahrheitsansprüchen verbindet[2]. Beispiele aus der Rechtsgeschichte zur Untermauerung solcher Rationalitätsansprüche gibt es viele. Im Beweisrecht des Mittelalters wurden etwa Anforderungen an rationale Beweiswürdigung und glaubwürdiges Zeugenverhalten als Voraussetzung für die Richtigkeit des Urteils formuliert[3]. Hier begegnet man eigenen Rationalitätskriterien für die juristisch relevante Bewertung menschlichen Verhaltens und individueller Beobachtungen. Aber auch ein Gottesurteil war juristisch gesehen rational, weil es auf eine höhere, weltlicher Legitimation entrückte Entscheidungsinstanz verweist. Insofern sind, je nach Rechtsauffassung, „Wunder und Beweis" keine Gegensätze, vielmehr kann das Wunder der Beweis sein[4]. Begriffe von Tatsachen, Evidenz und Objek-

---

1 Allgemein dazu *Bernhard Peters*. Rationalität, Recht und Gesellschaft. Frankfurt/M. 1991.

2 *Josef Esser*. Möglichkeiten und Grenzen dogmatischen Denkens im modernen Zivilrecht. In: Archiv für civilstische Praxis 172 (1972), S. 103 ff. (insbes. S. 111).

3 *Susanne Lepsius*. Von Zweifeln zur Überzeugung. Der Zeugenbeweis im gelehrten Recht ausgehend von einer Abhandlung des Bartolus von Sassoferrato. Frankfurt/M. 2003, S. 83 ff.

4 Vgl. *Lorraine Daston*. Wunder, Beweise und Tatsachen. Zur Geschichte der Rationalität. Frankfurt/M. 2001, S. 29 ff.

tivität[5] dienen der Nachvollziehbarkeit und Rückbindung von Normen an Bereiche, welche politische Herrschaftsansprüche mit logischen Überzeugungsmustern verbinden. Möglicherweise lassen sich verschiedene Rationalitäten des Rechts ausmachen, in aktueller Terminologie etwa auf sozialer oder prozeduraler Ebene; daneben wird eine wissenschaftliche oder formale Rechtsrationalität beschrieben[6]. Unabhängig davon, wie man die Rationalität des Rechts definiert, scheint eines fest zu stehen: Irrationale, rein emotionale Elemente haben darin offenbar keinen Platz. Sie sind in vieler Hinsicht Sand im Getriebe einer Legitimationsmaschinerie. Andererseits lässt sich aber auch in Aussagen von Rechtswissenschaftlern eine Entkopplung von Rechtswissen und rationalem Expertenwissen unter Verweis auf einen eigenen normativen Wert nicht unmittelbar rationaler Elemente beobachten. Seit dem 19. Jahrhundert war es ein gängiger Ausgangspunkt juristischer Argumente, menschliches, natürliches oder konkretes Recht einem kühlen Vernunftprodukt entgegenzusetzen. Anrufungen von Gefühl, Gemüt, Innerlichkeit und Seele gegen formale Strenge waren – ob explizit oder unterschwellig – in vielen rechtspolitischen oder -methodischen Argumentationsmustern erfolgreich. Zwar liefen die vielfältigen Rationalismus-Kritiken am Werk von Gelehrten[7], Gesetzgebern oder Richtern selten explizit auf den Vorwurf eines Mangels an Gefühl hinaus. Noch weniger verstanden sie sich als Plädoyers zugunsten „irrationalen Rechts". Dennoch schwingt im bekannten Klischee des „Juristen als solchen"[8] auch der Vorwurf der Gefühllosigkeit mit. Kritik an solchen Positionen äußerte etwa aus rechtssoziologischer Sicht Theodor Geiger, der als Emigrant während der NS-Zeit unter dem deutlichen Eindruck der Folgen eines sich irrational-gefühlsorientiert gebenden Rechtsdenkens stand. Er störte sich an der „Veneration" und „mystischen Feierlichkeit", mit dem Worte wie „Rechtsgefühl" ausgesprochen wurden und warf die Frage auf, ob sie nicht mehr als „farbenprächtige Wort-Kulissen für die Illusionsnummern behendiger Gedankenjongleure" seien[9]. Seine Skepsis

---

5 Zu diesen Begriffen als Kategorien des Rationalen *Daston*, a.a.O.
6 Aus kritischer Sicht *Bernhard Peters*. Rationalität, Recht und Gesellschaft. Frankfurt/M. 1991, insbes. S. 100-114.
7 Ausführlich in Bezug auf die Kritik des Systemdenkens Puchtas *Hans-Peter Haferkamp*. Georg Friedrich Puchta und die „Begriffsjurisprudenz". Frankfurt/M. 2004, S. 281-284.
8 Anschaulich *Ulrich Falk*. Ein Gelehrter wie Windscheid. Frankfurt/M. 1989, S. 112 ff.
9 *Theodor Geiger*. Vorstudien zu einer Soziologie des Rechts. 4. Aufl. Berlin 1987 (Erstauflage 1947). Hg. von Manfred Rehbinder, S. 340.

gegenüber dem „Rechtsbewusstsein", das er an diesem Punkt mit „Rechts-gefühl" gleichsetzt, beruht auf der Unmöglichkeit seiner unmittelbaren Er-kenntnis. „Gefühle" seien keine Erfahrungskategorien, sondern nur in Form von Reaktionen und Aussagen von außen erkennbar, wobei der Rückschluss von der äußeren Manifestation auf das ‚wahre' innere Gefühl stets zweifelhaft sei[10]. Das Trügerische der auf Gefühl oder Bewusstsein verweisenden Aussage oder Handlung führe also dazu, dass diese als juris-tische Kategorien ungeeignet seien. Was hier deutlich wird, ist ein Span-nungsfeld zwischen Emotionen, also unkontrollierbaren und nicht immer verlässlich ergründbaren Faktoren auf der einen und den Gewissheitsan-sprüchen des Rechts auf der anderen Seite. Auf dieser Ebene lassen sich Forschungsfragen für eine wertende Rechtswissenschaft der Gegenwart formulieren, aber auch für eine eher deskriptiv orientierte Rechtsgeschich-te. Diese kann sich an der Kategorie des „Rechtsgefühls" orientieren, ohne zu eng am Begriff haften zu bleiben.

II. Rechtsgefühl aus Sicht der Rechtsgeschichte

1. Aufgaben und Potenziale

Rechtsgeschichte kann den Erfahrungsschatz des Rechts in affektiver Hin-sicht deutlich machen, um Orientierungswissen für gegenwärtige Debat-ten zu erarbeiten. In der rechtshistorischen Forschung fand die Kategorie „Rechtsgefühl" nur in der hinlänglich bekannten „Privatrechtsgeschichte der Neuzeit" von Franz Wieacker Beachtung. Dort steht die Akzentuie-rung von „Rechtsgefühl" für eine Epochenbeschreibung, nämlich die des „juristischen Naturalismus", der gegen Ende des 19. Jahrhunderts durch empirisch orientierte Menschenbilder das Rechtssubjekt zum affekt- und triebgesteuerten Wesen enthumanisiert und damit das Recht – von den Werten isoliert – zur bloßen Wirklichkeitswissenschaft gemacht habe[11]. Natürlich ist Wieackers Meistererzählung kritisch zu lesen und gerade seine Polemik gegen den „Naturalismus" kann man als verschleierte Apo-logie seiner eigenen Rolle im Nationalsozialismus deuten[12]. Was fehlt,

---

10 *Geiger.* ebenda, S. 341.
11 *Franz Wieacker.* Privatrechtsgeschichte der Neuzeit. 2. Aufl. Göttingen 1968, S. 563 ff.
12 Zur Einordnung etwa *Joachim Rückert.* Geschichte des Privatrechts als Apologie des Juristen. In: Quaderni fiorentini 24 (1995), S. 531-562. Wieackers eigene Aus-führungen über das Recht der Volksgemeinschaft und die Anwendung des kon-

ist eine Auseinandersetzung mit Rechtsgefühl ohne den verzerrenden Kontext einer rechtshistorischen Meistererzählung, die mittlerweile selbst Teil der juristischen Zeitgeschichte ist.

Dennoch verweist die von Wieacker angesprochene Verbindung von Rechts- und Naturwissenschaften auf einen zentralen Kontext. „Rechtsgefühl", als Begriff und Konzept, hat mit dem Aufkommen der Psychologie zu tun. Die naturwissenschaftliche Entdeckung des Bewusstseins ließ die Frage entstehen, inwiefern sich Empfindungen von Recht individuell als innerer Kompass für bestimmte Verhaltensweisen formieren konnten. Auf der anderen Seite konnte „Rechtsgefühl" im 19. Jahrhundert im Zuge einer romantisch wirkenden Aufwertung des Irrationalen gegenüber dem scheinbar wissenschaftlich erfahrbaren und somit vorbestimmbaren Recht akzentuiert werden[13]. Motive einer aus der Natur entspringenden Gerechtigkeit ließen später Parallelen zur (ethologischen) Verhaltungsforschung deutlich werden, Rechtsinstinkte schienen nun bei Mensch und Tier gleichermaßen erkennbar[14].

Lange vor diesen modernen Verbindungen zwischen Naturwissenschaft und Recht war es die Disziplin des Naturrechts, welche das Rechtsgefühl thematisierte[15]. Ein Ziel der Wissenschaftsgeschichte ist es, hier die Unterschiede und Gemeinsamkeiten von Naturrecht und einer das Recht beeinflussenden Naturwissenschaft, wie sie im 19. Jahrhundert deutlicher hervortrat, herauszuarbeiten. Damit wären auch allgemeine Reflexionen über die Relevanz von Vorstellungen „menschlicher Natur" im Rechtssystem möglich, die Verbindungen zu aktuellen Debatten ermöglicht/en.

---

kreten Ordnungsdenkens wurden so als idealistische, an sozialen Wertvorstellungen orientierte Gegenentwürfe zu einer biologisch-rassisch definierten Volksgemeinschaft darstellbar, welche wiederum als entartete Form eines „juristischen Naturalismus" historisierbar wurde.

13 Ein eindringliches Beispiel für diese personalisierte Auffassung von Rechtsgefühl stammt von *Julius von Kirchmann*. Die Wertlosigkeit der Jurisprudenz als Wissenschaft. Ein Vortrag gehalten in der Juristischen Gesellschaft zu Berlin 1848. Neudruck Darmstadt 1966, S. 18: „Setzt man die Vergleichung fort, so zeigt sich eine neue Eigentümlichkeit des Gegenstandes der Jurisprudenz darin, dass alles Recht nicht bloß im Wissen, sondern auch im Fühlen ist, dass ihr Gegenstand nicht bloß im Kopfe, sondern auch in der Brust des Menschen seinen Sitz hat. Ob das Licht eine Wellenbewegung des Äthers oder die geradlinige Bewegung feiner Körperchen ist; ob die Vernunft und Verstand eins, oder unterschieden sind; ob die algebraischen Gleichungen vierten Grades direkt aufgelöst werden können oder nicht; das alles sind Fragen, aber das Gefühl hat dabei nirgends im voraus entschieden".

14 Vgl. *Giorgio Del Vecchio*. Die Gerechtigkeit. 2. Aufl. Basel 1950, S. 97 ff.

15 Dazu unten IV.

Ein anderes Thema ist die Geschichte der Praxis und der Reflexionen über die Rechtsanwendung. Noch heute nehmen Rechtsanwender für sich zuweilen in Anspruch, über ein „Judiz" zu verfügen, also die durch Fachkunde geschulte Fähigkeit zum eigenen rechtlichen Urteil ohne vorherige methodisch-systematische Normerkundung. Das „Judiz" verweist auf eine Art informellen Wissensbestand der Praxis. Als solcher ist es bislang unerforscht. Auf die Spur kommt man ihm mit soziologischen Methoden, da keine Texte darüber zu finden sind.

Für die Rechtsgeschichte spielte die gefühlsmäßige Rechtsfindung ebenfalls eine große Rolle. Den Schöffen des Mittelalters wurde bescheinigt, sie entschieden *„wenn auch nicht nach Willkür, so doch nach dem Rechtsgefühl oder Rechtsbewusstsein, welches in ihnen, welche einen besonderen Beruf aus der Anwendung des Rechts machten, lebhafter als in den übrigen Mitgliedern des Volkes existierte"* heißt es bei Otto Stobbe[16]. Später stellte Oskar von Bülow – nicht unkritisch – die Schöffen als Urteiler dar, welche „unter der Leitung des im Volke pulsierenden, freilich oft von gegensätzlichen Strömungen durchwogten Rechtsgefühls"[17] standen und daher nicht gänzlich gegen Willkür und Parteilichkeit gefeit waren. Herauszufinden gilt es, ob die heutigen Verweise auf ein Judiz alte Vorstellungen notwendig irrationaler Restbestände bei der Entscheidungsfindung konservieren und was damit konkret legitimiert wird.

Insgesamt zeigt der Blick auf die Rechtsgeschichte, dass Rechtsgefühl individuell, aber auch kollektiv, theoretisch, praktisch, oder politisch formuliert sein kann. In jedem der Bereiche transportiert es eine spezifische Normativität und kann gleichzeitig Indikator für ein bestimmtes Verständnis juristischer Rationalität sein, die eventuell als Gegenbild zu einer gefühlsmäßigen Normativität Konturen gewinnt.

2. Anregungen seitens der historischen Emotionsforschung

Berücksichtigt man, dass sich Teile der rechtshistorischen Disziplin primär als normativ orientierte Geschichtswissenschaft mit prinzipiell historischen Erkenntnisinteressen ohne erstrangigen Fokus auf das geltende Recht betrachten, muss erstaunen, dass das Thema der emotionalen Erkenntnis in dieser Forschungsrichtung bislang nicht vorkam. Tatsächlich ist das Thema der historischen Emotionsforschung in der letzten Zeit ein

---

16 *Otto Stobbe.* Geschichte der deutschen Rechtsquelle. Bd. 1. Leipzig 1860, S. 277.
17 *Oskar von Bülow.* Gesetz und Richteramt. Leipzig 1885, S. 17.

Thema mit großer Konjunktur im Bereich der Geschichtswissenschaften[18]. Ausgehend von einer Kritik am mangelnden historischen Bewusstsein aktueller Kognitionswissenschaften kennzeichnet etwa Ute Frevert einen Ansatz historischer Emotionsforschung, der sich als Teil einer historischen Semantik versteht[19]. Im Mittelpunkt steht dabei eine Rekonstruktion der zeitgenössischen Reflexionen und Argumentationsmuster über Gefühle, wie sie etwa von 1700 bis in die Gegenwart hervorgebracht worden sind[20]. Dabei soll es um mehr gehen als eine Geschichte politisch-sozialer Sprache, wie sie etwa im begriffsgeschichtlichen Pionierwerk „Geschichtliche Grundbegriffe" in Angriff genommen wurde. Die hier gekennzeichnete Form der Emotionsgeschichte sieht sich als Wissenschaft zur Erforschung einer Sprache, die sich auf die Beschreibung menschlicher Potenziale bezieht und ihre Anregungen daher eher bei einer historischen Anthropologie sucht[21]. In dem gekennzeichneten sprachgeschichtlichen Projekt ließe sich auch die Rechtswissenschaft berücksichtigen, handelt es sich doch um eine Disziplin, welche eine Beschreibung menschlicher Potenziale verwendet, um daraus Normen für menschliches Verhalten zu gestalten. Juristische Sprache könnte also in historischer Perspektive eine Schnittmenge zwischen soziopolitischer Sprache und anthropologisch sensibler Terminologie bilden. Auch wenn sich emotionsgeschichtliche Ansätze für die Rechtswissenschaft und Rechtsgeschichte stets offen zeigen, kommt Jurisprudenz in ihnen meistens nur am Rande vor. Als Verknüpfung von Rechtgeschichte und Emotionsgeschichte wurde etwa die Thematisierung von Emotionen bei Zeugenvernehmung und Beweisführung anhand des Lügendetektors vorgeschlagen[22]. Hier soll ein Beispiel für die, insofern noch zu erforschende, juristische Berücksichtigung von Gefühlen liegen; weitere Anhaltspunkte wären Strafe, Zurechnung oder ‚Verbrechen aus Leidenschaft'[23]. Nicht klar wird hier jedoch, welchen Begriff von Emoti-

---

18 Aus interdisziplinärer Sicht: *Dagmar Ellerbrock/Sylvia Kesper-Biermann*. Between Passions and Senses? Perspectives on Law and Emotions. Inter disciplines 2 (2015); siehe auch *Jan Plamper*. The History of Emotions. An introduction. Oxford 2015. Nicht selten mit Verbindungen zu Literaturwissenschaft siehe etwa *Sigrid G. Köhler/Sabine Müller-Mall/Florian Schmidt/Sandra Schnädelbach (Hrsg.)*. Recht fühlen. Paderborn 2017; *Hilge Landweer/Dirk Koppelberg (Hrsg.)*. Recht und Emotion (2 Bde.). Freiburg 2016.

19 *Ute Frevert*. Emotional Lexicons. Continuity and Chance in the Vocabulary of Feeling 1700-2000. Oxford 2014, S. 1 ff.

20 *Frevert*. ebenda, S. 2.

21 *Frevert*. ebenda, S. 11.

22 *Jan Plamper*. The History of Emotions. An Introduction. Oxford 2015, S. 284.

23 *Plamper*. ebenda.

on die Rechtsgeschichte dann zugrunde zu legen hätte. Problematisch erscheint vor allem die Konzentration auf Situationen, welche aus der Außenperspektive als emotionale Begegnungen von Menschen mit dem Rechtssystem oder der Justiz erscheinen[24].

Vielversprechend erscheint hingegen jeglicher Hinweis der Emotionsgeschichte auf semantische Veränderungen und das Aufkommen neuer Sprachmuster bei der Beschreibung menschlicher Handlungspotenziale. Solche sind für die Normgestaltungen unmittelbar relevant. Im Bereich der Emotionsgeschichte wurde etwa darauf hingewiesen, dass neben der bereits bekannten Beschreibung des Empfindsamkeitskultes des 18. Jahrhunderts in der Mitte dieses Jahrhunderts, auch in der politischen und philosophischen Sprache eine Entdeckung der Innerlichkeit und der Empfindungen nachweisbar ist[25]. Solche Zusammenfassungen und Sondierungen terminologischer Veränderungen sind ein wichtiger Fundus für die Bedingungen juristischer Reflexion in jener Zeit. Juristen hatten die philosophischen Werke ihrer Zeitgenossen oftmals rezipiert. Neue Erkenntnisse über Bewertungen von Gefühlen im Vokabular einer bestimmten Zeit ermöglichen vielleicht neue Zugänge zu juristischen Werken. Die Erkenntnisse der Gefühlsgeschichte wären hier also Kontext und Folie für die neue Analyse juristischer Schriften aus vergangenen Jahrhunderten. Andererseits können sie aber auch selbst rechtshistorische Fragestellungen anregen. So ist etwa im Bereich der Emotionsgeschichte von einer eigenen „Sattelzeit" die Rede, welche im späten 19. Jahrhundert angesetzt wird. Gekennzeichnet sei sie durch die Hinwendung der Psychologie zu den Naturwissenschaften und dem damit verbundenen Aufstieg der Psychologie als Leitwissenschaft, der sich im darauffolgenden Jahrhundert vollzog[26]. Rechtswissenschaftliche Auswirkungen dieser Wende sind bereits in einem Sammelband von Mathias Schmoeckel eingehend analysiert worden[27]. Es gäbe zahlreiche Ansätze, auf dieser Ebene weiter zu forschen und über die

---

24 Deutlich wird das vor allem bei Beiträgen wie von *Sandra Schnädelbach*. The jurist as manager of emotions. German debates on Rechtsgefühl in the late 19th and early 20th century as sites of negotiating the juristic treatment of emotions, Inter disciplines 2 (2015), S. 47 ff. mit dem Ergebnis, dass „Rechtsgefühl" bürgerlich-männliche Wertvorstellungen transportieren sollte. Wo es sich auf die damals von Männern dominierte Rechtsanwendung bezog, ist das wenig erstaunlich. Die Relevanz einer solchen Erkenntnis hängt von Alternativen ab, die historisch zu ermitteln wären.

25 *Frevert*. Lexicons, S. 5, in Bezug auf Herder.

26 *Frevert*. Lexicons, S. 11.

27 *Mathias Schmoeckel (Hrsg.)*. Psychologie als Argument in der juristischen Literatur des Kaiserreichs. Baden-Baden 2009.

bloße Impulsfunktion der Psychologie als Wissenschaft hinaus detaillierter nach den Auswirkungen der Verwissenschaftlichung menschlicher Gefühle zu fragen, die sich im späten 19. Jahrhundert entscheidend verändert hatte.

Insgesamt fällt also auf, dass ein Blick auf die Emotionsgeschichte die Rechtsgeschichte für bestimmte kulturelle Gegebenheiten sensibilisieren kann, welche dann auf ihre Relevanz für die Rechtsentwicklung zu überprüfen wären. Reflexionen über den Umgang mit Emotionen könnten für die Rechtsgeschichte neue Zäsuren deutlich machen, die bei der Konzentration auf politische Umbrüche, Gesetzgebungsverfahren, Organisation der Justiz und sonstiger Institutionen, oder Herausbildung wissenschaftlicher Theorien nicht ohne weiteres offensichtlich werden. Zum Teil können sich beim Fokus auf das Thema „Emotionalität" Verbindungen ergeben, die schon auf anderer Ebene diskutiert worden sind, etwa zwischen Recht und Wissenschaft. Emotionsgeschichte suggeriert also offenbar neue Themen, vielleicht auch neue Periodisierungen. Für eine „Geschichte des Rechtsgefühls" gäbe es also einige Anregungen.

3. Rechtsgefühl, Intuitive Rechterkenntnis und Wissenschaftsgeschichte des Rechts

Weiterhin stellt sich die Frage, wo eine solche Geschichte des Rechtsgefühls methodisch zu verorten wäre. Es geht dabei zunächst um eine Geschichte der emotionalen Erkenntnismöglichkeiten von Recht und damit um eine Art von Rechtswissen. Im Mittelpunkt steht die Frage, wie dies in verschiedenen historischen Kontexten, vielleicht sogar „Epochen", beurteilt, beschrieben oder konstruiert wurde. Für Kirchmann etwa lag in der Existenz eines Rechtsgefühls der entscheidende Unterschied zwischen Jurisprudenz und der exakten Wissenschaften:

> „Setzt man die Vergleichung fort, so zeigt sich eine neue Eigentümlichkeit des Gegenstandes der Jurisprudenz darin, dass alles Recht nicht bloß im Wissen, sondern auch im Fühlen ist, dass ihr Gegenstand nicht bloß im Kopfe, sondern auch in der Brust des Menschen seinen Sitz hat. Ob das Licht eine Wellenbewegung des Äthers oder die geradlinige Bewegung feiner Körperchen ist; ob die Vernunft und Verstand eins, oder unterschieden sind; ob die algebraischen Gleichungen vierten Grades direkt aufgelöst werden können oder nicht; das

alles sind Fragen, aber das Gefühl hat dabei nirgends im Voraus entschieden."[28]

Wo das „Gefühl sich schon für eine Antwort entschieden" habe, „ehe noch die wissenschaftliche Untersuchung begonnen", sei die Wissenschaftlichkeit von Rechterkenntnis erschwert, denn „Gefühl" sei kein Wahrheitskriterium, sondern „Produkt der Erziehung, der Gewohnheit, des Zufalls"[29].

Wenn man der These Kirchmanns folgt, dass Recht von Wissenschaft streng zu unterscheiden ist, weil sie eine emotionale Komponente ausschließt, welche im Recht notwendig vorhanden ist, könnte man thematische, vielleicht auch methodische Konsequenzen für die Rechtsgeschichte begründen. Konsens dürfte sein, dass Rechtsgeschichte sich als Geschichte der Praxis oder Geschichte der Wissenschaft betätigen kann[30]. In den aktuellen Methodendebatten des Fachs, wie sie zuletzt von Peter Oestmann angestoßen wurden, hat die Kategorie „Wissenschaftsgeschichte" ihren festen Platz und eindeutigen Stellenwert neben Normengeschichte und Praxisgeschichte. Die nicht nur von Kirchmann und nicht erst seit Kirchmann vorgebrachten Zweifel an der Wissenschaftlichkeit des Rechts werden dabei nicht diskutiert. Aus Sicht rechtshistorischer Methodik ist darin auch zunächst kein Versäumnis zu sehen. Wenn mit „Wissenschaftsgeschichte" gemeint ist, dass man sich juristischer Literaturproduktion, Verbreitung von Normkenntnissen an Universitäten, den wissenssoziologischen Bedingungen der Herausbildung juristischer Denkschulen und Traditionen, dem Dialog, dem Austausch untereinander oder der fachspezifischen Sozialisation von Juristen zum Nachdenken über Recht widmet[31], impliziert der Begriff keine Stellungnahme zum Erkenntnischarakter der Jurisprudenz. Ihre notwendig normativ-wertende Vorgehensweise ist damit nicht geleugnet, ein zu Recht kritikwürdiger Anspruch empirisch zweifelsfrei nachweisbarer Normativität wird der „Rechtswissenschaft" damit nicht zugewiesen. Der Unterschied zu Kirchmann liegt darin, dass dieser einen

---

28 *Julius von Kirchmann*. Die Wertlosigkeit der Jurisprudenz als Wissenschaft. Ein Vortrag gehalten in der Juristischen Gesellschaft zu Berlin 1848. Neudruck Darmstadt 1966, S. 18.

29 *Kirchmann*. ebenda, S. 19.

30 Zuletzt *Peter Oestmann*. Normengeschichte, Wissenschaftsgeschichte und Praxisgeschichte. Drei Blickwinkel auf das Recht der Vergangenheit (History of Legal Norms, Science and Practice. Three Perspectives on the Law of the Past) (October 31, 2014). Rechtsgeschichte – Legal History 23/2015; Max Planck Institute for European Legal History Research Paper Series No. 2014-06. SSRN: http://ssrn.com/abstract=2526811.

31 Dazu auch *Oestmann*. a.a.O., S. 4 f.

umfassenden, nicht zuletzt von der Naturwissenschaft als Leitdisziplin geprägten Wissenschaftsbegriff zugrunde legt und die Eigenschaften der Jurisprudenz damit vergleichend reflektiert, während die Methodik der Rechtsgeschichte ihren Wissenschaftsbegriff pragmatisch aus der Binnenperspektive heraus bestimmt. Die gewohnten Bemühungen um Wissenschaftsgeschichte des Rechts können also mit dieser Überlegung nicht in Frage gestellt werden.

Wenn Wissenschaftsgeschichte für die Rechtsgeschichte ein Orientierungsbegriff zur Beschreibung eines bestimmten Erkenntnisvorgangs ist, könnte man angesichts Kirchmanns These jedoch die Frage stellen, ob dieser nicht zu eng ist, wenn er nur die innerhalb professioneller Strukturen erfolgte Normproduktion ins Auge fasst. Ein Vorwurf könnte lauten, dass man bei Konzentration auf Recht von Juristen (seien es Gesetzgeber, Richter oder Gelehrte) Gefahr laufen könnte, das emotional erkennbare Recht[32] zu vernachlässigen oder zu übersehen, weil „Wissenschaftsgeschichte" Recht in seiner Darstellung auf die Analyse von Fachdiskursen beschränkt.

Dieser Anspruch einer Neubestimmung und Erweiterung des Fokus stimmt in seiner Zielrichtung zum Teil mit einer in der Geschichte zu beobachtenden Tendenz zur Ersetzung des Begriffs „Wissenschaftsgesichte" durch „Wissensgeschichte" überein. Hier handelt es sich um eine noch sehr heterogene Forschungsrichtung, bei der von unterschiedlichen Motiven getragene Ansätze zusammenkommen[33]. Theoretisch neutraler kann sich „Wissensgeschichte" auf die historische Beschreibung von durchaus europäisch geprägten Wissensspeichern wie Archiven beziehen[34]. Artikuliert wurde so etwa der Anspruch, sich einem „prekären", weil durch soziale Stigmata ausgegrenzten, vielleicht gar tabuisiertem Wissen der frühen Neuzeit widmen zu müssen[35]. Für Gebiete wie Magie und Rituale – denen übrigens bereits seit längerem unter dem Aspekt der Kulturgeschichte erhöhte Aufmerksamkeit zuteilwird[36] – mag das interessante neue Perspek-

---

32 Die Abgrenzung zu Recht, das von juristischen Laien, etwa vor der Professionalisierung des Juristenstandes im Mittelalter, erkannt und ausgesprochen wurde, sei hier dahingestellt.

33 Überblick bei *Achim Landwehr*. Wissensgeschichte. In: Handbuch Wissenssoziologie und Wissensforschung. Hg. von Rainer Schützeichel. Konstanz 2007, S. 801-813.

34 *Markus Friedrich*. Die Geburt des Archivs. Eine Wissensgeschichte. München 2013.

35 *Martin Mulsow*. Prekäres Wissen. Eine andere Ideengeschichte der Frühen Neuzeit. Berlin 2012.

36 Dazu auch *Renn*. History of Science, S. 38.

tiven eröffnen. Aus Sicht einer historischen Emotionsforschung des Rechts als Parallele zu fordern, man müsse das von den Fachleuten formalistisch verdrängte Gefühl als prekäres Rechtswissen historisch neu entdecken, wäre freilich in dieser Form zu undifferenziert und klischeehaft. Die Tendenz zur Entdeckung von „Nischen-Wissen"[37] umfasst freilich auch „Knowhow", also praktisches Wissen. Davon sind historisch neue Vorstellungen entstanden. „Von Postulaten zu Praktiken" lautet das Motto zahlreicher unterschiedlicher Forschungsansätze zur Geschichte der frühen Neuzeit[38]. Praktik wird dabei verstanden als „typisiertes, routiniertes und sozial verstehbares Bündel von Aktivitäten"[39]. Statt Geschichte einer Person oder eines Geistes wird die Frage relevant, „was Leute tun"[40]. Alltagsphänomene erhalten so ein eigenständiges historisches Gewicht und werden nicht nur als bloße Konsequenzen oder praktische Auswirkungen von etwas Höherem wie Normen oder Idealen erfahrbar[41]. Das wiederum eröffnet den Blick auf neue Kategorien eines „Alltagwissens" und führte überhaupt zu einer Reflexion über Formen des Wissens in der frühen Neuzeit. Berührungspunkte zwischen einer möglichen „Wissensgeschichte des Rechts" scheinen hier nicht ausgeschlossen zu sein. So könnte man etwa fragen, ob „Rechtsgefühl" als Alltagswissen von Normen über menschliches Zusammenleben in diesem Forschungsansatz zu verorten wäre, womit man dann eine Rationalitätsfixierung[42] der Rechtswissenschaft überwinden könnte. Auf der anderen Seite wären die neuen Wissenskonzepte mit rechtshistorischen Überlegungen zu Gewohnheitsrecht oder Rechtsgewohnheit in Dialog zu bringen.

Konkret stellt sich hier jedoch die Frage, ob man durch Einbeziehung der intuitiven, gefühlsbasierten, vielleicht gar irrationalen Erkenntnismög-

---

37 *Mulsow*. Prekäres Wissen, S. 20 ff.
38 Dazu aktuell der Sammelband *Arndt Brendecke (Hrsg.)*. Praktiken der frühen Neuzeit. Akteure – Handlungen – Artefakte. Köln, Weimar, Wien 2015. Zu einer Anwendung des Konzepts der Praktiken in der Rechtsgeschichte siehe *Thorsten Keiser*. Prozesse vor dem Reichskammergericht als Praktiken der frühen Neuzeit = Schriften der Gesellschaft für Reichskammergerichtsforschung, 48. Wetzlar 2020.
39 *Brendecke*. ebenda, S. 15.
40 *Brendecke*. ebenda, S. 16.
41 *Brendecke*. ebenda, S. 18, wonach der Alltag ist nicht mehr nur Prüfungsgegenstand im „Lichtkegel von Idealen und Normen" sei.
42 Zu Rationalität und Wissensgeschichte auch *Renn*. History of Science, S. 39, dort zu einem „dilemma of rationality", welches Wissenschaftsgeschichte begrenze.

lichkeiten des Rechts über die Wissenschaftsgeschichte hinaus[43] zu einer neuen Wissensgeschichte gelangen kann, welche zumindest manche der oben geschilderten Perspektiven im Sinne einer methodischen Neuorientierung fruchtbar umsetzen kann.

4. Quellen des Rechtsgefühls?

Auch wenn es anregend wäre, über neue Ansätze einer Wissensgeschichte des Rechts nachzudenken, ist einer solchen Überlegung auf methodischer Ebene mit Skepsis zu begegnen. Das hängt im Wesentlichen mit den Erkenntnismöglichkeiten der Rechtsgeschichte zusammen. Vergangenes Recht begegnet uns zumindest in der Regel als sprachliche Überlieferung, also in geronnener Form innerhalb eines grammatisch-logischen Systems[44]. Sichtbar werden in dieser Gestalt Rechtssätze, Regeln oder Urteile, aber kaum „Empfindungen". In den meisten Fällen liegen solchen Rechtsäußerungen Gefühlsregungen zugrunde. Rückschlüsse darauf sind aber nur indirekt möglich, so dass es hier keine analytisch verwertbaren Quellen gibt. Was Geiger 1947 aus Sicht einer das juristische Argumentationsreservoir seiner Zeit kritisch durchleuchtenden Rechtssoziologie konstatierte, trifft auf die Rechtsgeschichte heute noch genauso zu. Sie hat einzugestehen, dass ihre Quellen dieselben bleiben, auch wenn sich das Forschungsinteresse verschiebt.

Zweifel sind auch angebracht, ob sich die in manchen wissensgeschichtlichen Ansätzen mehr oder weniger zum Ausdruck kommende Forderung zur Überwindung der Fachdiskurse erfüllen lässt. Eine Konzentration auf Emotionalität im Recht bewirkt möglicherweise eine Hinwendung zu neuen Formen des Wissens, aber keine Abwendung des Fokus von den „Rechtsexperten"[45]. Im Gegenteil könnten diese gerade in den Mittelpunkt des Interesses treten, in ihrer Funktion als Entscheidungsträger, wobei

---

43 Davon abgesehen ist richtig, dass Wissenschaftsgeschichte des Rechts nie den Anspruch erhoben hat, das „materielle Recht" einer Epoche abzubilden. Darauf verweist aktuell *Oestmann*, S. 4.

44 Sofern man symbolische oder ritualhafte Formen von Normativität außer Acht lässt.

45 Als Beispiel für einen solchen wissensgeschichtlichen Anspruch im Bereich der Geschichte der Ökonomie: *Daniel Speich Chassé*. Die Erfindung des Bruttosozialprodukts. Globale Ungleichheit in der Wissensgeschichte der Ökonomie. Göttingen 2013, S. 12 ff., wobei es hier nicht zuletzt um eine politische Kontextualisierung der Wirtschaftsgeschichte geht, die gegen eine unpolitische Dogmengeschichte in Stellung gebracht wird.

die emotionale Motivation ihrer Entscheidungen die eigentlich relevante Aktivierung eines Rechtsgefühls ausmacht. Die aktuelle Law and Neuro-science-Bewegung[46] sieht etwa hierin eine, wenn nicht die entscheidende Rechtfertigung ihrer Ansätze, von denen man sich ein um hirnorganische Kenntnisse erweitertes Verständnis der Rechtsprechung erhofft[47].

„Empfindungen" können freilich ebenfalls wie „Expertenwissen" kulturell kodiert und in einen hierarchischen Zusammenhang gebracht werden. Abgesehen von der Frage, ob eine ohne normatives Vorverständnis und normative Prägung erfolgende Gefühlsbildung überhaupt vorstellbar ist[48], dürfte Gefühlswissen von Juristen ebenso hierarchisierbar sein und damit als Herrschaftswissen taugen[49], wenn nämlich Empfindungen steuerbar sind und, gleichsam als „Fühlen-Müssen", gemeinsamen Mustern folgen.

Auffindbar und rechtshistorisch von besonderem Interesse sind aber freilich sprachliche Zeugnisse juristischer Empfindungen. Wenn etwa Heinrich Hubmann 1954 „das Rechtsgefühl" zum „Mittler zwischen Rechtspraxis und Naturrecht" macht[50], sagt das zunächst weniger über das Rechtsgefühl selbst aus, sondern über seine Rolle im juristischen Diskurs der sogenannten „Naturrechtsrenaissance" der fünfziger Jahre. Ist der Forschungsgegenstand ein Gerichtsurteil aus der Vergangenheit, lässt sich nicht mehr rekonstruieren, was der Entscheidungsträger dabei empfunden haben mag. Heutige Ansätze, gerade aus den USA, welche dort von „Gefühl" reden, wo ungefilterte, impulsive, von erwarteten Mustern abweichende Handlungen auftreten und daraus auf die Abwesenheit einer Steuerung durch den Verstand schließen[51], sind zu unpräzise für historische Fragestellungen. Betrachtungsgegenstand können also nur solche Texte sein, die von einer intuitiven oder gefühlsmäßigen Erkenntnis-

---

46 Dazu unten III.
47 *Pardo/Patterson*. Minds, Brains and the Law, S. 53. Vgl. insgesamt auch: *Brian H. Bornstein/Richard Wiener (Hrsg.)*. Emotions and the Law. Psychological Perspectives. New York 2011.
48 Dazu *Jhering*. Entstehung des Rechtsgefühls, S. 32 ff.
49 Wenn man dieses definiert als „sämtliche Informationen, die innerhalb eines bestimmten gesellschaftlichen Handlungszusammenhangs dazu geeignet sind, herrschaftliche Ansprüche zu legitimieren, durchzusetzen und zu tradieren". *Thomas Hildebrand*. Herrschaft, Schrift und Gedächtnis. Das Kloster Allerheiligen und sein Umgang mit Wissen in Wirtschaft. Recht und Archiv (11.-16. Jahrhundert). Zürich 1996, zitiert nach *Achim Landwehr*. Wissensgeschichte. In: Handbuch Wissenssoziologie und Wissensforschung. Hg. von Rainer Schützeichel. Konstanz 2007, S. 801-813 (806).
50 *Heinrich Hubmann*. Naturrecht und Rechtsgefühl. In: AcP 153 (1954), S. 297-331.
51 *Susan A. Bandes*. The Passions of Law. New York and London 1999.

möglichkeit des Rechts berichten. Insofern muss der erste Schritt in der Auffindung von Texten bestehen, welche sich dem Rechtsgefühl widmen, oder seiner Kritik. Solche Aussagen erscheinen oft an wichtigen Stellen und haben eine große Tragweite. Sie sind aber regelmäßig Teil jenes Expertendiskurses, den die Wissensgeschichte gerade überwinden möchte. Das Besondere an einer Geschichte in diesem Sinne wäre aber gerade nicht, dass sie zu einem Verlassen des Expertendiskurses befähigen würde. Vielmehr sind die Stellen innerhalb des Expertendiskurses aufzufinden, welche eine Durchbrechung des Rechts zum Gefühl hin argumentativ untermauern.

Eine Zusammenschau solcher Texte und deren Analyse im kulturellen und politischen Kontext ihrer Zeit wäre ein lohnendes Unterfangen und ein neuer rechtshistorischer Forschungsansatz. Methodisch wäre eine solche „Geschichte des Rechtsgefühls" aber der Wissenschaftsgeschichte im hergebrachten Sinn zuzuordnen, eben als Geschichte der fachjuristischen Stellungnahmen, Analysen, Behauptungen zum emotionalen Recht und dessen Verortung im Zusammenhang mit anderen Rechtsquellen.

5. *Rechtsgefühle statt Rechtsgefühl – Pluralismus von Normen und Empfindungen*

Der soeben skizzierte Forschungsansatz bedarf allerdings einer Einschränkung. Möglicherweise ist es nicht ausreichend, „das Rechtsgefühl" zu untersuchen, sondern unterschiedliche Rechtsgefühle. Auf die Notwendigkeit einer differenzierenden Auffächerung des Konzepts hatte bereits 1923 Erwin Riezler verwiesen. Er beschrieb drei verschiedene Kategorien oder „Rechtsgefühle". Erstens das Gefühl für die richtige Falllösung als erlernbare juristische Fertigkeit, zweitens das Gefühl als Bedürfnis, das vorhandene gesetzte Recht auch zu verwirklichen und drittens das Gefühl, das den Menschen nach einem höheren Rechtsideal streben lässt[52]. Schon diese Dreiteilung lässt das Erkenntnispotenzial erahnen, das sich ergibt, wenn man unterschiedliche „Rechtsgefühle" als juristische Instrumente erfasst und untereinander vergleicht. Evident ist auch, dass sich Spannungen ergeben können, etwa zwischen Normdurchsetzungsdrang und dem Erfühlen einer Idee oder eines Ideals, das womöglich dem geltenden Recht gerade zuwiderläuft.

---

52 *Erwin Riezler.* Das Rechtsgefühl – Rechtspsychologische Betrachtungen. 1923. 3. Aufl. 1968.

In einer pluralen Dimension wird „Rechtsgefühl" auch bei Rudolf von Jhering erfasst. In seiner berühmten Schrift „Der Kampf ums Recht" beschreibt Jhering, wie eine „Reizung des Rechtsgefühls" den Einzelnen erst zur Ahndung der Rechtsverletzung antreibt und damit letztlich zum Kampf ums Recht[53]. Rechtsgefühl sei dabei ebenfalls viel mehr als bloß Trieb oder Affekt. Das Bemerkenswerte an Jherings Sichtweise ist, dass er dem Konzept des Rechtsgefühls eine soziale Dimension eröffnet. So ist das Rechtsgefühl verschiedener Stände unterscheidbar von dem Rechtsgefühl verschiedener Völker oder Individuen[54]. Hier lässt sich beobachten, wie der Begriff pluralistisch aufgefaltet wird. Rechtsgefühle können auch als kollektive Gefühle zu erfassen sein. Gerade Gustav Rümelin hat vor allem diese kollektive Seite theoretisch zu erfassen versucht, indem er Rechtsgefühl als eine Art Ordnungstrieb eines Volkes auffasste, das dem Ganzen als Triebfeder für neue Gesetze diente[55].

III. Exkurs: Rechtsgefühl aus Sicht von Hirnforschung und Psychologie

Betrachtet man die heutige Situation, scheint allerdings vor allem eine Vorstellung von Rechtsgefühl im Vordergrund zu stehen. Es ist weniger die Rede von den Konflikten verschiedener, individueller oder kollektiver Rechtsgefühle. ‚Das Rechtsgefühl' scheint derzeit, von dunklen-romantischen Verbrämungen vergangener Zeiten befreit, auf dem Boden naturwissenschaftlicher Tatsachen eine Renaissance zu erleben. Zu verdanken ist das den stark an Aufmerksamkeit gewinnenden Neurowissenschaften, welche zu einem gesteigerten Interesse der Rechtswissenschaft an affektiven Elementen führen, insbesondere auf dem Gebiet juristischer Entscheidungsfindung. Die Frage, ob und wie man ‚Recht fühlen kann'[56] beschäftigt Juristen und enthält gleichermaßen ein interdisziplinäres Dialog-

---

53 *Jhering*. Kampf ums Recht. zitiert nach Auswahl seiner Schriften, herausgegeben von Fritz Buchwald, S. 212.
54 Ebenda.
55 *Gustav Rümelin*. Über das Rechtsgefühl. In: ders. Reden und Aufsätze. Tübingen 1875, S. 62-87 (S. 84 ff).
56 Zuletzt etwa *Julia Hänni*. Gefühle als Basis juristischer Richtigkeitsentscheidungen. In: Thomas Hilgers u.a. (Hrsg.). Affekt und Urteil. Paderborn 2015, S. 133-142; *Sabine Müller-Mall*. Zwischen Fall und Urteil. Zur Verortung des Rechtsgefühls. ebenda, S. 117 ff.

angebot an Psychologie und Naturwissenschaften[57]. Forschungen in dieser Richtung stehen im Zusammenhang mit Versuchen zur naturwissenschaftlich neuronalen Lokalisierung von psychologischen oder kognitiven Phänomenen, welche andere Wissenschaften scheinbar gemäß ihrer eigenen Logik und Prämissen konstruiert haben. Über die naturwissenschaftliche Community hinaus bekannt wurde etwa die ursprüngliche Frage des Nobelpreisträgers Eric Kandel nach dem physischen Ort des freudschen Über-Ichs, welche umfangreiche Forschungen über Bewusstseinsphänomene anregte[58]. In den Bereich des naturwissenschaftlich Möglichen rückt damit auch die Frage nach der Erkennbarkeit eines für normative Wertungen zuständigen Hirnareals, oder allgemeiner, eines biologisch erkennbaren Gerechtigkeitssinns[59]. "Sense of justice", Rechtsgefühl oder Gerechtigkeitsempfinden wurden zum Gegenstand experimenteller Beweisführung[60]. Wird Rechtsgefühl zum naturwissenschaftlich belegbaren Faktum, verlieren Vorbehalte, wie Geiger sie äußerte, scheinbar an Plausibilität. Das ursprünglich Geheimnisvolle, nur mit Worten Fassbare, gerinnt zum Farbschema in den bildgebenden Verfahren der Hirnforschung. Damit erhält es eine eigene Logik, Plastizität und Überzeugungskraft, welche scheinbar einen direkten Zugang zum Gefühl eröffnet, welches zuvor nur indirekt aus Aussagen oder Handlungen rekonstruiert werden konnte. Die Sprache des 19. Jahrhunderts, kritikwürdige und anachronistische Begriffe wie Volk, Geist oder Bewusstsein, scheinen überwunden und ein neuer, unmittelbarer Zugang zu Tiefenebenen normativer Erkenntnis gefunden zu sein. Gleichzeitig lässt sich mit den bildgebenden Verfahren der Neurowissenschaften ein neues Spannungsverhältnis zwischen Sprache und Bild beobachten.

Auf visuell-physiologische Beschreibung normativer Empfindungen bezogene Verfahren haben in der Rechtswissenschaft Interesse, aber auch

---

57 Teilweise finden sich auch Schnittmengen mit ästhetischen Theorien oder der Kunstwissenschaft. Hier liegt der thematische Schwerpunkt von *Thomas Hilgers u.a.* (Hrsg.), Affekt und Urteil, Paderborn 2015.

58 *Eric Kandel*. Auf der Suche nach dem Gedächtnis: Die Entstehung einer neuen Wissenschaft des Geistes. München 2007.

59 Siehe dazu die Beiträge in *Roger D. Masters/Margaret Gruter (Hrsg.)*. The Sense of Justice. Biological Foundations of Law. Newbury Park 1992.

60 *Michael S. Pardo, Dennis Patterson*. Minds, Brains and the Law. The Conceptual foundation of Law and Neuroscience. Oxford 2013, S. 50 ff., siehe dort die Diskussion eines Aufsatzes über die hirnphysiologische Verortung von "legal reasoning" von *Oliver R. Goodenough*. Mapping Cortical Areas Associated with Legal Reasoning und Moral Intuition. In: Jurimetrics 41 (2001), S. 429-442.

scharfe Kritik hervorgerufen[61]. Problematisch erscheint bereits der Ausgangspunkt einer solchen Forschung, nämlich die Unterscheidung zwischen „rule based application of law" und „justice based application of law". Von beiden Bereichen wurde behauptet, dass sie in verschiedenen Arealen unterschiedliche Hirnfunktionen aktivieren, wenn Probanden Fragen aus der einen oder anderen Kategorie gestellt werden[62]. Wenn solche Erkenntnisse tatsächlich naturwissenschaftlich korrekt sind (was von Juristen freilich nicht überprüft werden kann), hätte man nicht weniger als ein Erkenntnisinstrument für den physiologischen Nachweis eines Rechtsgefühls. Es gäbe dann einen Sektor im Gehirn, welcher ein Gerechtigkeitsempfinden aktivieren könnte, das unabhängig von den Induktionen bereits vorhandener positiver Normen zu eigenen Ergebnissen kommen könnte. Die aus juristischer Sicht berechtigte Frage, ob und wie man zwischen ‚regelgeleiteter' und ‚gerechtigkeitsgeleiteter' Rechtserkenntnis unterscheiden kann, wäre von dem überwältigenden naturwissenschaftlichen Argument der Existenz solcher Instanzen im Gehirn scheinbar mühelos überwunden. Ein Rechtsgefühl wäre naturwissenschaftlich bewiesen und die Rechtswissenschaft hätte ihre Konsequenzen daraus zu ziehen – oder auch nicht. Denn bei jeder Bezugnahme von human- oder naturwissenschaftlichen Erkenntnissen auf die Jurisprudenz stellt sich die Grundfrage, inwiefern sie diese außerjuristischen Wahrheitsannahmen überhaupt in ihr eigenes Wertungssystem einbeziehen will. Eine Normativitätswissenschaft mit eigenen Legitimationsmustern stellt ihre Konzepte, Dogmen und Systeme in der Regel aufgrund immanenter Kritik infrage, aber nicht aufgrund von Erkenntnissen außerhalb des Rechtssystems. Diese werden meist nur in das System integriert, wenn sie bereits vorhandene juristische Argumentationsformen stützen können. Prinzipielle Abschottung und lediglich funktionale Öffnung prägt schon seit Jahrhunderten das Verhältnis der Rechtswissenschaften zur Naturwissenschaft. So konnte um 1900 die zivilrechtliche Willenslehre durch die Erkenntnisse der zeitgenössischen Psychologie genauso wenig erschüttert werden[63] wie einhundert Jahre später durch die Erkenntnisse der Hirnforschung. Gerechtigkeit und Wertung als Maßstäbe der Jurisprudenz sind von naturwissenschaftlicher Erkenntnis und empirischer Wahrheit prinzipiell zu trennen.

---

61 Differenziert und kritisch etwa *Pardo/Patterson*. Minds, Brains and the Law, S. 51 ff.
62 *Pardo/Patterson*. Minds, Brains and the Law, S. 50.
63 Mit signifikanten Beispielen *Hans-Peter Haferkamp*. Psychologismus bei Ernst Zitelmann. In: Mathias Schmoeckel (Hrsg.). Psychologie als Argument in der juristischen Literatur des Kaiserreichs. Baden-Baden 2009, S. 215-223 (223).

Dennoch ist das Thema des nicht von gesetzlicher Normativität gesteuerten Rechtsgefühls auf verschiedenen Ebenen relevant. Neben der Hirnforschung wird es auch von der Rechtspsychologie thematisiert[64]. Auffällig ist dabei eine gewisse Dominanz von strafrechtlichen Fragen wie Zurechnung oder von prozessualen Problemen, welchen die Aussagepsychologie sich schon seit etwa einem Jahrhundert der emotionalen Komponente des Strafverfahrens bei der Beweiserhebung gewidmet hatte. Die Rechtsgeschichte ist in diesen Diskursen bislang wenig vertreten. Autoren, die sich mit der Existenz eines Rechtsgefühls beschäftigen, verzichten meistens auf die Geschichte als Erfahrungskategorie und widmen sich eher soziologisch den aktuellen Problemen richterlicher Entscheidungsfindung, wobei die Ideengeschichte ‚des Rechtsgefühls' zwar vorkommt, aber eher als Kontext aktueller Fragen[65]. Rechtshistorisch bemerkenswert ist vor allem ein Sammelband über das Verhältnis von Psychologie und Rechtswissenschaft in der zweiten Hälfte des 19. Jahrhunderts[66]. Er enthält wertvolle Informationen über die Rolle von Gefühl und Intuition für das Rechtssystem vor dem Hintergrund der in jener Zeit an Bedeutung gewinnenden wissenschaftlichen Erkundung des Unbewussten.

Auffällig ist aus Sicht der Rechtsgeschichte ebenfalls, dass einzelne Fragestellungen der Neurowissenschaften bekannte Assoziationen hervorrufen. Rudolf von Jhering als der in Deutschland wohl berühmteste Autor, der sich explizit dem Rechtsgefühl gewidmet hatte[67], stellte bekanntlich die Frage nach dessen Herkunft. Als Alternativen diskutierte Jhering die „historische" Rückbindung an erlerntes Verhalten und die „nativistische" Theorie des angeborenen Rechtsgefühls, wobei er ersterer klar den Vorzug gab[68]. Für die heutige Neurowissenschaft ist diese Frage ebenfalls von zentraler Bedeutung. In der Hirnforschung wird etwa von einem nonverbalen Algorithmus gesprochen, in welchem ein genetischer Fingerabdruck, aber

---

64 *Brian H. Bornstein/Richard Wiener (Hrsg.)*. Emotions and the Law. Psychological Perspectives. New York 2011; in Deutschland zeitweise viel beachtet: *Erwin Riezler*. Das Rechtsgefühl – Rechtspsychologische Betrachtungen. 3. Aufl. München 1969.

65 So etwa die Beiträge in: *Ernst-Joachim Lampe (Hrsg.)*. Das sogenannte Rechtsgefühl (=Jahrbuch für Rechtssoziologie und Rechtstheorie, Bd. 10). Opladen 1985.

66 *Schmoeckel*. 2009.

67 Dazu *Klaus Luig*. Zur Bedeutung der Psychologie in Jherings Lehre vom Rechtsgefühl. In: Mathias Schmoeckel (Hrsg.). Psychologie als Argument in der juristischen Literatur des Kaiserreichs. Baden-Baden 2009, S. 209 ff.

68 *Rudolph von Jhering*. Über die Entstehung des Rechtsgefühls. Vortrag von 1884. In: Walter Barfuß (Hrsg.). 125 Jahre Wiener Juristische Gesellschaft. Wien 1992, S. 31-47 (32 ff.).

auch kulturelles Erbe und persönliche Erfahrung prägend für ein bestimmtes Programm seien, welches dann zur emotionalen Rechtserkenntnis befähige[69]. „Nativistische" Ansätze können heute durch die moderne Genetik gestützt werden. Daneben kann die „historische" Einstufung des Rechtsgefühls auf entwicklungspsychologische Erkenntnisse verweisen, welche ein Lernverhalten bezüglich normativer Vorgaben, der Wirkung von Sanktionen oder Ähnliches zu analysieren vermögen. Die historischen Verbindungen zu Autoren wie Jhering, der ohne die empirischen Erkenntnismöglichkeiten der Gegenwart auf einer ähnlichen Basis argumentierte, fehlen.

IV. Wende zum „Rechtsgefühl" seit dem 18. Jahrhundert?

Wenn man als Zwischenergebnis festhalten kann, dass eine historische Erforschung „des Rechtsgefühls" – unabhängig davon, wie man den Begriff definieren und von anderen Kategorien wie „Rechtsbewusstsein" etc. abgrenzen will – der Rechtsgeschichte zwar neue Forschungsperspektiven eröffnet, dabei aber einen Rückgriff auf hermeneutische Instrumente der den kulturellen Kontext der Rechtsprobleme berücksichtigenden Wissenschaftsgeschichte erfordert, muss man auf der sprachlichen Eben ansetzen. Eine historische Frage kann etwa lauten, ob und ab wann in juristischen Texten eine Möglichkeit zur emotionalen Rechtserkenntnis war, welche juristischen Implikationen damit verbunden sind und warum in einer bestimmten Zeit solche Konzepte auf eine bestimmte Art in der Rechtsterminologie verwendet wurde[70]. Die Emotionsgeschichte kann hier einige Orientierungen geben, indem sie Kontexte der juristischen Diskurse aufzeigt.

---

69 *Pardo/Patterson.* Minds, Brains and the Law. S. 50, m.w.N.

70 Ein aktueller eher von Historikern ausgehender Ansatz fragt dagegen weniger nach systemimmanenten Bedeutungen von „Rechtsgefühl", sondern vielmehr nach der Bedeutung des Rechts als „institution", welche in historischen Situationen „emotional scripts" hervorbringe. Recht ist in dieser analytischen Perspektive eher Faktor emotionaler oder affektiver Handlungsmuster. Zum Forschungsgegenstand werden dann z.B. menschliche Verhaltensweisen, welche mit normativen Mustern in Verbindung stehen, etwa wenn es um emotionale Reaktionen von Beteiligten in Prozessen geht. Im Gegensatz zu Rechtsgefühl stehen hier von rechtlichen Faktoren oder im Zusammenhang mit Prozessen entstehende Gefühle im Mittelpunkt. Siehe dazu den Bericht über die Berliner Konferenz „Criminal Law and Emotions in European Legal Cultures: From the 16th Century to the present". In: https://www.h-net.org/reviews/showrev.php?id=44736. Von diesem historischen Forschungsinteresse ist das rechthistorische eindeutig zu unterscheiden.

Von Interesse sind hier insbesondere die sprach- und kulturgeschichtlichen Initiativen dieser Forschungsrichtung. So wurde etwa betont, dass „im Zeitalter der Aufklärung" eine Diskussion um Sinne, Gefühle und Gemütslagen eingesetzt hatte, deren Spuren in den Nachschlagewerken dieser Zeit deutlich sichtbar sind[71]. Dabei handelte es sich um ein Phänomen mit Ausprägungen in verschiedenen europäischen Ländern. „Sentimentalism" konnte zum Stichwort der Moralphilosophie werden, wobei vor allem die in Deutschland kritisch aufgenommene Gefühlsethik von Hume oder Hutcheson zu nennen ist[72]. Auch die Kunstgeschichte widmete sich in letzter Zeit dem Thema der „Gefühle" im 18. Jahrhundert, das im Rokoko besondere Ausprägungen gefunden hat. Hier kann man von einer künstlerischen Neuentdeckung von Leidenschaft und Gefühl sprechen, die dann in eine bestimmte Formensprache übersetzte standardisierte Ausdrucksformen einer gemessenen, leidenschaftsarmen Sentimentalität hervorbrachte, die später als epochenspezifisch beschrieben wurde[73]. Literarischer Sentimentalismus wird mit den Romanen Samuel Richardsons oder mit Rousseau assoziiert[74] und fand in Goethes Werther einen so individuellen Nachklang, dass der kurze Briefroman als Auseinandersetzung mit einem zeitgenössischen Genre gelesen werden kann.

Was hat die Rechtsgeschichte zu dieser Art von Epocheneinteilung beizutragen, die – wenn man eine sehr pauschale Einteilung zugrunde legt – etwa ab der Mitte des 18. Jahrhunderts grundlegende kulturelle Neuerscheinungen im Hinblick auf die Bedeutung menschlicher Gefühle in den Fokus rückt? Auf den ersten Blick scheint eine Veränderung des kulturellen Klimas im Hinblick auf „Gefühle" zumindest keine schnellen und unmittelbaren Spuren in der Jurisprudenz hinterlassen zu haben, zumindest nicht, wenn man den Naturrechtsdiskurs der damaligen Zeit beobachtet. Empfindungen, Affekte oder Triebe spielten für Theorien des Naturrechts nicht erst seit der Zeit des Rokoko oder der literarischen Empfindsamkeit eine Rolle, sondern bereits vor Beginn des 18. Jahrhunderts. Auch im Bereich der Erkenntnismöglichkeiten des Rechts, welche für die Frage nach „Rechtsgefühl" maßgeblich sind, findet man eher Stabilität

---

71 *Frever*. Emotional Lexicons, S. 12 ff.
72 Zu Inhalten und Rezeption *Günter Gawlick/Lothar Kreimendahl*. Hume in der Deutschen Aufklärung. Umrisse einer Rezeptionsgeschichte. Stuttgart 1987, S. 115-119.
73 Zuletzt etwa *Maraike Bückling (Hrsg.)*. Gefährliche Liebschaften. Die Kunst des französischen Rokoko. München 2015.
74 Zur Rezeption, auch sozialhistorisch *Frevert*. Emotional Lexicons, S. 14 ff.

und Kontinuität von Vorstellungen aus dem 17. Jahrhundert[75]. Eine pauschale Kategorie der gefühlsmäßigen Erkenntnis von Richtig und Falsch, Gut und Böse, Recht und Unrecht, ist kaum zu finden. „Affekte", Begierden und Leidenschaften sind etwa bei Pufendorf Gefahrenquellen, die es zu unterdrücken gilt, weil sie Schäden und Unfrieden verursachen können[76]. Ihr Wert zur Normerkenntnis liegt lediglich darin, dass der Mensch als defizitäres Wesen im Rahmen des Naturrechtsmodells konzipiert und dessen Regeln danach geformt werden müssen, als Ausgleich der durch Leidenschaft drohenden Gefahren. Eine individuell-kognitive Funktion, die dem Einzelnen bei der Normerkenntnis als eine Art emotionaler Kompass für Recht und Unrecht zugutekommen kann, ist mit dem Affekt nicht verbunden. Für Pufendorf ist Naturrecht dem Menschen „ins Herz geschrieben" und „angeboren" wie die Muttersprache[77]. Freilich spielt sinnliche Erkenntnis eine Rolle für Pufendorf, wenn es um die Moralität von Handlungen geht. Handlungswahrnehmung, auch auf sinnlicher Ebene, ist mit Voraussetzung für vernünftige Urteile[78].

Eine ähnliche Bewertung der Sinne als Erkenntnisinstrumente findet sich in Zedlers Universallexikon von 1743. Dort wird unter dem Lemma „Sinne" behauptet, dass „der Anfang" aller (!) menschlichen „Erkenntnis" die „Empfindung" sei[79]. Empfindung wird hier freilich nicht als „Gefühl" im psychologischen Sinne, sondern als konkreter sensorischer Eindruck (d.h. Hören, Sehen etc.) angesprochen. Als Voraussetzungen für das Nachdenken ebneten die Sinne somit den „Weg zu der judiciösen und gelehrten Erkenntnis der Wahrheit". Die juristische Funktionsbestimmung der Sinneseindrücke nach „natürlichem Recht" folgt jedoch einem klassischen Schema, wie man es im Naturrecht etwa bei Pufendorf findet: Wenn die Fähigkeit sinnlicher Wahrnehmung zur „Wahrheit" oder der „vernünftigen Einrichtung des Gemüthes" notwendig erscheint, gehört die Erhaltung der sinnlichen Wahrnehmungsmöglichkeiten zu den Pflichten des Menschen gegen sich selbst[80]. Sinnliche Empfindung schafft hier also die

---

75 Zur naturrechtlichen Erkenntnistheorie immer noch lesenswert *Walter Euchner*. Naturrecht und Politik bei John Locke. Frankfurt/M. 1969, S. 19 ff.

76 *Samuel von Pufendorf*. Über die Pflicht des Menschen und des Bürgers nach dem Gesetz der Natur (1673). Hg. von Klaus Luig. Frankfurt/M., 1994, S. 31 (§ 14), 46 (§ 4).

77 *Pufendorf*. ebenda, S. 49 f. (§ 12).

78 Ausführlich *Horst Denzer*. Moralphilosophie und Naturrecht bei Samuel Pufendorf. München 1972, 42-49.

79 *Zedler*. Universallexikon, Bd. 37. Art. „Sinne", Sp. 1691-1699 (1694). Hinweis auf das Zitat bei *Frevert*. Emotional Lexicons, S. 12.

80 Ebenda, Sp. 1696.

Basis für durch Vernunft oder andere Instanzen zu vermittelnden Wertungen, wird aber nicht Quelle von Wertungen an sich. Der Schritt zum Gefühl als Erkenntnisinstrument für Recht im Sinne eines psychologisch konnotierten „Rechtsgefühls", unmittelbarer Rechtsintuition, oder eines Judiz, wie man es aus dem 19. Jahrhundert kennt, ist hier nicht vollzogen. Aus Sicht der Rechtsgeschichte können die kulturellen Veränderungen des 18. Jahrhunderts in diesem Bereich also offenbar weniger deutlich als Zäsur wahrgenommen werden.

Terminologisch bemerkenswert in Bezug auf Rechtsgefühl und Emotion sind allerdings die Schriften Feuerbachs, die gegen Ende des 18. Jahrhunderts erschienen sind. Bei Feuerbach erhält die emotionale Erkenntnis von Rechten eine teilweise zentrale Bedeutung, wenn es um die naturrechtliche Begründung der Menschenrechte geht. Dieser Frage widmete sich Feuerbach in seinem Frühwerk, etwa in der Schrift „Über die einzig möglichen Beweisgründe gegen das Dasein und die Gültigkeit der natürlichen Rechte" von 1795. Zur Begründung der Existenz von Menschenrechten verweist der junge Feuerbach auf menschliche „Gefühle von Recht"[81]. Eingeführt wird das Konzept im Rahmen einer Reflexion über die Prägung des Menschen durch Staat und Erziehung. Diese führten zu „Vorurteilen", welche die „natürlichen Gefühle von Recht und Nicht-Recht" hemmen oder unterdrücken könnten[82]. Anders als in vorhergehenden naturrechtlichen Schriften, erscheint „Gefühl" (nicht „Sinn", „Wahrnehmung" oder „Empfindung") hier auf den ersten Blick als unmittelbarer Zugang zum Recht, nicht bloß als Eingangsvoraussetzung eines sich dann vollziehenden Erkenntnisprozesses, der seine Grundlagen in einer näher definierten Rationalitätsvorstellung hat. So schreibt Feuerbach: „In dem menschlichen Geist, sobald wir alle äußere zufällige Hindernisse seiner vollkommnen Wirksamkeit von ihm entfernen und ihn uns ohne alle künstlich hinzugekommenen Modifikationen denken, müssen sich die ursprünglichen Gefühle von Recht vollkommen rein ankündigen. – Denn die Gefühle an und für sich selbst irren nicht."[83] Dem Gefühl scheint hier also eine eigene normative Wahrheit zuzukommen. Interessant ist die Aussage Feuerbachs auch im Zusammenhang der neusten Erkenntnisse der historischen Emotionsforschung. Hier wird darauf hingewiesen, dass

---

81 *Paul Johann Anselm Feuerbach*. Über die einzig möglichen Beweisgründe gegen das Dasein und die Gültigkeit der natürlichen Rechte. Zitiert nach: Naturrecht und positives Recht, ausgewählte Texte von Paul Johann Anselm Feuerbach. Hg. von Gerhard Haney. Freiburg/Berlin 1993, S. 7-55.

82 *Feuerbach*. ebenda, S. 14.

83 *Feuerbach*. ebenda, S. 15.

„Gefühl" als selbständiger Begriff um 1775 erstmalig in einem deutschen Lexikon auftaucht und dann ab 1800 allmählich einen Bedeutungswandel erfährt, von der bloß mechanischen Wahrnehmung hin zur elementaren, das subjektive Bewusstsein des Menschen prägenden Instanz[84]. Dieser Schritt von der auf mechanische Kausalmodelle beschränkten Physiologie des 18. Jahrhunderts zur komplexen Psychologie des 19. Jahrhunderts, scheint sich bei Feuerbach schon anzudeuten. Der Mensch kann demnach auch vom Recht subjektive Empfindungen ausbilden, die dann der Modifikation durch Erziehung oder Konventionen unterliegen[85]. Feuerbach ist jedoch weit entfernt davon, eine populäre und triviale Differenzierung von Gefühl und Verstand vorzunehmen. Auch die durch Gefühl gewonnenen Erkenntnisse müssen einen logischen Filter durchlaufen und werden letztlich doch Teil eines rationalen Prozesses. In einer anderen frühen Schrift von 1796, in der Feuerbach seine Thesen zu den Menschenrechten und Naturrecht nochmals aufgreift und vertieft, kommt die Notwendigkeit einer harmonischen Verbindung von Gefühl und Vernunft deutlich zum Ausdruck. Dieses geschieht im Zuge einer philosophischen Erörterung[86] über den „gemeinen Menschenverstand" und dessen Bedeutung für die Möglichkeit „philosophierender Vernunft". Feuerbach merkt diesbezüglich an: „Die Gründe für die Realität der Urtheile des gemeinen Menschenverstandes, können aber nicht in den Gefühlen selbst gefunden werden; wir dürfen nicht sagen, unsere Gefühle haben Wahrheit darum, weil wir es fühlen; – denn dies ist es ja eben, was die Vernunft bezweifelt und in Anspruch nimmt."[87] In diesem philosophischen Prozess räsonierender Vernunft haben die Gefühle keinen unmittelbar-subjektiven juristischen Erkenntniswert. An anderer Stelle wird dieser dann auch in Bezug auf „Rechte" in Zweifel gezogen:

„Ich habe daher nicht allein das Bewusstseyn von Rechten schlechthin, sondern bin mir auch solcher Rechte bewusst, die aus einer andern

---

84 So die Beobachtung von *Frevert*. Emotional Lexicons, S. 19. Vgl. auch *Johannes F. Lehmann*. Geschichte der Gefühle. Wissensgeschichte, Begriffsgeschichte, Diskursgeschichte. In: Handbuch Literatur & Emotionen. Hg. von Martin von Koppenfels und Cornelia Zumbusch, Berlin 2016, S. 150 ff.

85 *Feuerbach*. Beweisgründe, S. 15.

86 Überhaupt ging es Feuerbach bei seiner zweiten Schrift primär um die philosophische Begründung natürlicher Rechte. Vgl. dazu *Wilhelm Gallas*. P.J.A. Feuerbachs „Kritik des natürlichen Rechts". Heidelberg 1964, S. 7.

87 *Paul Johann Anselm Feuerbach*. Kritik des natürlichen Rechts als einer Propädeutik zu einer Wissenschaft der natürlichen Rechte. Altona 1796 (Nachdruck Hildesheim 1963), S. 25.

Quelle als den Gesetzbüchern des Staats entsprungen sind. Das Daseyn dieser Rechte soll aber gerechtfertigt werden; ich kann bei den Aussprüchen des gemeinen Menschenverstandes und der Reflexion über die mir durch das Gefühl vorgelegten Rechte nicht stehen bleiben; und muß also der philosophierenden Vernunft die Frage vorlegen:
– 1) giebt es überhaupt Rechte? Täuscht mich nicht das Gefühl über das Vorhandenseyn nicht positiver und in so ferne natürlicher Rechte?
– 2) täusche ich mich nicht bei Bestimmung einzelner Rechte, ist das, was ich durch mein bloßes Gefühl geleitet für ein Recht halte, wirklich ein Recht? Oder mit anderen Worten: welches sind die natürlichen Rechte?"[88]

Gefühltes Recht bedarf also der verstandesmäßigen Überprüfung. Insofern stimmt Feuerbachs Ansatz mit dem anderer Naturrechtsautoren vor ihm überein. Dennoch fällt auf, dass das Gefühl mehr ist als bloß mechanische Sensorik. Die Option eines Bewusstseins außerpositiven Rechts ist zumindest vorhanden. Mit „Bewusstsein" von Recht außerhalb der Gesetzbücher verwendet Feuerbach schließlich auch einen Begriff, der wie ein Vorgriff auf das 19. Jahrhundert mit seinen vielfältigen Beschwörungen individuellen wie kollektiven Rechtsbewusstseins wirkt[89].

Zusammenfassend kann man sagen: Das 18. Jahrhundert ist in Bezug auf das Problem der Rechterkenntnis von einer komplexen Verhältnisbestimmung zwischen Sensorik, Emotion, Wissen und Vernunft geprägt. Die hier genannten Beispiele können nur einen sehr kleinen Eindruck der komplexen Probleme und Verhältnisbestimmungen in diesem Bereich geben. Es gibt jedoch gewisse Anzeichen für eine Entwicklung der „Empfindung" von der bloß sinnlichen Faktenwahrnehmung zu einer eigenen Instanz mit Relevanz für die Rechtserkenntnis.

V. Fazit und Ausblick: Politischer Sentimentalismus und Rechtsgefühle in der Gegenwart

Das Thema „Emotionalität im Recht" bietet für die Rechtsgeschichte noch einige vielversprechende Forschungsansätze. Schriften aus dem Bereich der Emotionsgeschichte könnten dazu anregen, sich einer Geschichte juristischer Argumente über Erkenntnismöglichkeiten des Rechts in historischer

---

88 *Feuerbach*. Kritik, S. 28.
89 Etwa bei *Friedrich Carl von Savigny*. Vom Beruf unserer Zeit für Gesetzgebung und Rechtswissenschaft. Heidelberg 1814, S. 9 oder S. 11.

Perspektive zu nähern. Anders als in der allgemeinen Emotionsgeschichte wird dabei aber eine Besonderheit des Rechts zutage treten: Für das Recht der Vergangenheit waren die Kategorien von Verstand, Vernunft und Gefühl oftmals keine Gegensätze[90], teilweise waren sie sogar unmittelbar aneinandergekoppelt und sollten produktive Verbindungen eingehen. Geschichte des Rechtsgefühls ist also auch Geschichte der Aussagen über die Möglichkeit rationalen Umgangs mit Empfindungen als Voraussetzung für gerechte Normen.

Auf der anderen Seite liefert die Rechtsgeschichte einer heutigen, auf die aktuelle Rechtsordnung gerichteten Analyse des Themas, notwendiges Orientierungswissen. In der historischen Perspektive zeigt sich, dass Rechtsgefühl individuell, aber auch kollektiv, theoretisch, praktisch oder politisch formuliert sein kann. In jedem der Bereiche transportiert es eine spezifische Normativität und kann gleichzeitig Indikator für ein bestimmtes Verständnis juristischer Rationalität sein.

Bei Betrachtung der gegenwärtigen Situation fällt auf, dass „Gefühle" im politischen Diskurs eine immer größere Rolle spielen. Sie sind nicht individuell und konkret, sondern abstrakt und allgemein formuliert. Anders als im 19. Jahrhundert spielt die Betrachtung und Sublimierung nationaler Empfindungen natürlich keine Rolle mehr[91], stattdessen treten heute gruppenspezifische Gefühle in den Vordergrund. Es geht dabei auch nicht um „Rechtsgefühle", etwa dem bei Feuerbach vorkommenden Sinn der Erforschung eines Rechtsbewusstseins. Vielmehr werden die heute politisch relevanten Empfindungen durchaus als Affekt angesehen und gerade als solcher in einer politischen Relevanz anerkannt, ja geradezu in ähnlicher Form sublimiert wie im 19. Jahrhundert das Nationalgefühl. In der heutigen Spielart eines politischen Sentimentalismus werden „Gruppen von Menschen zu Opfergemeinschaften erklärt"[92], denen in den verschiedensten Situationen verletzte Gefühle zugeschrieben werden. Verweise auf solche Kränkungen, die mit der Identität der Gruppen zu tun haben und oft von nicht gruppenzugehörigen Personen vorgebracht werden, die sich zu Anwälten der Beleidigten machen, führen regelmäßig zu durch das Internet als Kommunikationsmedium befeuerten Skandalisierungen. Diese sind wiederum Vorgaben für politische Forderungen, die als kollektive Rechte von Gruppen formuliert werden. Solche Rechtsbehauptungen wer-

---

90 Vgl. dazu: *Nancy E. Johnson.* Impassioned Jurisprudence. Law, Literature and Emotion 1760-1848. Lewisburg 2015.

91 Wie etwa bei *Gustav Rümelin.* Recht und Rechtsgefühl, S. 84 ff.

92 So die Formulierung aus feministischer Sicht von *Caroline Fourest.* Generation beleidigt. Von der Sprachpolizei zur Gedankenpolizei. Berlin 2020, S. 65.

den dann wieder als Freibriefe für in hohem Maße affektgesteuerte Diffamierungen genutzt. Wie in der Geschichte zeigt sich auch hier, dass der Zusammenhang von Recht und Gefühl immer eine politische Dimension hat.

Auf der anderen Seite gibt es einen philosophischen Ansatz, der bestimmte Gefühle als negativ zu konnotieren und als politische Gefahr zu stigmatisieren versucht. „Gerechtigkeit" sei nur mit „Liebe", nicht aber mit „Angst" oder „Abscheu" zu erreichen[93]. Wer wann auf welche Weise was und wen zu lieben hat, ist die normative Projektionsfläche der philosophischen Beobachterin. Hier versucht Rechtsphilosophie kontrollierend und wertend in die Welt der Gefühle einzudringen und damit ein Gebiet zu betreten, das der liberale Rechtsstaat mit guten Gründen als exklusiven Raum des Individuums normativ abgesichert hat. Der national gefärbte oder psychologisierende Gefühlskitsch der Rechtswissenschaft des 19. Jahrhunderts, die Mystifizierungen von Interessen über die Kategorie des Rechtsgefühls, aber auch die elitäre Behauptung von nicht erlern- und erklärbaren emotionalen Fähigkeiten zur Rechtsfindung, sollten genügend lehrreiche Beispiele zur kritischen Einordnung solcher Konzepte bieten. Ein Blick in die Rechtsgeschichte verhilft so vielleicht zu der heute besonders notwendigen Erkenntnis, dass Gefühle im Recht stets eine Rolle spielten, aber nur im sicheren Rahmen rechtsstaatlicher Rationalität Anerkennung verdienen.

---

93 *Martha Nussbaum*. Politische Emotionen. Berlin 2014, S. 471 ff.

Rechtsgefühl(e) und Menschenrechte.
Die Freiheit von Folter im langen 19. Jahrhundert

Sylvia Kesper-Biermann

Der Menschenrechtsgeschichte wurde jüngst bescheinigt, sie habe „a human rights scholarship without the humans" hervorgebracht[1]; statt Menschen würden Vertrags- und Rechtstexte sowie Strukturen im Vordergrund einer vor allem von Jurist:innen und Politikwissenschaftler:innen betriebenen Geschichtsschreibung stehen. Das führt der australische Historiker Roland Burke in seinem Forschungsüberblick von 2017 unter anderem darauf zurück, dass emotionshistorische Ansätze in der Menschenrechtshistoriographie zur zweiten Hälfte des 20. Jahrhunderts kaum berücksichtigt worden seien. Tatsächlich spielen Gefühle bislang vor allem in der Analyse zivilgesellschaftlicher Menschenrechtsorganisationen wie *Amnesty International* und deren Mobilisierungen in den 1970er und 1980er Jahren eine Rolle[2]. Je weiter das Untersuchungsobjekt jedoch zeitlich zurückliege, so Burke weiter, desto stärker werde die Emotionsgeschichte als notwendiger Bestandteil einer Geschichte der Menschenrechte verstanden und angewandt[3]. Dabei sind beispielhaft das Buch von Lynn Hunt über die ‚Erfindung' der Menschenrechte im 18. Jahrhundert[4] oder Studien zum Humanitarismus und zu humanitären Interventionen in den internationalen Beziehungen des 19. Jahrhunderts zu nennen[5].

Auch wenn also bereits ein Anfang gemacht ist, lohnt es sich, Menschenrechte und Emotionen vom späten 18. bis zum frühen 20. Jahrhundert erneut in den Blick zu nehmen – nicht zuletzt deshalb, weil das 19. Jahrhundert unlängst als „Zeitalter des Gefühls" bezeichnet worden

---

1 *Roland Burke.* Flat affect? Revisiting emotion in the historiography of human rights (S. 125). In: Journal of Human Rights (16). 2. 2017, S. 123-141. DOI: 10.1080/14754835.2015.1103168.
2 Ebenda, S. 131-136.
3 Ebenda, S. 126.
4 *Lynn Hunt.* Inventing Human Rights. A History. New York / London 2007.
5 z.B. *Fabian Klose.* "In the Cause of Humanity". Eine Geschichte der humanitären Intervention im langen 19. Jahrhundert. Göttingen 2019.

ist[6]. Ferner erscheint es weiterführend, statt wie bisher von Menschenrechten vornehmlich im Plural zu sprechen, einzelne der sehr unterschiedlichen unter diesem Oberbegriff zusammengefassten Individualrechte in den Blick zu nehmen und ihrer je eigenen Entwicklung nachzugehen. So können auch die damit verbundenen spezifischen Gefühle einbezogen werden. Bislang dominiert in diesem Kontext die Berücksichtigung von Empathie[7]; eine Differenzierung im Hinblick auf unterschiedliche Emotionen und deren Zusammenhang mit einzelnen Menschenrechten fehlt hingegen. Die vorgeschlagene Herangehensweise macht es darüber hinaus möglich, die Einbindung einzelner Individualrechte in die jeweiligen Rechtskulturen zu untersuchen.

Die folgenden Ausführungen gehen diesen Fragen anhand der Freiheit von Folter nach. Diese Schwerpunktsetzung bietet sich an, weil Folter nach wie vor als „eines der größten Verbrechen gegen Menschenrechte"[8] gilt. Dem Folterverbot wird also elementare und archetypische Bedeutung zugemessen, so dass es stellvertretend für die Menschenrechte insgesamt stehen kann[9]. Dementsprechend ist es mit starken Gefühlen verbunden[10]. Der Beitrag geht in vier Schritten vor. Zunächst geht es *erstens* um die Entstehung des Folterverbots und um einige systematische Bemerkungen über sein Verhältnis zu Menschenrechten und Menschenwürde. Der *zweite* Teil untersucht, welche Emotionen mit der Freiheit von Folter während des 19. Jahrhunderts verbunden waren. Im Einzelnen gehörten Empathie, Rechtsgefühl und Ekel dazu. *Drittens* stehen die Erscheinungsformen des Folterverbots in der deutschen Rechtskultur des 19. Jahrhunderts im Mittelpunkt. Das Fazit fasst *viertens* die Ergebnisse zusammen und gibt einen Ausblick über Deutschland hinaus.

---

6 *Richard Evans.* Das europäische Jahrhundert. Ein Kontinent im Umbruch 1815-1914. München 2018, S. 605.

7 z.B. *Frederik von Harbou.* Empathie als Element einer rekonstruktiven Theorie der Menschenrechte. Baden-Baden 2014.

8 *Holger Furtmayr/Bianca Schmolze/Mechthild Wenk-Ansohn.* Ärztliche Dokumentation der Folgen von Folter. Verpflichtung im Namen der Menschenrechte. In: Deutsches Ärzteblatt 111, 20, S. 882 f.

9 vgl. *John T. Parry.* Understanding Torture. Law, Violence, and Political Identity. Ann Arbor 2010, S. 82; *Markus Kotzur.* Folterverbot (S. 242). In: Arnd Pollmann/ Georg Lohmann (Hrsg.). Menschenrechte. Ein interdisziplinäres Handbuch. Stuttgart / Weimar, S. 242-244.

10 *Sylvia Kesper-Biermann.* Menschenwürde, Rechtsstaat und Emotionen. Der Foltervorwurf als (rechts)politische Herausforderung in Deutschland vom 18. bis 20. Jahrhundert. In: Jens Eisfeld/Martin Otto/Louis Pahlow/Michael Zwanzger (Hrsg.). Naturrecht und Staat in der Neuzeit. Tübingen 2013, S. 269-294.

1. Freiheit von Folter: Menschenwürde und Menschenrecht

„Folter ist verboten. Immer und überall. [...] Es gibt keine Abwägung mit anderen Menschenrechten oder staatlichen Interessen, keine Ausnahmen, keine Relativierung. Das Folterverbot gilt absolut und immer, weil Folter die Menschenwürde verletzt, also den Menschen in seinem Menschsein angreift", erklärt *Amnesty International* Deutschland auf seiner Internetseite[11]. Die Organisation verweist unter anderem auf die Allgemeine Erklärung der Menschenrechte von 1948, deren Artikel 5 lautet: „Niemand darf der Folter oder grausamer, unmenschlicher oder erniedrigender Behandlung oder Strafe unterworfen werden", sowie auf rechtlich bindende Normen wie die UN-Antifolterkonvention von 1984[12]. Eine solche Sichtweise, welche das Folterverbot vorrangig im Kontext international anerkannter und durch Rechtstexte abgesicherter Menschenrechte verortet, ist vergleichsweise jung. Sie etablierte sich erst seit den 1940er Jahren[13]. In den älteren, klassischen Grund- und Menschenrechtskatalogen des 18. und 19. Jahrhunderts findet sich die Freiheit von Folter als Abwehrrecht gegen den Staat hingegen nicht. Weder die französische Erklärung der Menschen- und Bürgerrechte von 1789 noch die Grundrechte des deutschen Volkes von 1848 beispielsweise erwähnen es.

Daraus lässt sich jedoch nicht schließen, das Folterverbot habe generell in Rechtstexten der Zeit keine Rolle gespielt. Im Gegenteil: In Deutschland wie in ganz Kontinentaleuropa erfolgte die formale Abschaffung der Folter zwischen der Mitte des 18. und dem ersten Drittel des 19. Jahrhunderts. Schweden (1734/1772) und Preußen (1740/1754) gehörten zu den ersten Territorien, welche diesen Schritt unternahmen, unter den letzten befanden sich Portugal (1826) und Baden (1831)[14]. Die Einzel- bzw. Nationalstaaten normierten das Folterverbot im Verlauf des 19. Jahrhunderts weiterhin meist im Rahmen der Strafgesetzgebung bzw. der

---

11 Amnesty International o.J: Hintergrundinformationen zu Folter, URL: https://www.amnesty.de/informieren/hintergrundinformationen-zu-folter [26.3.2021].

12 vgl. *Jan-Maximilian Zeller*. Folter vor dem Forum des Rechts. Frankfurt/M. u.a. 2014.

13 Die folgenden Ausführungen basieren auf *Sylvia Kesper-Biermann*. Menschenrechte sehen lernen. Medialisierungen der Folter im Europa des 19. Jahrhunderts (S. 101-106). In: Birgit Hofmann (Hrsg.). Menschenrecht als Nachricht. Medien, Öffentlichkeit und Moral seit dem 19. Jahrhundert. Frankfurt a.M. 2020, S. 99-131.

14 *Mathias Schmoeckel*. Humanität und Staatsraison. Die Abschaffung der Folter in Europa und die Entwicklung des gemeinen Strafprozeß- und Beweisrechts seit dem hohen Mittelalter. Köln/Weimar/Wien 2000, S. 50-74.

Regelung des Strafprozesses - und zwar ohne dezidierte Verbindungen zu den Menschenrechten herzustellen[15]. Im Deutschen Reich enthielten allerdings weder das Reichsstrafgesetzbuch von 1871 noch die Reichsstrafprozessordnung von 1877 ein explizites Folterverbot. Zu den Gründen dafür gehörte die Einführung des reformierten Strafprozesses sowie das lineare Fortschrittsdenken des 19. Jahrhunderts. Man ging davon aus, die Folter sei ohnehin nur noch von historischer Bedeutung und für die Zukunft endgültig überwunden[16]. Ihre Abschaffung stand dementsprechend bei deutschen (Kriminal-)Juristen seit der Jahrhundertmitte kaum noch auf der Tagesordnung, während das Thema in der zweiten Hälfte des 18. und im frühen 19. Jahrhundert Gegenstand eines umfangreichen, europaweiten Expertendiskurses von Juristen, Staatsbeamten und Philosophen gewesen war[17].

Besondere Verbreitung auch im deutschsprachigen Raum hatte in diesem Zusammenhang die Schrift *Über Verbrechen und Strafen* aus dem Jahr 1764 gefunden. Es handelte sich, wie schon der Titel deutlich macht, um ein „kriminalpolitisches Manifest"[18], in dem sich der Italiener Cesare Beccaria für ein Verbot der Folter als Maßnahme innerhalb umfassender Reformen der Strafjustiz aussprach. Wie Lynn Hunt zutreffend feststellt, betonte er selbst dabei nicht „the connection between his views on torture and nascent rights language"[19]. Seine Argumente für ein Ende der Folter richteten sich unter anderem auf Zweifel an deren Nützlichkeit und Zweckmäßigkeit und auf die allgemeine Sicherheit, nicht auf die Beachtung der Menschenrechte[20]. Insofern lässt sich der Schlussfolgerung Hunts, „by the 1780s, the abolition of torture and barbarous forms of corporal punishment had become essential articles in the new human rights doctrine"[21], auch über das Beispiel Beccaria hinaus für die gesamte Abschaffungsdiskussion, nicht folgen.

---

15 *Sylvia Kesper-Biermann.* Grausamkeit, Barbarei und Seelen-Tortur. Die symbolische Funktion der Folter in den Strafrechtsreformdebatten des 19. Jahrhunderts. In: Karsten Altenhain/Nicola Willenberg (Hrsg.). Die Geschichte der Folter seit ihrer Abschaffung. Göttingen 2011, S. 147-167.

16 *Kesper-Biermann.* 2013, S. 277.

17 *Schmoeckel.* 2000.

18 *Kai Ambos.* Cesare Beccaria und die Folter – Kritische Anmerkungen aus heutiger Sicht (S. 504). In: Zeitschrift für die gesamte Strafrechtswissenschaft. 122, 3, 2010, S. 504-520 (im Original hervorgehoben).

19 *Hunt.* 2007, S. 102.

20 *Ambos.* 2010, S. 511.

21 *Hunt.* 2007, S. 31.

Bereits an anderer Stelle ist darauf hingewiesen worden, dass die Geschichte der Menschenrechte nicht mit der Geschichte des Humanitarismus gleichgesetzt werden kann, sondern „eine klare methodische Unterscheidung zwischen einem Diskurs um die Gewährung von gleichen menschlichen Rechten einerseits und einem Diskurs um die Beendigung menschlichen Leids andererseits" erforderlich ist[22]. Das zeigt sich gerade im Hinblick auf das Folterverbot. Denn obwohl die Freiheit von Folter nicht als Menschenrecht eingefordert wurde, spielten bei ihrer Legitimation seit dem 18. Jahrhundert humanitäre Überlegungen eine wichtige Rolle. Folter wurde regelmäßig als Verletzung der Menschlichkeit bzw. der Menschenwürde, als grausam und unmenschlich bezeichnet; der Verzicht auf sie erfolgte „im Namen der Humanität"[23]. Johann Adam Bergk stellte in seiner Übersetzung von Beccarias Schrift fest: „Kein Mensch, er mag schuldig oder unschuldig sein, darf gemartert werden, weil er eine Person und Subjekt des Sittengesetzes, also heilig ist, und weil sein Körper als Bedingung der Wirksamkeit der moralischen Natur unverletzlich gehalten werden soll"[24]. Es wird deutlich, dass der Körper zunehmend als geschützter und unverletzbarer Bereich des Individuums angesehen wurde, auf den der Staat keinen Zugriff haben sollte[25]. Schmerz und Leiden wurden zudem generell nicht mehr als unausweichlich, sondern im Gegenteil als inakzeptabel angesehen[26] – allerdings im strafrechtlichen Kontext bis in die zweite Hälfte des 19. Jahrhunderts hinein vielfach nur dann, wenn es sich um exzessive oder so genannte ‚unnötige' Schmerzzufügung handelte. Darunter fiel auf jeden Fall die Folter; sie galt als „Inbegriff herzloser Grausamkeit"[27]. Ihre Abschaffung wurde im 19. Jahrhundert als wichtiger Schritt im Hinblick auf die Verwirklichung aufgeklärter, humanitärer Prinzipien interpretiert. „Vernunft und Menschlichkeit" hätten die Tortur „schon größtentheils im Laufe des vorigen Jahrh[underts, SKB] aus dem Gerichtsverfahren verbannt", hieß es beispielsweise in einem Konversati-

---

22 *Klose.* 2019, S. 78; vgl. *Samuel Moyn.* Substance, Scale and Salience. The Recent Historiography of Human Rights (S. 130 f.). In: Annu. Rev. Law Soc. Sci. 8, 2012, S. 123-140.

23 *Schmoeckel.* 2000, S. 572; vgl. *Harbou.* 2014, S. 322.

24 *Johann Adam Bergk.* Des Marchese Beccaria's Abhandlung über Verbrechen und Strafen. Von neuem aus dem Italienischen übersetzt, Bd. 1. Leipzig 1798, S. 135.

25 *Schmoeckel.* 2000. S. 516 f.

26 *Karen Halttunen.* Humanitarianism and the Pornography of Pain in Anglo-American Culture (S. 303 f.). In: The American Historical Review 100, 1995, S. 303-334.

27 *Franz Helbing.* Die Tortur. Geschichte der Folter im Kriminalverfahren aller Völker und Zeiten, Bd. 2, Ndr. d. Ausg. Gross-Lichterfelde-Ost 1910. Augsburg 1999, S. 256.

onslexikon aus dem Jahr 1838[28]. Um 1900 hatte sich dieser Zusammenhang als so selbstverständlich etabliert, dass der Schriftsteller Rudolf Quanter in seiner Abhandlung über *Die Folter in der deutschen Rechtspflege sonst und jetzt* mit ironischem Unterton bemerken konnte: „Dem modernen Menschen geht es wie dem Automaten: wirft man oben das Wort Folter hinein, dann fällt mit tötlicher [!] Sicherheit eine faustdicke Humanitätsphrase unten heraus"[29]. Vor diesem Hintergrund und angesichts der massiven Menschenrechtsverbrechen während des Zweiten Weltkriegs erschien dann 1948 die Aufnahme der Freiheit von Folter in die Allgemeine Erklärung der Menschenrechte, platziert unter den Abwehrrechten gegen den Staat, nur folgerichtig[30]. Die Phase vom ausgehenden 18. zum frühen 20. Jahrhundert wirkte demnach als notwendige Transformationsphase[31], in der von einem Verschwinden des Folterverbots, wie es für die Menschenrechte allgemein behauptet wurde[32], keine Rede sein kann. Den damit verbundenen Gefühlen kam dabei eine wesentliche Rolle zu.

2. Folterverbot und Emotionen: Empathie, Rechtsgefühl, Ekel

Wenn Juristen, aber auch Angehörige anderer Berufs- und Bevölkerungsgruppen im langen 19. Jahrhundert über die Folter bzw. das Folterverbot redeten, taten sie das fast durchweg in einer hoch emotionalen Sprache. Adjektive wie ,unmenschlich', ,grausam', ,barbarisch', ,schrecklich' sowie ,abscheulich' und ,ekelhaft' tauchten dabei regelmäßig auf[33]. Der Schriftsteller George Hiltl schilderte zum Beispiel in einem Artikel für die Familienzeitschrift *Gartenlaube* 1864 die „Anwendung der gebräuchlichsten Folter- und Strafwerkzeuge" der Vergangenheit anhand eines fiktiven Hexenprozesses aus dem 17. Jahrhundert. Er stellte fest: „Die in den Protokollen enthaltenen Vorschriften bezüglich der Abnahme der Bekenntnisse, so

---

28 Art. Folter. In: Brockhaus Bilder-Conversations-Lexikon, Bd. 2: Leipzig 1838, S. 68 f.

29 *Rudolf Quanter*. Die Folter in der deutschen Rechtspflege sonst und jetzt. Ein Beitrag zur Geschichte des deutschen Strafrechts. Dresden 1900 (ND, Aalen 1970), S. 1 f.

30 *Johannes Morsink*. World War Two and the Universal Declaration (S. 369 f.). In: Human Rights Quarterly 15, 1993, S. 357-405.

31 *Kesper-Biermann*. 2020 S. 106.

32 *Stefan-Ludwig Hoffmann*. Einführung. Zur Genealogie der Menschenrechte (S. 14). In: ders. (Hrsg.). Moralpolitik. Zur Geschichte der Menschenrechte im 20. Jahrhundert. Göttingen 2010, S. 7-37.

33 *Kesper-Biermann*. 2020. S. 107.

wie diese selbst, sind fast stets dieselben. Sie sind so haarsträubender Art, so fürchterlichen Inhaltes, daß Mitleid, Schauer über die schreckenerregende Verfinsterung der Geister und Unwillen über die Willkür der geistig beschränkten Richter mit einander wechseln, wenn man die Acten durchliest"[34]. Die hier beschriebene Gefühlsmischung galt als selbstverständliche und gesellschaftlich erwartete Reaktion auf Berichte über oder Bilder von Folterungen. Bemerkenswert dabei ist, dass diese Emotionen erst mit der Umbewertung der Tortur von einem legalen Element des Strafverfahrens zu einem absolut unzulässigen Mittel staatlicher Gewalt seit der zweiten Hälfte des 18. Jahrhunderts mit der Folter verbunden wurden. Die Abschaffungsbefürworter hatten innerhalb des Expertendiskurses nicht nur juristische Argumente angeführt, sondern auch an Gefühle appelliert, um ihre Forderung zu untermauern. So wie sich das Folterverbot als unbestreitbare rechtliche und moralische Norm im beginnenden 19. Jahrhundert allgemein durchsetzte, erschienen auch die damit nun verbundenen Emotionen als ‚natürlich'[35].

Systematisiert man die von Hiltl mit der Folter bzw. dem Folterverbot im langen 19. Jahrhundert in Zusammenhang gebrachten Gefühle, so lassen sich Empathie („Mitleid"), Rechtsgefühl („Unwillen") und Ekel („Schauer") unterscheiden. Auf die Bedeutung von (individueller) Empathie für die Geschichte der Menschenrechte insgesamt hat die Forschung wiederholt hingewiesen[36]. „Imagined empathy", also das Mitgefühl mit dem Leiden anderer, weit entfernter, unbekannter Menschen, gewann als zentraler Bestandteil der „humanitären Revolution" im Verlauf des langen 19. Jahrhunderts an Bedeutung[37]. Diese Entwicklung spielte auch für das Folterverbot eine zentrale Rolle, indem sich die humanitäre Sensibilität auf – in der Regel körperliche – Leiden und Schmerzen der grundsätzlich als unschuldig angesehenen, der Tortur unterworfenen Opfer bezog. Schon in seiner berühmten *Theorie der ethischen Gefühle* wählte Adam Smith gerade das Einfühlen in die Qualen eines Menschen auf der Folterbank als Beispiel für Empathie („sympathy"), also das „Erbarmen oder das Mitleid, das Gefühl, das wir für das Elend anderer empfinden, sobald wir dieses entweder selbst sehen, oder sobald es uns so lebhaft geschildert

---

34 *Georg Hiltl.* Die Anwendung der gebräuchlichsten Folter- und Strafwerkzeuge (S. 604). In: Die Gartenlaube. 1864, S. 539-542, 603-606.
35 *Kesper-Biermann.* 2013. S. 271f.
36 vgl. *Burke.* 2017.
37 *Klose.* 2019, S. 70-76.

wird, daß wir es nachfühlen können"[38]. Das ,Nachspüren' des Schmerzes von realen, aber auch fiktiven Personen führte zu einer Abwehrreaktion und zum Wunsch, eine Wiederholung zu vermeiden, also zu einer affektiven Untermauerung des Folterverbots[39]. Voltaire schrieb beispielsweise 1766 in seinem Kommentar zu Beccarias Werk[40]: „[...] und dennoch empören sich alle, durch ein von Gott, in unsre Herzen eingepflanztes Mitleiden, wider die Marter". Spätere Übersetzungen sprachen teilweise in säkularisierter Form von einem natürlichen Mitgefühl jedes Menschen, das die Illegitimität der Folter deutlich mache[41].

Weniger intensiv als die Empathie ist bislang das Rechtsgefühl im Zusammenhang mit den Menschenrechten betrachtet worden, auch wenn gerade die Kombination von Mitgefühl und einem „sense of injustice when governments resort to measures which invade the perceived natural rights of mankind" als „real seed of the human rights movement" gilt[42]. Beccaria habe „das Rechts- und Schamgefühl gegen die Tortur" aufgerüttelt, erklärte etwa der Rechtsprofessor Carl Theodor Welcker 1834 und leitete daraus eine sich notwendig ergebende einhellige Ablehnung der Folter ab: "Die Tortur nun aber wagt ja heut zu Tage auch nicht ein Jurist, nicht ein Regierungsmann mehr zu vertheidigen"[43]. Der Begriff ,Rechtsgefühl' tauchte im deutschen Sprachraum erstmals in den 1790er Jahren auf[44] und blieb über das gesamte lange 19. Jahrhundert hinweg von Bedeutung. Eine besondere Konjunktur erlebte er in Deutschland in den Jahrzehnten um 1900[45]. Obwohl - oder gerade weil - er facettenreich war und keineswegs einheitlich verwendet wurde, spielte er insbesondere in rechtspolitischen

---

38 *Adam Smith.* Theorie der ethischen Gefühle. Auf der Grundlage der Übersetzung von Walther Eckstein neu herausgegeben von Horst D. Brandt. Hamburg 2010 [1759], S. 5.

39 vgl. *Harbou.* 2014, S. 308f.

40 Des Herrn Marquis von Beccaria unsterbliches Werk von Verbrechen und Strafen (1788). Neueste Ausgabe von neuem verbessert und vermehrt nebst dem Commentar des Voltaire, Widerlegungen und andern interessanten Werken verschiedner Verfasser, Bd. 1, Breslau, S. 237.

41 *Harbou.* 2014, S. 323.

42 *Andrew Clapham.* Human Rights. A Very Short Introduction. Oxford 2007, S. 9.

43 *Carl Theodor Welcker.* Anklage (S. 584). In: Carl von Rotteck/ders. Staats-Lexikon oder Encyclopädie der Staatswissenschaften, Bd. 1. Altona 1834, S. 573-584.

44 *Johannes F. Lehmann.* ,Rechtsgefühl'. Zur Diskursgeschichte eines Begriffs um 1800. In: Sigrid G. Köhler/Sabine Müller-Mall/Florian Schmidt/Sandra Schnädelbach (Hrsg.). Recht fühlen. Paderborn 2017, S. 33-41.

45 *Sandra Schnädelbach.* Entscheidende Gefühle. Rechtsgefühl und juristische Emotionalität vom Kaiserreich bis in die Weimarer Republik. Göttingen 2020, S. 15-18.

Debatten eine wichtige Rolle[46]. Der Juraprofessor Eduard Osenbrüggen stellte 1854 fest, „daß die Bezeichnungen: allgemeines Rechtsbewußtsein des Volks, allgemeines Rechtsgefühl, natürliches Gefühl und gesunder Menschenverstand neben und durch einander, als identisch oder doch als verschwistert gebraucht werden"[47].

Der Begriff des Rechtsgefühls wurde um 1800 zunächst von der Strafrechtstheorie aufgegriffen[48]. Da gleichzeitig die Diskussion über die Folter als Verletzung der Menschlichkeit in erster Linie in strafrechtlichen Kontexten erfolgte, verwundert es nicht, dass Rechtsgefühl, Menschenwürde und Tortur schnell in einen engen Zusammenhang gebracht wurden. Im Hinblick auf das Folterverbot war das Verständnis von Rechtsgefühl als einer allgemeinmenschlichen Fähigkeit zentral, intuitiv zu fühlen, was Recht ist bzw. was Recht sein sollte. So war der Kriminalrechtswissenschaftler Carl Grolmann 1798 von einem „jedem, auch dem rohesten Menschen […] beywohnende[n] Rechtsgefühl" überzeugt[49]. Der Jurist Jodocus Temme stellte fest: „Das allgemeine sittliche und rechtliche Bewußtsein trägt jeder Mensch in sich"[50]. In eher populärwissenschaftlichen Kontexten formulierte der bereits erwähnte Schriftsteller Rudolf Quanter 1900: „Instinktiv kann nur das gefühlt werden, was natürlich ist", nur „das natürliche Recht kann deshalb instinktiv empfunden werden". In Bezug auf die Tortur folgerte er dementsprechend, sie widerspreche dem „natürlichen Rechtsgefühl"[51]. Nicht nur in diesem Beispiel wurde das Empfinden von Recht vor allem mit dem Naturrecht in Verbindung gebracht. Gustav Rümelin etwa nannte zuerst in einer Rede von 1871 das Natur- und Vernunftrecht in einer Reihe mit Rechtsbewusstsein und Rechtsgefühl[52]. Die Menschrechte wiederum standen ebenfalls in enger Beziehung zum Naturrecht[53] und erschienen als so elementar, dass sie über das Rechtsgefühl besonders gut zu erfassen seien. Die um 1900 allgemein zu beobachtende „Medikalisierung des Rechtsgefühls"[54] war demgegenüber für das Folterverbot nicht von Bedeutung.

---

46 vgl. auch *Schnädelbach*. 2020, S. 35f.
47 *Eduard Osenbrüggen*. Die Berufung auf das Rechtsbewußtsein im Volke (S. 166). In: Archiv des Criminalrechts. NF 1854, 1, 1854, S. 152-170.
48 *Lehmann*. 2017, S. 36.
49 zit. nach *Lehmann*. 2017, S. 37.
50 zit. nach *Osenbrügge*n. 1854, S. 168.
51 *Quanter*. 1970 [1900], S. 17f.
52 *Gustav Rümelin*. Rechtsgefühl und Gerechtigkeit. Frankfurt/M. 1948 [1907], S. 5.
53 *Moyn*. 2012, S. 126.
54 *Schnädelbach*. 2020, S. 79.

Nach Ansicht vieler Juristen des 19. Jahrhunderts bedurfte es einer allmählichen Kultivierung des Rechtsgefühls im Verlauf der Menschheitsgeschichte, und zwar unter anderem durch verstandesmäßige Einsichten, Fortschritt und ‚Zivilisation'. Das „Rechtsgefühl des Naturmenschen", erklärte Rudolf von Jhering 1867, stand noch „ganz unter der Herrschaft des Schmerzes". Erst wenn „diese Stufe des noch im Affect befangenen Rechtsgefühls überwunden ist [...] gewinnt das Urtheil den richtigen Masstab für eine gerechte Würdigung des Unrechts"[55]. Folgt man dieser Auffassung, dann war es nicht überraschend, sondern lediglich folgerichtig, dass sich erst im Zuge der Aufklärung, als man in der Lage war zu erkennen, Folter sei unmenschlich und unrechtmäßig, das Rechtsgefühl gegen diese Praxis regte. Wie sich den Ausführungen Hiltls, aber auch vieler anderer entnehmen lässt, zeigte sich die vom kultivierten Rechtsgefühl hervorgerufene Ablehnung der Tortur in Emotionen wie Empörung und Entrüstung[56]. Menschenrechte als universell gültige Rechte des Individuums gegen den Staat wurden in erster Linie durch ihre Verletzung und damit durch die Verletzung des Rechtsgefühls, das sich dagegen sträubte, sichtbar[57].

Schließlich ist als weitere, von Hiltl erwähnte und mit der Folter verbundene Emotion Ekel zu nennen[58]. „Ein heisser Ekel steigt in uns auf und weicht allmählich einem bitteren Weh, wenn wir sehen, [...] wie von der Justizverwaltung die ärgsten Quälereien der Folter betrieben wurden." So leitete der Jurist und Journalist Richard Wrede[59] seine kulturhistorischen Studien über *Die Körperstrafen bei allen Völkern* ein. Ekel ist kein unveränderlicher, angeborener Instinkt, sondern die Emotion ist das Ergebnis von Sozialisations- und Akkulturationsprozessen. Was als ekelhaft und abscheulich empfunden wird, variiert von Kultur zu Kultur und ist historischem Wandel unterworfen. Das zeigt sich deutlich am Beispiel der Folter, denn sie verwandelte sich in der öffentlichen Wahrnehmung von einem lange allgemein akzeptierten Bestandteil des Strafverfahrens in eine grausame, verabscheuungswürdige Verletzung der Menschenwürde.

---

55 *Rudolf von Jhering*. Das Schuldmoment im römischen Privatrecht. Eine Festschrift. Gießen 1867, S. 9f.

56 vgl. *Schnädelbach*. 2020, S. 59.

57 *Sigrid G. Köhler*. Menschenrecht fühlen, Gräuel der Versklavung zeigen. Zur transnationalen Abolitionsdebatte im populären deutschsprachigen Theater um 1800 (S. 71). In: dies./Sabine Müller-Mall/Florian Schmidt/Sandra Schnädelbach (Hrsg.). Recht fühlen. Paderborn 2017, S. 63-79.

58 Zum Folgenden *Kesper-Biermann*. 2020, S. 107-109.

59 *Richard Wrede*. Die Körperstrafen bei allen Völkern von den ältesten Zeiten bis auf die Gegenwart. Kulturgeschichtliche Studien. Dresden 1898, S. 1.

Ekel ist nicht nur für das Individuum und seinen Körper von Bedeutung, sondern bezieht sich auch auf Verhaltensweisen im zwischenmenschlichen Umgang. Als verkörpertes moralisches Urteil geht die Ablehnung dessen, was als unangemessenes Handeln verstanden wird, mit emotionalen bis hin zu physischen Reaktionen wie beispielsweise Übelkeit einher. Häufig steht dabei ein Verhalten, das als Verletzung bzw. Missbrauch des menschlichen Körpers verstanden wird, im Mittelpunkt.

Wie Ekel gelten auch Rechtsgefühl und Empathie als soziale Emotionen, das heißt sie werden für das gesellschaftliche Zusammenleben als wichtig, wenn nicht gar als notwendig angesehen. So spricht man beispielsweise vom moralischen Ekel[60], der als soziales Gefühl für die Schaffung und Aufrechterhaltung sozialer Ordnungen von Bedeutung ist. Das Rechtsgefühl sei im 19. Jahrhundert als „moralischer Sinn", als moralisches Gefühl verstanden worden, erklärt Sandra Schnädelbach[61]. Das macht die Verbindung zu den Menschenrechten, die man ebenfalls als moralische Rechte ansah[62], deutlich. Nimmt man also die drei mit der Folter verbundenen Gefühle gemeinsam in den Blick, fällt auf, dass sie eng miteinander verbunden waren. Aus unterschiedlichen Richtungen wirkten sie zusammen, das heißt die als ‚natürlich' wahrgenommenen Gefühlsreaktionen untermauerten das Folterverbot als Gebot der Menschlichkeit, wenn auch nicht als Menschenrecht. Das verweist auf seine Bedeutung in der deutschen Rechtskultur des langen 19. Jahrhunderts.

3. Die Freiheit von Folter in der deutschen Rechtskultur

Das Folterverbot verschwand zwar während des 19. Jahrhunderts aus den juristischen Expertendiskursen in Deutschland, blieb aber in anderen Kontexten überaus präsent[63]. So bildete Folter ein verbreitetes Element (historischer) Romane beispielsweise der Schauerromantik. Illustrierte (Familien-)Zeitschriften wie die *Gartenlaube* publizierten Artikel zum Thema und es erschienen insbesondere um 1900 populärwissenschaftliche Darstellungen, beispielsweise die von Rudolf Quanter[64]. Folterinstrumente waren in öffentlichen kulturhistorischen Museen, in Schaubuden auf Jahrmärkten,

---

60 *Christoph Demmerling/Hilge Landweer*. Ekel (S. 94). In: Philosophie der Gefühle. Von Achtung bis Zorn. Stuttgart/Weimar 2007, S. 93-110.
61 *Schnädelbach*. 2020, S. 63.
62 *Harbou*. 2014, S. 305.
63 zum Folgenden *Kesper-Biermann*. 2020, S. 112-126.
64 *Quanter*. 1970 [1900].

in Wachsfigurenkabinetten sowie auf Weltausstellungen und in Sammlungen von Privatpersonen gegen Eintrittsgeld zu sehen; ferner konnten frühneuzeitliche Folterkeller besichtigt werden. Die von der Forschung hervorgehobene Bedeutung von Literatur, Theater und weiteren Formen (populärer) Kultur für die Etablierung der Menschenrechte seit dem 18. Jahrhundert[65] bestätigt sich auch im Hinblick auf die Freiheit von Folter. Deren Sichtbarmachung mithilfe von Sprache, Bildern oder Objekten bekräftigte ihre Ablehnung als schwerwiegende Verletzung der Menschenwürde. Das entsprach einem Muster, das für die Menschenrechte insgesamt als typisch herausgestellt und von Cornelia Vismann als „Sprechweise der Deklaration" bezeichnet wurde: „Jemand, der gefoltert wurde, beruft sich daher auf kein Recht, er beschreibt, was ihm angetan wurde - in allen Details. Er zeigt die Spuren seiner Verletzungen [...] Die Beurteilung als Unrecht fällt mit der empirischen Beschreibung der Unrechtshandlung zusammen"[66]. Texte, Bilder und andere (populäre) Repräsentationen waren für diese „Deklarationen" deutlich besser geeignet als die nüchternen Rechtstexte, in denen das Folterverbot um 1800 ursprünglich formuliert worden war. Wie bereits erwähnt, fehlten diese in Deutschland dann mit der Vereinheitlichung des Straf- und Strafprozessrechts im Kaiserreich seit den 1870er Jahren zudem vollständig.

Romane oder Zeitschriftenartikel, beispielsweise der von George Hiltl aus dem Jahr 1864, ermöglichten „radikal individualisierte Erzählungen" von Menschenrechtsverletzungen[67]. Hiltl erklärte, die Anwendung der Folter werde „am anschaulichsten, wenn wir es versuchen einem peinlichen Verhöre beizuwohnen, in dessen Verlauf die gebräuchlichsten Instrumente in Thätigkeit gesetzt werden"[68]. Im Artikel für die *Gartenlaube* folgte eine entsprechend eindringliche, auf das Jahr 1693 datierte Schilderung, in der eine fiktive, der Hexerei beschuldigte Frau im Mittelpunkt stand. Im Sinne der Individualisierung durften auch ihre Gedanken und Empfindungen nicht fehlen: „Schon bemächtigt sich der Angeklagten eine entsetzliche Furcht, sie blickt mit halbverdrehten Augen die schauerlichen

65 z.B. *Hunt*. 2007; *Köhler*. 2017.

66 *Cornelia Vismann*. Menschenrechte: Instanz des Sprechens – Instrument der Politik (S. 287). In: Hauke Brunkhorst (Hrsg.). Demokratischer Experimentalismus. Politik in der komplexen Gesellschaft. Frankfurt a.M. 1998, S. 279-304.

67 *Peter Schneck*. Das Recht der Entrechteten. Literatur und die Erfindung der Menschenrechte (S. 452). In: Radhika Natarajan (Hrsg.). Sprache, Flucht, Migration. Kritische, historische und pädagogische Annäherungen. Wiesbaden 2019, S. 447-470.

68 *Hiltl*. 1864, S. 540.

Vorbereitungen an. [...] Sie will versuchen, wie lange sie die Marter ertragen kann, die ihrer wartet"[69]. Wichtiger noch als die Gefühlsbeschreibungen der Folteropfer waren die Gefühle, die in den Leser:innen, den Besucher:innen von Foltermuseen und den Betrachter:innen von entsprechenden Visualisierungen hervorgerufen wurden. Empathie, Rechtsgefühl und Ekel konnten durch diese populären Repräsentationen, für die zudem eine hoch emotionale Gestaltung charakteristisch war, besonders effektiv adressiert werden. Ein Beispiel ist die Erzählung „Ein Ehemann als Marterknecht". Sie erschien 1868 in einer Sammlung von „Dunklen Geschichten aus Österreich" mit einer ganzseitigen Illustration des Malers und Grafikers Vinzenz Katzler (Abb. 1)[70].

Abb. 1: Ein Ehemann als Marterknecht, in: Hermann 1868

---

69 *Hiltl*. 1864, S. 541.
70 *Moriz Hermann*. Dunkle Geschichten aus Österreich. Mit Illustrationen von Vinzenz Katzler. Wien 1868, nach S. 224.

Darin möchte ein krankhaft eifersüchtiger Ehemann von seiner Frau den Namen ihres vermeintlichen vorehelichen Liebhabers erfahren. Als Assessor des Wiener Kriminalgerichts mit den Verhörtechniken der Vergangenheit vertraut, bringt er im Keller des Gerichtshauses gelagerte frühneuzeitliche Folterwerkzeuge wie Daumen- und Beinschrauben mit nach Hause und foltert seine Gattin, die sich nichts vorzuwerfen hat und insofern auch nicht das geforderte „offene[s] Bekenntniß"[71] ablegen kann, zu Tode. Die Szene wird im Text ausführlich über mehrere Seiten beschrieben und mithilfe der Illustration visualisiert. Die Anklänge an zeitgenössische Vorstellungen über Hexenprozesse, wie sie Hiltl in seinem Artikel exemplarisch beschrieben hat, sind unübersehbar. Die Fenster im Haus des Ehepaares sind verbarrikadiert, nur Kerzenschein erhellt den Raum und die Schreie des Opfers können nicht nach außen dringen. Zudem erklärt der Peiniger vor der Anwendung erst ausführlich die Wirkungsweise jedes einzelnen Instruments. Die körperlichen und auch seelischen Leiden der jungen Frau, ablesbar in der Illustration unter anderem an ihrer Körperhaltung und ihrem Gesichtsausdruck, sollen Empathie, die Schilderung der dem Rechtsgefühl widersprechenden Grausamkeit Entrüstung und Empörung hervorrufen.

Die Unvereinbarkeit der Marterhandlungen mit dem Rechtsempfinden der zweiten Hälfte des 19. Jahrhunderts wird ferner durch weitere Mittel unterstrichen. So ist der folternde Ehemann von Beruf (Straf-)Jurist und sollte sich deshalb besonders an Recht und Gesetz orientieren sowie die Menschenwürde respektieren. Stattdessen zeigt er sich vollkommen empathielos, „von dem Jammer und Wehgeschreie der armen Gemarterten gänzlich ungerührt"[72]. Die Folterwerkzeuge musste er aus dem Keller des Gerichtsgebäudes holen; sie waren schmutzig, alt und rostbefleckt, weil sie schon sehr lange nicht mehr benutzt worden waren. Diese „entsetzlichen Erfindungen des Mittelalters"[73] gehörten also einer voraufklärerischen, vergangenen Zeit an, in der das Rechtsgefühl, wie von Jhering beschrieben, in Deutschland noch nicht entsprechend kultiviert war. Schließlich thematisiert der Verfasser explizit die Emotion Ekel. Nach der Festnahme des Täters beginnt die Untersuchung des Falls „und die Details derselben erfüllten Richter und Beisitzer mit Schauder und Abscheu vor dem gefühllosen, entmenschten Bösewichte"[74]. Die Stilisierung des „Bösewichts",

---

71 *Hermann*. 1868, S. 232.
72 Ebenda, S. 234.
73 Ebenda, S. 234.
74 Ebenda, S. 236.

der zuvor schon als grausamer Verbrecher charakterisiert worden war, zum Gegenbild wird auf diese Weise fortgesetzt. Seine Tat zeige, dass er selbst über keines der als natürlich angesehenen Gefühle verfüge; das allein genügte deutlich zu machen, dass bei ihm keinerlei Menschlichkeit anzutreffen ist. Die Popularität solcher weit verbreiteten Schilderungen und Visualisierungen von Folter und Folterverbot hing unter anderem damit zusammen, dass Ekel als ambivalente Emotion beschrieben wird[75]. Sie enthält als eine Facette Faszination und Lust, unter anderem die Lust an der Überschreitung auch moralischer Grenzen. Folterrepräsentationen ermöglichten den Zeitgenossen so ein unterhaltendes emotionales Erlebnis, das als Ambivalenz von Abscheu und Vergnügen beschrieben und von Karen Halttunen als „pornography of pain" bezeichnet wurde[76].

Die mit der Folter bzw. dem Folterverbot verbundenen Gefühle waren zum einen auf das Individuum bezogen, zum anderen wirkten sie als soziale Emotionen kollektiv. Die Freiheit von Folter bildete einen wesentlichen Bestandteil der Rechtskultur im Deutschland des 19. Jahrhunderts, verstanden als „Inbegriff der in einer Gesellschaft bestehenden, auf das Recht bezogenen Wertvorstellungen, Normen, Institutionen, Verfahrensregeln und Verhaltensweisen"[77]. Sie galt als selbstverständlicher, nicht hinterfragbarer Grundpfeiler der politischen Ordnung und des Zusammenlebens, als Indikator für Fortschritt, Modernität und Rechtsstaat. Erzählungen wie die von Hermann, Visualisierungen und Foltermuseen wiederholten diese Sichtweise immer wieder in emotionalisierender Art und Weise, denn Rechtskultur wurde und wird „auch und gerade durch ihre mediale Vermittlung geprägt"[78]. Konkurrierende Normvorstellungen, wie sie in verwandten Fragen, beispielsweise der Todesstrafe[79], zutage traten, waren in Bezug auf die Folter grundsätzlich nicht denk- bzw. sagbar. Dieser über alle politischen, konfessionellen oder sozialen Gruppen hinweg geteilte Konsens ermöglichte es dem Folterverbot, als Bestandteil der Rechtskultur eine wichtige Rolle für die Selbstdeutung und Selbstreflexivität[80] der deut-

---

75 vgl. *Kesper-Biermann*. 2020, S. 109.

76 *Halttunen*. 1995.

77 *Thomas Raiser*. Grundlagen der Rechtssoziologie, 6., durchges. U. erw. Aufl. Tübingen 2013, S. 330.

78 *Peter Mankowski*. Rechtskultur. Tübingen 2016, S. 279.

79 *Richard Evans*. Rituale der Vergeltung. Die Todesstrafe in der deutschen Geschichte 1532-1987. Berlin 2001.

80 *Georg Mohr*. Rechtskultur. In: Handbuch der Politischen Philosophie und Sozialphilosophie. Hrsg. von Stefan Gosepath/Wilfried Hisch/Beate Rössler. Berlin 2009. URL: https://www.degruyter.com/document/database/HPPS/entry/HPPSID _287/html.

schen Gesellschaft einzunehmen. Die mit ihm als ‚natürlich' verbundenen Emotionen konnten dazu beitragen, die Menschen zu einer „Gefühlsgemeinschaft" zusammenzubinden[81] und innergesellschaftliche Trenn- und Konfliktlinien zu überwinden.

Als in erster Linie relevante Gemeinschaft betrachtete man im 19. Jahrhundert die (deutsche) Nation[82]. Das Strafrecht, in dessen Kontext das Folterverbot ja rechtlich normiert worden war, wies nach Ansicht der Juristen eine besonders enge Verbindung zu ihr auf. Rudolf von Jhering stellte stellvertretend für viele fest: „Aber das Strafrecht ist der Knotenpunkt, wo die feinsten und zartesten Nerven und Adern zusammenlaufen, und wo jeder Eindruck, jede Empfindung sich fühlbar macht und äusserlich sichtbar wird, das Antlitz des Rechts, auf dem die ganze Individualität des Volks, sein Denken und Fühlen, sein Gemüth und seine Leidenschaft, seine Gesittung und seine Rohheit sich kund gibt, kurz auf dem seine Seele sich wiederspiegelt – das Strafrecht ist das Volk selbst"[83]. Gleichermaßen wurde der Zusammenhang des Rechtsgefühls mit Nation bzw. Volk betont[84]. Im Hinblick auf die Folter bzw. das Folterverbot spielte das jedoch keine Rolle. Aufgrund des engen Zusammenhangs mit der Menschenwürde galt die Freiheit von Folter als allumfassendes Gebot der Menschlichkeit und nicht als Ausdruck des spezifischen Rechtsempfindens einer Nation. Die beiden anderen mit ihr verknüpften Emotionen, Empathie und Ekel, erschienen ebenfalls als allgemein menschlich und unterstrichen so dessen universellen, für alle Menschen gleichermaßen geltenden Charakter.

4. Fazit und Ausblick

Das Folterverbot war im langen 19. Jahrhundert in Deutschland mit den Emotionen Empathie, Rechtsgefühl und Ekel verbunden. Es war in verschiedenen (populären) Formaten und Medien sehr präsent und bildete einen wichtigen Bestandteil der Rechtskultur. So konnte es die Deutschen zu einer „Gefühlsgemeinschaft" zusammenbinden und die Funktion identitätsbildender Sinnstiftung nach innen übernehmen. Damit einher ging gleichzeitig die Abgrenzung von anderen Rechtskulturen nach außen[85].

---

81 *Köhler.* 2017, S. 70.
82 Zur gegenwartsbezogenen These, dass „jedwede Rechtskultur national ist", vgl. auch *Mankowski.* 2016, S. 279.
83 *Jhering.* 1867, S. 2f.
84 z.B. *Osenbrüggen.* 1854, S. 161.
85 *Mankowski.* 2016, S. 279.

Die Abschaffung der Tortur und vor allem die Einhaltung dieser Norm diente als Gradmesser für ‚Zivilisation' und konnte unter anderem dazu genutzt werden zu beurteilen, welche Staaten, Nationen oder Weltregionen sich noch in einem ‚primitiven' Zustand befanden[86]. Daran zeigt sich, dass sich das Folterverbot im 19. Jahrhundert in einem Spannungsverhältnis zwischen universellem Anspruch und zivilisatorisch-kulturellen Zuschreibungen befand. Es sollte einerseits prinzipiell für jedes Individuum ohne Unterschied gültig sein und verfügte so über das Potential, Trennlinien auch über große Entfernungen zu überwinden. Andererseits bedeuteten Empathie, Rechtsgefühl und Ekel angesichts der Verletzung der Menschenwürde nicht, dass für alle Menschen selbstverständlich Rechtsgleichheit gefordert worden wäre[87]. Vielmehr konnte gerade der Verweis auf Emotionen und deren (fehlende) Kultivierung, wie schon bei Adam Smith, Ungleichheit legitimieren. „Ein zivilisiertes Volk", argumentierte er in der *Theorie der ethischen Gefühle*, „das gewohnt ist, seinen natürlichen Gemütsbewegungen einigermaßen freien Lauf zu lassen, wird dadurch freimütig, offen und aufrichtig. Barbaren dagegen, die die Äußerungen eines jeden Affektes ersticken und verbergen müssen, erwerben dadurch notwendig die Gewohnheit der Falschheit und der Verstellung. [...] Selbst die Folter ist nicht imstande, sie dahin zu bringen, daß sie etwas gestehen würden, was sie nun einmal nicht sagen wollen[88].

Der Blick auf das Folterverbot zeigt zudem, dass es sich lohnt, einzelne Menschenrechte gesondert in den Blick zu nehmen, ihre Entwicklung zu verfolgen und die Kontexte, in denen sie diskutiert wurden, differenziert zu betrachten. Das lange 19. Jahrhundert wird in diesem Zusammenhang als Transformationsepoche in der Geschichte der Menschenrechte erkennbar. Juristische Fachdiskussionen über die Freiheit von Folter verschwanden weitgehend; es kam aber zu einer breiten Popularisierung und Verankerung der Norm im Werte- und Gefühlshaushalt breiter Bevölkerungsschichten, an welche unter anderem die Menschenrechtskataloge in der zweiten Hälfte des 20. Jahrhunderts anknüpfen konnten.

---

86 *Kesper-Biermann*. 2020, S. 104f.
87 vgl. *Klose*. 2019, S. 79; Köhler. 2017, S. 70.
88 *Smith*. 2010 [1759], S. 337f.

III: *Rechtsgefühle* in Legal Theory and Practice

III: Rechtsgefühle in juristischer Theorie und Praxis

Consulting One's Legal Consciousness: Unsimple Fact or Dangerous Fiction?

Jeanne Gaakeer

'Absolutely just law cannot be had'

'Multi-faceted and difficult to translate, this concept's [*Rechtsgefühl's*] spectrum of meaning ranges from an innate feeling for justice or an inner moral sense to a trained feeling from the written law and for legal right. It is also related to the process of making a judgment in a case, understood as a juridical intuition or hunch. Even concepts like *Rechtsbewusstsein* (consciousness of justice) and *Gewissen* (conscience) were used synonymously with the term.[1]

I. Nature or Nurture

1. Nature

As my starting point for a discussion of the relevance of the concepts of '*Rechtsbewusstsein*' and '*Rechtsgefühl*' as legal consciousness and/or feeling or sense of justice and right(s) in contemporary legal theory and legal practice, I turn to Ulpian's definition of law, *ius*, which, as he claims, is derived from justice, *iustitia*: 'unde nomen iuris descendat. Est autem a iustitiam appellatum: nam ... ius est ars boni et aequi'[2]: law is the art of knowing what is good and equitable. Ulpian then distinguishes between public law and private law, the latter consisting, firstly, of civil law as the law of a specific community, secondly, of *ius gentium* or what we would now call international law, and, thirdly and lastly, of natural law as the

---

1 Adolf Lasson, *System der Rechtsphilosophie* (Berlin & Leipzig: Guttentag, 1882, 243, my translation of 'Das absolut gerechte Recht ist nicht zu haben'; Sandra Schnädelbach, 'The jurist as manager of emotions: German debates on *Rechtsgefühl* in the late 19th and early 20th century as sites of negotiating the juristic treatment of emotions', trans. Adam Bresnahan, *InterDisciplines* 2 (2015): 47-73, 47.

2 *Digests*, I.1.1 (Ulpian).

precepts that are innate to all human beings[3] and the norms for human conduct that are good and equitable at all times, i.e., irrespective of the place and the situation.[4] The inclusion of natural law in the concept of law is relevant for a first distinction between meanings of legal consciousness. This distinction pertains to the question whether a sense of justice is innate or not, that is to say either in an individual or a group or people, and if it is relevant for contemporary jurisprudence. First, however, a note on terminology. The term I will use throughout this essay, not out of terminological carelessness, at least I hope, but because of the huge differences in disciplinary, definitional outlooks and/or translations of the works of prominent German legal scholars discussed below, is legal consciousness.

Proponents of the 'nativist approach' claim that justice is planted in the human heart by nature. This biological-anthropological-psychological view comes in different forms, starting with the Historical School of Jurisprudence. Its main theorists Friedrich Carl von Savigny (1779-1861) and Georg Friedrich Puchta (1798-1846) not only vehemently opposed the very idea of the codification of law but also rejected the prioritising of human reason as the means to understand law that had been advocated by Enlightenment thinkers, on the ground that this was ahistorical. The Historical School aimed to understand law by looking for the true legislator and found it in the spirit of the people, the *Volksgeist*, a term coined by Johann Gottfried Herder (1744-1803). The thesis that the root of law is to be found in the people builds on Herder's views on the organic relation between language and culture.[5] Von Savigny argued that the development of Roman law could be traced back throughout the centuries since the rediscovery of the *Corpus Iuris Civilis* and that law had therefore organically developed from the consciousness of the people. Thus, to von Savigny, the Roman *Pandects* could be reconceived as contemporary German law, that is, as Roman law's natural synthesis. If the seat of ethical consciousness is transferred from the individual to the people, the *Volksgeist* is the collective

---

3 *Digests*, I.1.3 (Ulpian).
4 *Digests*, I.2.1.1 (Paulus).
5 For an analysis of Herder's thought, see Jeanne Gaakeer, 'Close Encounters of the "Third" Kind', in *Diaspora, Law and Literature*, ed. Daniela Carpi and Klaus Stierstorfer (Berlin: De Gruyter, 2016), 41-67; see also Jeanne Gaakeer, *Judging from Experience. Law, Praxis, Humanities* (Edinburgh: Edinburgh University Press, 2019), chapters 2 and 11.

legal consciousness implanted in the heart of the people and it determines what (the) law is and how to act with it.[6]

Another, yet different, nativist approach to legal consciousness can be found in the Free Law Movement of the late nineteenth and early twentieth century. A first instance of it is already clear in the fierce debate between Rudolf von Jhering (1818-1892) and Joseph Kohler (1849-1919) about the meaning of the bond in Shakespeare's *The Merchant of Venice*. This debate deserves mention because it revolves around Portia's judicial interpretive position and her subjective legal consciousness, and both are important for the relationship between legal consciousness and equitable justice. Von Jhering initially adhered to the Romanist strand of the Historical School but later on developed a proto-sociological jurisprudence.[7] The starting point for this legal theory was found in the interests of individual persons within a given society, the so-called *Interessenjurisprudenz*.[8] The Free Law Movement, by contrast, took its leave from a sociological starting point to view law as a whole and from the concomitant idea that the judge should take into consideration the principles of justice as well as law; this included the lawgiver's intention in the sense of the purpose of a specific piece of legislation in favour of a discretionary, i.e., a free form of judicial interpretation. To von Jhering, Shylock did not get justice because Portia wrongly failed or deliberately refused to deny the validity of the bond on the ground that it was unconscionable.[9] To Kohler, Portia

---

6 A view expressed by the Dutch legal philosopher Hendrik Jacobus Hamaker, 'Het rechtsbewustzijn en de rechtsphilosophie', in *Opstellen over Recht*, n. ed. (Amsterdam: Müller, 1907), 1-35, 20-21. For nativist approaches, see also Wolfgang Fikentscher, 'The Sense of Justice and the Concept of Cultural Justice', in *The Sense of Justice, Biological Foundations of Law*, ed. Roger D. Masters and Margaret Gruter (Newbury Park/London/New Delhi: Sage Publications, 1992), 106-127.

7 In his three-volume *Der Zweck im Recht* (1877-1840); in English translation, Rudolf von Jhering, *Law as a Means to an End*, trans. Isaac Husik (Boston: Boston Book Company, 1913).

8 It is comparable to the Benthamite sociological idea of law as a means to an end and is echoed in Oliver Wendell Holmes Jr.'s 'The life of the law has not been logic: it has been experience', Oliver Wendell Holmes Jr., *The Common Law* [1881] (Cambridge/Mass.: Belknap Press, 2009), 3.

9 For purposes of citation I use the 4th edition in German and the 5th edition in English:
Rudolf von Jhering, *Der Kampf ums Recht*, 4th edition, in *Rudolf von Jhering Ausgewählte Schriften*, ed. Christian Rusche (Nürnberg: Glock und Lutz Verlag, 1965); Rudolph von Jhering, *The Struggle for Law*, trans. from the 5th edition in German John J. Lalor (Chicago: Callaghan and Co., 1879); here von Jhering, *Struggle for Law*, 81, note 1: 'The eminently tragic interest which we feel in Shylock, I find

deserves praise for her legal consciousness that makes her aware of the fact that the old law needs to be set aside. Obviously, Kohler argues, the lawgiver should be aware of the instincts of the people and preferably change the law accordingly. But, since this is not always possible, the judge should act as the intermediary between the lawgiver and the people. She should grasp the straw she needs to legitimise her decision, i.e., her instinctive judicial legal consciousness and conscience as the foundation of her decision, which she then clothes in the legal garb of interpretation, as Portia does.[10] This is the herald of the Free Law Movement, or so Kohler claims in a self-congratulatory vein.[11] What matters in the context of this essay is that Kohler prioritises the legal consciousness of a people and a society, as well as that of the individual judge as the starting point for judicial decision-making. The idea that subjective judicial consciousness is the decisive factor in the judicial construction of the applicable norm sits uneasily with the principles of equality before the law and legal certainty. And, even though Kohler insisted that the judge's discretionary power was not absolute in the sense that it could go *contra legem* (against the law), the Free Law Movement was increasingly criticised during the first decade of the twentieth century. Whereas Hermann Kantorowicz had argued that the progress of the law ultimately depends on culture and the will of the

---

to have its basis precisely in the fact that justice is not done to him; for this is the conclusion to which the lawyer must come. . . . when the jurist submits the question to a critical examination, he can only say that the bond was in itself null and void because its provisions were contrary to good morals. The judge should, therefore, have refused to enforce its terms on this ground from the first'.

10 Joseph Kohler, *Shakespeare vor dem Forum der Jurisprudenz* (Würzburg: Verlag der Stahel'schen Universitäts Buch- und Kunsthandlung, 1883), 83, 'the legal consciousness of the judge, the legal instinct that lives in him, that has not yet developed into a complete and clear insight and therefore hides itself behind the mock argument of the wise Daniel', my translation of 'das Rechtsbewusstsein des Richters, der im Richter lebende Rechtsinstinkt, der sich noch nicht zur vollständig klaren Erkenntnis heraufgearbeitet hat und sich daher hinter den Scheingründen des weisen Daniels verbirgt'.

11 Josef Kohler, *Shakespeare vor dem Forum der Jurisprudenz*, 2nd ed. (Berlin: Rothschild, 1919), iii, 'Was sind meine Ausführungen über den Spruch der Porzia anders als die Morgenröte der Freirechtsbewegung, welche hier und in meinem Aufsatz über die Interpretation der Gesetze zuerst zu Tage getreten ist?' My translation: 'What are my explanations of Portia's decision other than the dawn of the Free Law Movement, that is brought to light here and in my essay on the interpretation of the laws?'.

(individual) judge,[12] attendees of the second Conference of German Judges in 1911 restricted the freedom that the Free Law Movement assigned to judges. The Free Law Movement subsequently petered out and was discontinued in 1933.[13] The year is as significant as it is ominous, because by then what the Free Law theorists had propagated had been trumped by the very instincts of the people (healthy as these supposedly are) as the new, formal and sole guideline for judicial decision making, 'das gesunde Empfinden des Volkes', as the National Socialist creed had it.[14]

Because of the stark contrast between their views on legal consciousness, the debate between von Jhering and the nativist Gustav Rümelin is of related interest. Rümelin viewed legal consciousness when denoting the feeling for law and justice as an innate, psychological property, i.e. an inner source of law;[15] because to Rümelin, such form of legal consciousness starts as a form of sympathy for one's fellow human being and then becomes a general principle,[16] the notion of the organic growth of law follows out of it. This brings to mind contemporary discussions on the

---

12 Gnaeus Flavius [pseud.], [Hermann Kantorowicz], *Der Kampf um die Rechtswissenschaft* (Heidelberg: Winter, 1906), 34; Gnaeus Flavius [pseud.], 'The Battle for Legal Science', trans. Cory Merill, *German Law Review* 12, no. 11 (2006): 2005-2030, 2025 (my italics), 'We therefore demand that the judge ... decide a case as much as a case can be decided according to the clear wording of the code. He may and should abandon this, first, the moment the code appears to him not to offer an undisputed decision; secondly, if it, according to his free and conscientious conviction, is not likely that the state authority *in power at the time of the decision* would have come to the decision as required by law. In both cases he ought to arrive at the decision that, according to his conviction, the present state power would have arrived at had it the individual case in mind. Should he be unable to produce such conviction, he should then decide according to *free law*. Finally, in desperately involved or only quantitatively questionable cases such as indemnity for emotional damages, he should – and he must – decide according to *free will*'.

13 Klaus Riebschläger, *Die Freirechtsbewegung* (Berlin: Duncker und Humblot, 1968), 89.

14 See also Jeanne Gaakeer, 'Fuss about a Footnote, or the Struggle for (the) Law in German Legal Theory', in *As You Law it – Negotiating Shakespeare*, eds. Daniela Carpi and François Ost (Berlin: De Gruyter, 2018), 155-181.

15 Gustav Rümelin, 'Über das Rechtsgefühl', in *Rechtsgefühl und Gerechtigkeit* [1871], ed. Erik Wolf, *Deutsches Rechtsdenken*, no. 9 (Frankfurt am Main: Vittorio Klostermann, 1948), 5-22, 5, 'in dem Innern des Menschen enthaltenen Wurzel oder Quelle des Rechts'.

16 Rümelin, *supra* note 15, at 13, 'Jener erste unter den humanen Trieben, das Mitgefühl, welches uns fremdes Wohl und fremden Schmerz sympathisch mitempfinden heisst, verdichtet und verklärt sich im Rechtsgefühl zu einem allgemeinen Prinzip, zu dem Satz von der Gleichwertigkeit aller Individuen'.

role of empathy in judicial decision-making that I turn to below in section III.1. According to Rümelin, we would have to consult psychologists to find out what it is in us that makes us create law and where it can be located. This view is interesting in light of recent findings in psychology, for example, a Chicago psychologist's insight that some people have a highly developed 'justice sensitivity' that is rooted in reason rather than emotion,[17] or the view that young children develop a sense of justice at around the age of six.[18] If we return to the topic of empathy, findings in the neurosciences suggest that empathy is an embodied capability. To Rümelin, conscience and legal consciousness, meant as a sense of justice, are related concepts in which the human quest for an ethical-moral order finds its form.[19]

2. Nurture

But, as Hegel noted, we should be cautious lest

> the Idea of right and its further determinations, are taken up and asserted in immediate fashion as facts of consciousness, and our natural or intensified feelings, our own heart and enthusiasm, are made source of right. If this is the most convenient method of all, it is also

---

17 See Mark Prigg, 'The Superhuman Tendency', *Mail Online*, 21 January 2019, available at https://www.dailymail.co.uk/sciencetech/article-2601994/, last accessed 25 January 2019, referring to a test by Chicago psychologists using functional magnetic resonance imaging (fMRI) as a brain scanning device to study what happens in the individual's brain as he or she judges videos depicting behaviour that was either morally good or morally bad. For an evolutionary view on the human sense of justice, see Dennis L. Krebs, 'The Evolution of a Sense of Justice', in *Evolutionary Forensic Psychology: Darwinian Foundations of Crime and Law*, eds. Joshua Duntley and Todd K. Shackelford (Oxford: Oxford University Press, 2008), 229-245, 231, claiming that 'the key to understanding the origin of a sense of justice lies in identifying the adaptive functions it evolved to serve', i.e., 'to induce members of groups to uphold fitness-enhancing forms of cooperation'.

18 See Angela Chen, 'At age six, children develop a sense of justice', *The Verge*, 18 December 2017, last accessed 1 February 2019, https://www.theverge.com/2017/1 2/18/16789966/justice-fairness-psychology-children.

19 Rümelin, *supra* note 15, at 12, 'Gewissen und Rechtsgefühl sind die zwei einander koordinierten, verschwisterten Gestalten, in welche sich der sittliche Ordnungstrieb ausprägt'.

the least philosophical ... [it] makes the subjectivity, contingency, and arbitrariness of knowledge into its principle.[20]

What is more, despite the attractions of nativist positions, it should be noted that for the Romans, who also understood that 'every definition in law is hazardous',[21] legal consciousness was first and foremost a reaction to what was perceived as a concrete injustice. Such a reaction implies the existence of norms and rules that regulate the relations between human beings, i.e., private law that is valid for any society, whether it is handed down orally or (ultimately) laid down in legal codes or discovered on the basis of a concrete case by a judge who knows that his or her sense of justice is in conformity with that of the people he or she represents. Roman law already understood then that without private law no community of people can exist.[22] In other words, legal consciousness presupposes law.

The contextual approach that claims that legal consciousness is culture-dependent was espoused by von Jhering in 'Über die Entstehung des Rechtsgefühles'.[23] It followed out of John Locke's work, who, as von Jhering points out, had been undeservedly forgotten. While von Jhering admits that, originally at least, he was charmed by the idea of legal consciousness as an innate property to be elaborated on by means of psychological viewpoints, his knowledge of Roman law made him deny the possibility of an innate sense of justice. The criterion for the proper judgment of human behaviour in cases that are not yet covered by law

---

20 Georg Wilhelm Friedrich Hegel, *Elements of the Philosophy of Right*, ed. A. W. Wood and trans. H. B. Nisbet (Cambridge: Cambridge University Press, 2003), 27-28. Georg Wilhelm Friedrich Hegel, *Grundlinien der Philosophie des Rechts*, ed. Johannes Hoffmeister (Hamburg: Felix Meiner, 1955) 21, 'Die Ideen ... so auch die des Rechts und dessen weiterer Bestimmungen als Tatsachen des Bewusstseins unmittelbar aufzugreifen und zu behaupten, und das natürliche oder ein gesteigertes Gefühl, die eigen Brust und die Begeisterung zur Quelle des Rechts zu machen . . . wenn diese Methode die bequemste unter allen ist, so ist sie zugleich die unphilosophischste . . . so macht die Manier des unmittelbaren Bewusstseins und Gefühls die Subjektivität, Zufälligkeit und Willkür des Wissens zum Prinzip'.
21 *Digests*, 50, 17, 202 (Iavolenus), my translation of 'omnis definitio in iure periculoso est'.
22 Cf., the Dutch legal philosopher Henri van der Hoeven, *De vraag: mag het Wetboek van Strafrecht ongewijzigd ingevoerd worden* (Leiden: E.J. Brill, 1884), 43, for the view that however sophisticated a sense of justice may be, its existence depends on prior law; in other words, an acceptance of it in legal norms or codes. This is obviously of great importance for criminal law and the principle of *nullum crimen sine lege*, and it implies the rule of law.
23 Rudolf von Jhering, *Über die Entstehung des Rechtsgefühles* [1884], ed. Okko Behrends (Napels, Jovene Editore, 1986).

is to seek guidance in existing law. The example that von Jhering gives is that of taking away objects from a deceased person's estate: in the sense that these objects no longer have an owner they could theoretically be taken by anyone, but since theft is prohibited, the rights of the heir should prevail.[24] Through this analogous form of reasoning, new law is made. In other words, for von Jhering legal consciousness develops against the background of institutional law and equitable justice, and needs their nourishment: 'Our sense of justice therefore depends on the real facts and circumstances that have been realised throughout history'.[25] This comes as no surprise, of course, given that von Jhering's starting point in *The Struggle for Law* is the struggle by the individual person for his or her interests within a society. In his view:

> It is not the sense of right that has produced law, but it is law that has produced the sense of right. Law knows only one source, and that is the practical one of purpose.[26]

Comparable to Hegel, von Jhering points to the role of legal philosophy and legal theory in elaborating the relationship between law, justice (distributive as well as punitive) and legal consciousness. From the perspective of legal philosophy and legal theory, concepts such as equality, as far as claims and rights are concerned, need to be entered into the debate, according to Jhering. This includes measuring an individual's interests also in terms of their obligations, on the view that the individual as a member of society bears responsibility for what he or she creates in the way of good and bad.[27] The echoes of the three fundamental principles of justice in Roman law are obvious. What matters in society is '*honeste vivere, alterum non laedere, suum cuique tribuere*', i.e., to live honourably, to not harm or injure other people, and to render to each his or her own. These notions are not only the legal, but also the moral precepts of a general,

---

24 Von Jhering, *supra* note 23, at 48.
25 Von Jhering, *supra* note 23, at 54, my translation of 'Unser Rechtsgefühl ist also abhängig von den realen Thatsachen, die sich in die Geschichte verwirklicht haben'.
26 Von Jhering, *Struggle for Law, supra* note 9, Author's Preface, lix.
27 Cf. the Dutch legal philosopher Rudolf Kranenburg, *Positief Recht en Rechtsbewustzijn, inleiding in de rechtsphilosophie*, 2nd ed. (Groningen: P. Noordhoff, 1928), pp. 129-135, for the claim that there necessarily is and should be correspondence between the individual sense of right/legal consciousness and the law that binds all.

broadly applicable concept of good faith in human relations, with justice understood as the quest for harmonious human relations.

II. Culture

It is precisely because the *quidditas* or whatness of law is hard to define, as Immanuel Kant noted, that *'Rechtsgefühl'* and *'Rechtsbewusstsein'* remain important though contested topics in jurisprudence. That is to say, is law a state institution, a power structure, a system of rules, or an instrument of justice or oppression? Is it a theoretical structure or a practice? Or, is it all of the above?[28] The same goes for culture. The number of definitions of culture that have vagueness as their most common characteristic is abundant.[29] This surplus of definitions obviously leads to a number of conceptual Babels when considering the cultural location from which to best start research on legal consciousness. Given the replication of the problem of contradictory definitions in cultural studies of law as well as investigations into the cultural lives of law, i.e., when law deals with cultures,[30] it is important to specify how and where legal research and culture meet. This might be, for example, on the site of what Roger Cotterrell calls 'law as a cultural projection'.[31] This would imply asking, 'How ought law

---

28 See Jeanne Gaakeer, 'The Future of Literary-Legal Jurisprudence: Mere Theory or Just Practice?' *Law and Humanities* 5, no.1 (2011): 185-196.

29 See Austin Sarat and Thomas R. Kearns, 'The Cultural Lives of Law' in *Law in the Domains of Culture*, eds. Austin Sarat and Thomas R. Kearns (Ann Arbor: University of Michigan Press, 1998), 1-20, 3 for the view that traditionally the study of culture was the study of 'that complex whole which includes knowledge, belief, art, morals, law, custom, and any other capabilities and habits acquired by man as a member of society'. Such a definition is a broad umbrella under which practically every topic finds shelter. It disregards aspects of socialisation and acculturation connected to culture. Peter Burke, on the other hand, defends a broad definition that includes '... attitudes, mentalities and values and their expression, embodiment or symbolization in artefacts, practices and representations', *Cultural Hybridity* (Cambridge: Polity Press, 2009), 5. See also Jeanne Gaakeer, 'Reverent Rites of Legal Theory: unity-diversity-interdisciplinarity', *Australian Feminist Law Journal* 36 (2012): 19-43.

30 See Priska Gisler, Sara Steinert Borella and Caroline Wiedmer, 'Setting the Stage: Reading Law and Culture', in *Intersections of Law and Culture*, eds. Priska Gisler, Sara Steinert Borella and Caroline Wiedmer (Houndmills/UK: Palgrave MacMillan, 2012), 1-13.

31 Roger Cotterrell, 'Law in Culture', *Ratio Juris* 17, no. 1 (2004): 1-14, 5.

to be understood as a cultural system?'[32] With this in mind, I turn to the second distinction that needs to be made in the various conceptualizations of legal consciousness.

With its focus on the *fons et origo* of legal consciousness, the first distinction fails to address the relationship between the individual and society when seen in terms of what Rehbinder calls the '*Rechtsbewusstsein*', as a consciousness of (the) law, versus '*Rechtsgefühl*', as an individual's innermost feelings.[33] The point was already noted in 1919 by the Dutch legal philosopher Boasson, who attributed both an intellectual and an emotional function to the term '*rechtsbewustzijn*', i.e., '*Rechtsbewusstsein*'. He claimed therefore that, on the one hand, the individual should consult with himself or herself and, when deciding how to act, ask whether he or she is required to take the interests of others into consideration. (This is important, for example, in terms of criminal law for discerning the difference between intent (*malus*) and guilt and/or culpability.) On the other hand, from a legal-judicial perspective, one should ask whether the individual's view deserves protection as opposed to the state as a whole.[34] In short, the cognitive versus the emotional aspect is important when it comes to dealing with spontaneous feelings of citizens juridically. That is to say, in the situation, whether rightly so or not, that their feeling for what is right and just appears to have been violated, either by fellow citizens or by the state or local administration. It is with this second distinction that the role of the judge becomes prominent in democratic societies under the rule of law. Whether a conflict regarding a point of law or conflicting views on what is just are at stake, a court proceeding and a judicial decision are required in order to arrive at a solution, and, it is important to note, that 'the decision of the judge is implemented by the force of public power', as Paul Ricoeur emphasises.[35] What is more, the meaning of legal consciousness in a concrete case or situation depends both on the concept of the 'rule of law' and the *Rechtsstaat* in which

---

32 Austin Sarat, 'Situating Legal Scholarship in the Liberal Arts', in *Law in the Liberal Arts*, ed. Austin Sarat (Ithaca: Cornell University Press, 2004), 1-13, 4.

33 Manfred Rehbinder, *Rechtssoziologie*, 2nd ed. (Berlin and New York: De Gruyter, 1989), 169.

34 Johan Jozef Boasson, *Het Rechtsbewustzijn, een onderzoek naar het leven der rechts-idee in het individueel bewustzijn* (Den Haag: Martinus Nijhoff, 1919), 41.

35 Paul Ricoeur, *Hermeneutics and the Human Sciences,* trans. and ed. J. B. Thompson (Cambridge: Cambridge University Press, 1981), 215.

this concept is used, and which, in turn, influences this very concept; the relationship is reciprocal.[36]

The role of public debate on matters that (may) divide a society also comes into play with the second distinction. People may experience a sense of alienation and powerlessness when there is too large a discrepancy between the individual's internal view and the institutional view of what is right and just, a Kafkaesque gap between '*Rechtsnähe*' and '*Rechtsferne*', what is close to or distant from the letter of the law, as Marc Hertogh notes in his analysis of the Belgian Dutroux affair. This affair involved the kidnapping and murder of four girls during the 1990s and the recusal of the examining magistrate Connerotte after he attended a fund-raising dinner for the families of the missing children and accepted a spaghetti dinner and a pencil there.[37] This recusal created 'a deep divide between the official world of the Belgian legal system and that of the ordinary citizen. In many cases this was explicitly linked to different opinions about the *Rechtsstaat*'.[38] Some citizens vehemently protested against the recusal, which they saw as a violation of their sense of rightness and the law.

My second example is that of a recent Dutch case. This involved the '*Blockade-Frisians*', citizens from the province of Friesland who blocked a major road, making it impossible for demonstrators from other parts of the Netherlands to reach the Frisian capital of Leeuwarden. Demonstrators had wanted to block the ritual entry of Saint Nicholas and Black Peter into the city and 'Kick Out Zwarte Piet'. They had wanted to raise their voices against the presumed racism and colonialism of this Dutch December tradition in the Netherlands. In court, it turned out that neither group felt itself to have been heard or recognised: the '*Blockade-Frisians*' assumed that the authorities lacked appreciation for 'real' Dutch people who merely wanted an event for their children to not be disturbed by the violence that was to be expected from leftist demonstrators; and, as victims of the intimidating road block, the demonstrators felt unheard by a Dutch society that they perceived to be racist. While the court duly noted the

---

36 Cf., Marc Hertogh, 'A "European" Concept of Legal Consciousness: Rediscovering Eugen Ehrlich', *Journal of Law and Society*, 31, no. 4 (2004): 457-481, for the differences in the European and American conception of legal consciousness.

37 Hertogh, *supra* note 36, at 458-459. See the Belgian Court of Cassation, 14 October 1996, no. 379.

38 Hertogh, *supra* note 36, at 459.

antagonists' differing motivations in its written decision, it did not bring about a mutual understanding between the two groups.[39]

Thus, a people's idea of what is law and what is right may differ significantly, as was already noted by Eugen Ehrlich (1862-1922). His work remains important because he was one of the first to point out that any degree of freedom in a judicial interpretive act and the decision that results from it, is not 'arbitrary ... it grows out of the principles of juridical tradition'.[40] These principles include respect for the legal code, but that respect does not imply an interpretive restriction because even the 'simple' application of a legal rule 'is by its very nature creative'.[41] It should be noted that the judicial movement from facts to legal norms is always dialectical; it involves a going hither and thither between the facts and the norm, so to speak, as coined by the German jurist Karl Engisch in the phrase *das Hin-und Herwandern des Blickes*.[42] In performing this movement, judges need to constantly bear in mind the influence of their own interpretive frameworks on both the facts and the norm. As humans, we cannot escape our hermeneutic situation of being culturally determined, professionally as well as personally. That too is important to note in relation to the application of legal consciousness in legal judgment.[43]

What matters to me here are two things. The first is that Ehrlich emphasises '*the element of creative thought*', the second is that 'each application of a general rule to a particular case is necessarily influenced by the personality of the judge who makes it'; in other words,

> the administration of justice has always contained a personal element ... The point is that this fact should not be tolerated as something unavoidable, but should gladly be welcomed. For the one important desideratum is that his personality must be great enough to be properly entrusted with such functions.[44]

---

39 ECLI:NL:RBNNE:2018:4555; ECLI:NL:RBNNE:2018:4557; ECLI:NL:RBNNE: 2018:4558; ECLI:NL:RBNNE:2018:4559; ECLL:NL:RBNNE:2018:4561. European decisions that have a European Case Law Identifier (ECLI) can be accessed via the European e-justice portal <e-justice.europa.eu>.

40 Eugen Ehrlich, 'Judicial Freedom of Decision: Its Principles and Objects', trans. Ernest Bruncken and Layton B. Register, in *Science of Legal Method* [1917] (New York: A.M. Kelley, 1969), 47-83, 71.

41 Ehrlich, *supra* note 40, at 73.

42 Karl Engisch, *Logische Studien zur Gesetzanwendung* [1943] (Heidelberg: Winter, 1963), 15.

43 See also Gaakeer, *Judging from Experience*, *supra* note 5, chapter 6.

44 Ehrlich, *supra* note 40, at 73 (italics in the original).

One thing is certain, ever since the term *'Rechtsgefühl'* was first used in von Kleist's *Michael Kohlhaas* (1810),[45] justice and the quest for justice have remained central to discussions in jurisprudence. As with the concepts of law and culture, *'Rechtsgefühl'* too remains an umbrella concept. This circumstance forces us to consider the 'whatness' of *'Rechtsgefühl'*, the *quidditas* question in our research. As Christoph Meier notes, there are at least fourteen different ways in which the term can be used, and each of these specific perspectives will guide our research and its possible outcomes.[46] This goes to show that, in the spirit of Kurt Lewin, there is nothing more practical than a good theory.

In what follows, I will focus on the second distinction that was noted in this section, specifically on the differentiation between the elements that help guide the act of judging and its outcome, and the individual person's legal consciousness as compared to the legal consciousness that prevails in one's society. I do so because personal values and valuations of other people's actions (biases included) and expectations that people have of the state and of judges are intimately related to the topic of empathy prominent in *Law and Literature*, an interdisciplinary field in legal theory that started in the U.S. in the 1970s and heralded a renaissance of the humanistic study of law. By now, *Law and Literature* has morphed into the field of *Law and the Humanities* in which, not incidentally, current topics are affect and emotion in law and legal theory.

III. A Nimble Mind

1. Empathy and Emotion

As Sandra Schnädelbach rightly notes, the early 'debates on *Rechtsgefühl* gave emotions an epistemological function'; with this the main question in terms of legal practice in the twentieth century became 'Could a jurist

---

45 Cf. Katharina Döderlein, *Die Diskrepanz zwischen Recht und Rechtsgefühl in der Literatur. Ein dramatischer Dualismus von Heinrich von Kleist bis Martin Walser* (Würzburg: Königshausen und Neumann, 2017), 18 and 67 n. 228. *Michael Kohlhaas* marks the ultimate shift from divine to human-made law, and the brothers Grimm called the novella the oldest source for the use of the term *'Rechtsgefühl'* (see Jacob Grimm and Wilhelm Grimm, *Deutsches Wörterbuch*, Band 8 [Leipzig: Hirzel, 1893], 432).

46 Christoph Meier, *Zur Diskussion über das Rechtsgefühl* (Berlin: Duncker & Humblot, 1986), 44-45 and 137-155.

consult his *Rechtsgefühl* when making a judgment? Should he? Was he permitted to do so?'[47] As I have suggested elsewhere,[48] jurists generally and judges more specifically all necessarily combine the practical and the theoretical, i.e., legal doctrine and the findings of the academic study of and research into law. To reach the outcome of a specific case, legal practice always reflects on the consequences of any theoretical, doctrinal assumption. This reflection includes attention to the possible theoretical justification of the position that could be taken when viewed against the background of the wider significance of the combined legal and cultural framework, for example, in high-profile cases that attract societal and/or media attention. In turn, theoretical knowledge, in the sense of academic legal scholarship, is augmented by the actual *quid-iuris* questions that legal practice raises, for instance, what is the law? These often go far beyond what academic doctrinal discourse can even begin to fathom. Again, the relationship between the two is a reciprocal one. Whereas practice turns to theory for justification, theory thrives on practical input. So, it matters a great deal whether or not one's '*Rechtsgefühl*' is part of this process, and if so, which form it then takes.

The struggle for a place for '*Rechtsgefühl*' was the topic of Max Rümelin's 1925 study of *Rechtsgefühl und Rechtsbewusstsein*.[49] Unlike his father Gustav, Max Rümelin rejected the nativist view of '*Rechtsgefühl*'. In contradistinction, he focuses on how the legal professional develops knowledge by means of experience. For a judge, at least, this results in developing an intuitive feel for the right decision, on the basis of

> the totality of the representations of (the) law present in a person's consciousness, either on the basis of education or accumulated in the mind on the basis of one's own experiences, in other words . . . the sum total of all experience as a unity.[50]

Rümelin notes that such legal intuition stands in contrast with conceptual thought. This observation anticipates, I suggest, the attention to what, in the field of *Law and the Humanities*, has been emphasised as essential ability for any judge. James Boyd White first drew attention to this abil-

---

47 Schnädelbach, *supra* note 1, at 48-49.
48 Gaakeer, *Judging from Experience, supra* note 5, at chapter 6.
49 Max Rümelin, *Rechtsgefühl und Rechtsbewusstsein* (Tübingen: Mohr-Siebeck, 1925).
50 Max Rümelin, *supra* note 49, at 20, 'die Gesamtheit der in einem Bewusstsein vorhandenen, auf Grund von Unterweisung oder von eigenen Erlebnissen im Gedächtnis aufgespeicherten Rechtsvorstellungen, oder ... die Summe aller Erfahrungen als Einheit' (my translation).

ity to bridge the fundamental difference between the narrative and the analytical, or the literary and the conceptual in the judge and what she recognises as the competing pulls in other people's texts. White calls this the difference between 'the mind that tells a story, and the mind that gives reason', because 'one finds its meaning in representations of events as they occur in time, in imagined experience; the other, in systematic or theoretical explanations, in the exposition of conceptual order or structure'.[51] This is especially important in the stage of justification, when the judge acts as the narrator of her own authorial act of comprehending the facts and circumstances of the case, and deciding what is and what is not relevant for the legal plot in the presented succession of events. This plotting in the form of a selection is always done with the aim of arriving at a decision, or, as Ricoeur put it succinctly, 'To tell and to follow a story is already to reflect upon events in order to encompass them in successive wholes'.[52] This also means, to me at least, that the way in which the outcome of this process is written down and then pronounced in an open courtroom is crucial for the acceptance of the decision by the parties involved, particularly in cases that draw attention in society at large and require people's acceptance.

Rümelin emphasises the importance of qualities that Aristotle had attributed to ethos and virtue long before him, when he claims that one does not become a good judge via intellectual achievements alone; rather, one needs a specific character and disposition for this.[53] In other words, a judge's ethos in the sense of her professional attitude cannot be separated from the persuasiveness of her judgement. A lack of reflection on this bond is an ethical and a professional defect. This means that knowledge of the law alone does not suffice. It needs to be complemented by love for the law and love for one's fellow human beings. The latter should not be confused with sympathy; on the contrary, as Rümelin claims, it is precisely because a judge should not lapse into feelings of sympathy that she needs '*Rechtsgefühl*' to do justice to the human condition in an individual case.[54] Rümelin's emphasis on the individual case is connected not only to '*Billigkeitsrecht*', or equity, a topic to which I will return, but

---

51 James Boyd White, *The Legal Imagination: Studies in the Nature of Legal Thought and Expression* (Boston: Little, Brown and Company, 1973), 859.

52 Paul Ricoeur, 'Narrative Time', *Critical Inquiry* 7, no. 1 (1980): 167-190, 178.

53 Max Rümelin, *supra* note 49, at 76, 'Zu einen guten Richter wird man nicht bloss durch Eigenschaften des Intellekts. Ebenso wesentlich sind Gemüt und Charakter'.

54 Max Rümelin, *supra* note 49, at 76.

also to the empathic imagination. More recently, this type of imagination was eloquently promoted by U.S. Supreme Court Justice Stephen Breyer when he writes that

> Law requires both a head and a heart. You need a good head to read all those words and figure out how they apply. But when you are representing human beings or deciding things that affect them, you need to understand, as best you can, the workings of human life.

This is particularly so in hard cases,

> where perfectly good judges come to different conclusions on the meaning of the same words . . . it is very important to imaginatively understand how other people live and how your decisions might affect them, so you can take that into account when you write.[55]

The success of professional empathy, therefore, is intimately connected to readers' response to the texts of law, and such a response, in turn, co-constitutes the legitimacy and authority of the judge as author.[56] When the judicial text is perceived as logocentric and cold, it can evoke violent emotions. A recent example in the Netherlands concerns a father who was present to hear the decision of a lower court with respect to the defendant, the driver of a car that ran over and killed his two-year-old daughter and both her grandparents, who were cycling on a bicycle track. Out of sheer disappointment and frustration, he threw a chair at the judge who read the decision in a public courtroom. The decision itself was correct in terms of traffic law and criminal law, also as far as the sentencing was concerned: the punishment did not involve a jail sentence, since the text of the relevant article of the Road Traffic Act does not include criminal intent. Yet the decision did not at all, or not explicitly, acknowledge the enormous suffering of the couple who had lost both a child and a set of parents.[57] In other words, the judicial decision performed its legal function in criminal law dispute resolution only in the abstract sense. It failed in

---

55 Eve Gerber, 'Stephen Breyer on Intellectual Influences', available at https://five books.com/best-books/stephen-breyer-on-intellectual-influences/ [last accessed 12 January 2018]. Cf. John Rawls, 'The Sense of Justice', *The Philosophical Review* 72, (1963): 281-305, 281, that Jean-Jacques Rousseau in his *Émile* 'asserts that the sense of justice is no mere moral conception formed by the understanding alone, but a true sentiment of the heart enlightened by reason, the natural outcome of our primitive affections'.

56 Gaakeer, *Judging from Experience, supra* note 5, at chapter 11.

57 Rechtbank Limburg, 21 November 2014, ECLI:NL:RBLIM:2014:10041.

its communicative and societal function, because it did not demonstrate an empathic stance towards the bereft parents, who had understandably hoped that a severe punishment would be given to the offender in the form of a jail sentence as a form of retribution. Nor did the decision explain why the law did not allow for such punishment in light of the court's qualification of the criminal act.

As a concomitant result, the general public felt similarly to the parents; it did not accept the decision as fair. Therefore, the performativity of the text of the judicial decision is intimately connected to the professional ethos that the judge who is taking the decision shows in his or her narrative, whether or not this ethos as narrative identity is consciously chosen.[58] In the appeal, the defendant was sentenced to jail. But in 2017, when he was released temporarily in order to visit his pregnant girlfriend in Poland, public emotions again ran high, because the specific terms of the release did not include guarantees with respect to his having to return to the Netherlands to serve the rest of his sentence.

For all of these reasons, the legal narrative and its rhetorical form, whether deliberately chosen or not, cannot be treated as separate from one another. Ideally, the justification of the decision is geared to a specific audience. Rhetorically speaking, the judge must try and gauge the expectations this audience has and which emotions are involved. Hence judicial ethos depends on this judicial incorporation of both logos and pathos.[59] For this reason, we need to carefully consider the role of '*Rechtsgefühl*', both as the emotion that guides the person who applies the law and as the emotion that her decision sparks in her audience.[60] This is even more the case because, as the findings of neurosciences suggest, empathy may well

---

58 For law as performance and event, see Julie S. Peters, 'Legal Performance Good and Bad', *Law, Culture and the Humanities* 4, no. 2 (2008): 179-200; 'Law as Performance: Historical Interpretation, Objects, Lexicons, and other Methodological Problems', in *New Directions in Law and Literature*, eds. Elizabeth S. Anker and Bernadette Meyler (Oxford: Oxford University Press, 2017), 193-209.

59 Willem Witteveen, 'Wat doet de rechter als hij recht vindt: de formule van het algemeen rechtsbewustzijn', *Recht en Kritiek* 9, (1983): 192-208, 204.

60 See also Julia Haenni, 'Emotion and Law: How Pre-Rational Cognition Influences Judgment', *German Law Journal* 13, no. 3 (2012): 369-380, for a Kantian, phenomenological approach, concluding, at 380, that 'The phenomenon of intuitive evaluation is therefore not to be understood as a factor interfering with the application of the law, but as an insight into the interaction of rational and emotional factors in the emergence of a moral, but also juridical, decision'.

be an embodied emotion.[61] As such, it has a basis in '*mirror neurons*, which fire both when a person performs an action or feels an emotion when she views someone else having the same experience'.[62] This also suggests that the understanding of '*Rechtsgefühl*' as innate may not be as far away as we thought it was, given the development of the term during the last century. What is more, the findings of the natural sciences need to be taken into careful consideration in interdisciplinary legal research on '*Rechtsgefühle*' because law is a value-laden discipline.

2. Seeing the Decision Intuitively

The question of whether '*Rechtsgefühl*' could be a building block in rendering judgement was also answered affirmatively by Ernst Weigelin, who attached significance to three relevant meanings of '*Rechtsgefühl*'.[63] These are, firstly, a sense of what the law requires, or which individual entitlements exist in a specific case. This includes a *sensus juridicus*, as the ability to intuitively see what the case requires so that the judge arrives at the decision on this basis first and then seeks its legal justification. And as the greatest Dutch legal theorist of the twentieth century, Paul Scholten, noted,

> the judge, who intuitively 'sees' the decision immediately after the case is presented to him, even though he doesn't know precisely yet, how he will motivate it, uses his knowledge of law – his complete experience – in this intuitive view.[64]

Secondly, '*Rechtsgefühl*', according to Weigelin, implies a feeling for what law ought to be, that is, a keen sense for the ideal of law and an inclination

---

61 See Gail Bruner Murrow and Richard W. Murrow, 'A Biosemiotic *Body* of Law: The Neurobiology of Justice', *International Journal for the Semiotics of Law* 26, no. 2 (2013): 275-314, 298, 'embodied empathy, broadly defined, involves the sharing, or automatic neural simulation, of the actual neural affective, neural somatosensory, or neural motor states of others with whom one "empathizes"'.

62 See Ann Jurecic, 'Empathy and the Critic', *College English* 74, no. 1 (2011): 10-27, 10 (italics in the original).

63 Ernst Weigelin, 'Das Rechtsgefühl in seiner ablehnenden Funktion', *Juristische Rundschau* 1950, no. 12 (1950): 361-362, 361, citing Erwin Riezler.

64 Paul Scholten, *General Method of Private Law. Mr. C. Asser's Manual for the Practice of Dutch Civil Law* [1931] (Amsterdam: Digital Paul Scholten Project, 2014), vol. 1, Chapter 1, available at General-Method-of-Private-Law-3.pdf (paulscholten.eu) [last accessed 13 March 2021], Section 28 'The decision'.

to help materialise this ideal of (the) law. This view is comparable to Gustav Radbruch's understanding of jurisprudence as a cultural discipline, and law as an activity that strives to make its idea and ideals happen, i.e., the view that

> From the concept of law, a cultural concept, that is, a concept related to value, we were pressed on to the value of the law, the idea of the law: Law is what, according to its meaning, is intended to serve the idea of the law.[65]

Radbruch speaks in terms of the fundamental principles of law. In western culture these principles include human dignity, freedom, equality and solidarity. They are the products of the work of humans throughout the ages, and are bound by their cultural contexts and, as such, are open to change. But, these principles are also stronger than any purely rule-oriented form of law so that a positive law that runs contrary to these principles must be denied its validity, a topic I turn to below in section IV. Thus, Radbruch offers a humanistic, intermediate position between the value-absolutism of natural law and the value-relativism of legal positivism. Furthermore, in that Radbruch explicitly thinks of law and jurisprudence as belonging to the domain of the Humanities, his view is also interesting for a methodological discussion of the place of law in the disciplinary spectrum.[66] And,

---

65 Gustav Radbruch, *The Legal Philosophies of Lask, Radbruch, and Dabin*, The 20th century legal philosophy series vol. IV, trans. Kurt Wilk and intro. Edwin W. Patterson (Cambridge/Mass.: Harvard University Press, 1950), 47-224, Section 9, 107 (the translation of the 3rd edition [1932] of Gustav Radbruch, *Rechtsphilosophie*, 3rd ed. [1914] (Leipzig: Quelle & Meyer, 1932). I also use Gustav Radbruch, *Rechtsphilosophie*, 8th ed., ed. Erik Wolf and Hans-Peter Schneider [Stuttgart: K. F. Koehler Verlag, 1973]).

66 See Gustav Radbruch, *Literatur- und kunsthistorische Schriften*, in *Gesamtausgabe*, volume 5, ed. Hermann Klenner (Heidelberg: C.E. Müller, 1997). For a discussion of Radbruch's literary analyses, see Hans-Albrecht Koch, '"Aber bald gewannen meine literarische Neigungen wieder die Oberhand": Gustav Radbruch als Literaturhistoriker', in *Grenzfrevel, Rechtskultur und literarische Kultur*, eds. Hans-Albrecht Koch, Gabriella Rovagni und Bernd H. Oppermann (Bonn: Bouvier Verlag, 1998), 153-166. Max Rümelin, *supra* note 49, at 75, also advances the interdisciplinary argument that in order to understand the distinctive elements and possible impact of 'Rechtsgefühl', we need to combine the findings of the behavioural sciences, sociology, (cultural) history, and the narratives of 'Rechtsgefühl' in literary works such a Shakespeare's *Measure for Measure*, *Hamlet* and *King Lear*, and those of Ibsen, Tolstoy, and Dostoevsky. See also Friedrich Kübl, *Das Rechtsgefühl* (Berlin: Putkammer & Mülbrecht, 1913), chapters 10 and 11 for 'Rechtsgefühl' in the works of Shakespeare, Goethe, and Schiller.

I would add that the realisation of law's values is indissolubly connected to the furthering of (social) justice and the struggle necessary to obtain that goal in concrete cases, for example, in the case of the right to vote, and all kinds of social rights that were fought for at the end of the nineteenth century and the early twentieth century. This includes the U.S. civil rights movement of the 1960s, and, more recently, the fight for gender equality. Finally, Weigelin points to the necessary understanding of the legal order and its institutions, including their limitations as part of *Rechtsgefühl*. To me, such an understanding includes a good working knowledge of procedural law.

In those cases in which the legal norm should be put aside on the basis of a judicial '*Rechtsgefühl*', we are also squarely in the domain of the *sensus juridicus*. There, the judge either seeks a solution that satisfies her '*Rechtsgefühl*' through extensive or restrictive interpretation, or, contrastingly, by making it explicit that existing law forces her to come to a specific decision that is undesirable and unjust and leads her to therefore ask legislators to take up the task of changing that law. As far as this second solution is concerned, the judge also faces a professional moral-formal dilemma that ensues on the basis of her decision, and she may experience an incompatibility between her cognitions, i.e. a cognitive dissonance between the claims of her professional and private self. What is she to do when the law that she has to uphold becomes repugnant to her '*Rechtsgefühl*'? As Robert Cover noted, the judge can either retreat into a mechanistic application of the law, or try to find a justification for her adherence to formal obligations, for example, by claiming that the responsibility is that of a different power, such as the lawgiver.[67] This obviously clashes with the principle that judicial independence entails that judges are liberated from hierarchical subordination when deciding cases. This independence obviously implies that one cannot hide behind the order of a supposedly superior state power, be it the lawgiver or the political administration. Hence the need for judicial daring. The point is eloquently addressed by Piero Calamandrei, arguing that in those situations

> when the judge's sense of justice is not in harmony with that of the legislator; when as a result of abrupt political changes and a break in juridical continuity, the judge is called on to apply a law that he believes unjust. It is very well to say that under the rule of law the principle of *dura lex sed lex* applies and that consequently the judge

---

67 Robert Cover, *Justice Accused, Antislavery and the Judicial Process* (New Haven: Yale University Press, 1975), 1-7 and 226-229.

must take the law as he finds it, without judging it. But the judge is a human being, and as such he automatically judges the law before applying it; even if he is willing to obey it, he cannot avoid making a moral and political evaluation according to the dictates of his *conscience*. And even if he *stifles the voice of his conscience*, when he is obliged to apply a law in which he does not believe, it is only natural that he will apply it mechanically, as an official duty, with a cold bureaucratic pedantry; he cannot be expected to vivify or to re-create a law that is extraneous or actually hostile to his philosophy.[68]

Judicial solutions remain in the domain of law in the sense that their outward appearance complies with what Rudolf Stammler calls the natural feeling for the law in hard cases, which is not a subjective feeling but an objectively valid art of contemplating things juridical.[69] Yet it is obvious that the methodological struggle with respect to the place of judicial '*Rechtsgefühl*' remains in full swing precisely because of its wide-ranging *quidditas*. Since this is unavoidable, conceptual clarity is of the utmost importance, even more so in interdisciplinary settings. I emphasise this point because there is broad consensus, theoretically at least, that the job specification for judges comprises at least three criteria: firstly, integrity as the combined result of impartiality, candour and daring – understood here as the guts to take unpopular decisions that may cause societal disapproval and/or unrest –; secondly, craftsmanship, i.e., both knowledge of the law and the imagination necessary to gauge what is at stake for the parties in an individual case; and, lastly, the ability to assess autonomously what is just (and act on that).[70]

From a methodological point of view, this means that the judge must be able to acknowledge the views of the opposing parties in a case as valid

---

68 Piero Calamandrei, 'The Crisis in the Reasoned Opinion', in *Procedure and Democracy*, trans. John Clarke Adams and Helen Adams (New York: New York University Press, 1956), 683-696, 692 (italics mine).

69 Rudolf Stammler, *Die Lehre vom dem richtigen Rechte* (Berlin: Guttentag, 1902), 146, 'das natürliche Rechtsgefühl' and 'eine *objektiv* gültige Art der Betrachtung rechtlicher Dinge' (my translation).

70 See Hans F.M. Hofhuis, 'De rechtspraak van binnen en van buiten', Speech held on 10 June 2011 for the Dutch Association of Jurists. The judicial panel which Hofhuis presided showed such daring in the Urgenda case (ECLI:NL:RBDHA: 2015:7145) when it ordered the Dutch government to take measures in order to reduce the emission of greenhouse gas by 25% (compared to the level of 1990) before 2020, a decision that was confirmed in appeal (ECLI:NL:GHDHA: 2018:2591).

propositions against the background of the legal order, and the demands of the society in which law performs its authoritative function. Legal rationality is more prominent, of course, in the phase of legitimisation, when the grounds for the decision are stated by giving reasons, i.e., the justification of the decision on the basis of the relevant facts and applicable law, in interaction with each other. In this way, the parties involved in a case, and society more widely, including legal scholarship, can reconstruct the line of reasoning which led to the decision. So obviously judicial decision making thus encompasses an appeal to the decision maker's legal conscience and consciousness.

Acknowledging different views requires an empathic attitude and an ability to move from the facts to the legal norm and back again that requires both insight into what makes a specific fact (and that includes insight into similarities and dissimilarities, in short: the metaphorical) and a keen sense of when to deviate from the legal certainty that law's interest in '*Normgerechtigkeit*' seeks to accomplish. I mean by this, the notion that justice follows from the application of the legal norm. In short, when it is correct to seek the equitable solution of '*Einzelfallgerechtigkeit*' in the individual case. As Boasson already noted in 1919, each judicial decision is an expression of the judge's combined consciousness of what the law is and what the facts and circumstances of a case are. According to Boasson, to arrive at this stage, the judge needs to use her 'productive imagination'[71] to understand and gauge what others tell her, and, more importantly, where it is necessary to bring forth novel, yet convincing interpretations of the case at hand. Such interpretations are nourished by experience and knowledge of the human condition. Boasson also warns the judge that her expectations on the basis of her productive imagination need to be mitigated by her maintaining a keen sense of the mistakes that professional and private biases may provoke.[72]

3. Grasping the Singularity of the Situation

The demand that a judge be able to see intuitively and correctly what the case requires brings me to the topics of practical wisdom or *phronèsis*,

---

71 Boasson, *supra* note 34, at 135 (my translation of the Dutch 'eigen produktieve fantasie').
72 Boasson, *supra* note 34, at 135.

metaphorical insight and imagination, and the equitable, all in connection to '*Rechtsgefühl*' as a *sensus juridicus*.

In the Aristotelian spectrum of the intellectual and moral virtues, *phronèsis* is placed in the category of intellectual virtues. It is distinguished from *épistèmè*, theoretical knowledge aimed at 'knowing that'. *Phronèsis* is the virtue of knowing not only human beings' ultimate goals but also how to secure them. In other words, the virtue includes the application of good judgement to human conduct, and that is a 'knowing how' rather than a 'knowing that'.[73] Yet although *phronèsis* is categorised as an intellectual virtue, i.e. a virtue in the sense of a dispositional quality that one acquires, for example, through instruction or one's education generally, it is nevertheless a matter of *ethos* or character. *Phronèsis* is more than a combination of knowledge (for example, the knowledge of widely accepted moral rules) and deliberative technique. It entails instead the ability to apply insight – gained in specific situations, and context-dependent, as such insight necessarily is – to new questions as they crop up. Ethics and epistemology thus go hand in hand in *phronèsis* as a *praxis* of concrete action in specific situations. To Aristotle, the critical quality of human 'understanding' answers the imperative quality inherent in and posed by *phronèsis*. This means that 'its end is a statement of what we ought to do or not to do'.[74] While not identical, understanding and *phronèsis* concern the same objects,[75] as Aristotle points out, because understanding is also about those things that are subject to questioning and deliberation rather than the strictly defined, universal givens of scientific knowledge. In examining the nature of human actions, Aristotle says that

> matters of conduct and expediency have nothing fixed or invariable about them ... the agents themselves have to consider what is suited to the circumstances of each occasion (πρоσ τоν καίρον), just as is the case with the art of medicine or of navigation.[76]

That the demands of legal practice include the need to do whatever is necessary under the circumstances requires insight into the nature of ac-

---

73 See also Gilbert Ryle, 'Knowing How and Knowing That', *Proceedings of the Aristotelian Society* 46 (1945): 1-16.

74 Aristotle, *The Nicomachean Ethics* [1926], trans. H. Rackman, ed. J. Henderson (Cambridge/MA and London: Harvard University Press, 2003), VI.x.2, 1143a9-10, 359.

75 Aristotle, *supra* note 74, at VI.x.2, 1143a8, 359, 'it [understanding] is concerned with the same objects as Prudence' [i.e., *phronèsis*].

76 Aristotle, *supra* note 74, at II.ii.3-5, 1104a4-10, 77.

tions to find how we ought to do them. This is also a point made by Paul Ricoeur, who insists on the input of the Humanities when it comes to developing judicial *phronetic* intelligence. What matters to me here is that Ricoeur connects a discussion of the deliberative aspect of *phronèsis* with the idea of hermeneutic movement as circular, as the 'back-and-forth motion' between the idea that we have about, for example, the good life or justice, and the decision to be made.[77] This ties in neatly with the legal methodology of connecting the facts and the relevant norm, the hermeneutic movement between norm and fact, to which Ricoeur approvingly refers when he writes that 'the man of wise judgement determines at the same time the rule and the case, by grasping the situation in its singularity.'[78] Or, as Radbruch notes, 'the sense of law requires a nimble mind that is able to shift from the specific to the general and back again from the general to the specific'.[79] Thus, *phronèsis* is perceived as an essential component in actual judging, in the sense that to judge is to act. As Paul Scholten observes,

> The judge does something other than observing in favor of whom the scales turn, he decides. That decision is an act, it is rooted in the conscience of he who performs the act. That which is expected of a judge is a deed ... It is the task of the judge to deliver judgment. ... It is not a scientific proposition, but a declaration of will: this is how it should be. In the end it is a leap, just like any deed, any moral judgment is.[80]

So the judge must choose. In connection to what this means for the judicial narrative, this means to choose between events and human acts considered to be – or not to be – legally relevant facts; between stories that are plausible in a legal context and those that are not; between narratives to which a legal value can be attached, or not, and for what reason. Because at the end of the day, the judge as reader-narrator tells the world how she interprets and evaluates what others have told her; lastly, this includes

---

77 Paul Ricoeur, *Oneself as Another* [1990], trans. K. Blamey (Chicago and London: University of Chicago Press, 1992), 179.

78 Ricoeur, *supra* note 77, at 175.

79 Radbruch, *supra* note 65, at Section 13, 'The Psychology of the Man of the Law', 130-136, 135; Radbruch *supra* note 65, 1973 edition, 199, 'Das Rechtsgefühl verlangt also einen behenden Geist, der vom Besondern zum Allgemeinen und vom Allgemeinen wieder zum Besondern hinüberzuwechseln vermag' (my translation).

80 Scholten, *supra* note 64, at Section 28.

a decision on the consequences of different choices. What weight should be attached to specific facts? What pieces of evidence should be valued as sufficient proof? Does, as the premise of the theory of anchored narratives claims, a 'good story' in criminal law have to be compatible not only with the available evidence but also anchored in our general knowledge of the world?[81] As Scholten notes, in the sense that each decision is rooted in the judge's legal consciousness, this consciousness '… speaks only then when a person who is aware of his responsibility forms his judgment'. Scholten also acknowledges that because the judge

> is always an agent of the community — his decision is not an individual moral judgment, but a statement given by somebody with power that binds the community. This implies that he has to be well informed about the conceptions held by those who are subjected to his jurisdiction.[82]

It is important to note that Scholten writes 'well informed'. Being informed does not imply that the judge is required to take people's *'Rechtsgefühl'* into consideration, particularly in the heat of the moment in socially controversial matters.

4. Intuitive Perception of (Dis)similars

The quality of the judge's phronetic discernment is important for the success of the process of interpretation and the evaluation of the circumstances of a given case. If we follow Kant in his *Critique of Judgment*, the first stage of any judgement is the imaginative one. In the sense that this includes reflecting upon what is 'not immediately there before our eyes', it suggests that judicial intuition as 'seeing' is also connected to metaphoric insight. That is because *phronèsis* and understandings of metaphor share an emphasis on the ability to see similarities and dissimilarities in a particular situation. In other words, a successful metaphorical performance makes us say, 'Oh, but now I see'. Secondly, because *phronèsis* implies the judge's professionally trained intuition of 'knowing by doing', it includes the immediate perception of what matters in a given situation.

---

81 Willem A. Wagenaar et al., *Anchored Narratives: The Psychology of Criminal Evidence* (Harvester Wheatsheaf: St. Martin's Press, 1993).
82 Scholten, *supra* note 64, at Section 28.

As Ricoeur notes, '"To metaphorize well", said Aristotle, "implies an *intuitive* perception of the similarity in dissimilars"'.[83] When he elaborates on the combination of metaphor and imagination, Ricoeur suggests that the first step to be taken is to ask us to understand imagination as the insight that metaphor offers when it asks us to contemplate on resemblance. This insight is both cognitive and perceptual when the imagination is viewed as the 'ability to produce new kinds by assimilation and to produce them not above the differences, as in the concept, but in spite of and through the differences'.[84] What matters then is the phronètic combination of thinking – in judicial *phronèsis* this obviously includes recognising the relevant legal aspects – and then understanding by grasping the particularity of the new situation that metaphor suggests.

The second step is that of incorporating the pictorial dimension of the imagination. Both *phronèsis* and metaphor depend on the capability to see what precisely this specific thing is that connects that which we already know to the new significance of the particular that we have discerned. This is the productive step, i.e., when we move from the semantic aspect of the metaphor to our literally figuring out what the new thing is. It is the moment in which the ordinary reference of a word is discarded in favour of the new meaning produced by the metaphor? This requires not only imagination but – in order to preclude jumping to conclusions about the legal meaning of it all, both new and old – also Coleridgean poetic faith, i.e. 'that willing suspension of disbelief', and what John Keats called a 'negative capability', i.e. 'when man is capable of being in uncertainties'.[85] This ability to be in uncertainties resembles an ideal judge's being open to contingency and ambiguity more generally. Methodologically, the suspension of judgement – or ἐποχή, epoché in Greek philosophy – is normative for the legal profession. In the sense claimed here, it also points to an articulation of the conjunction in *Law and Literature*, when insights from literary theory can be transported to law to clarify existing notions.

---

83 Paul Ricoeur, *The Rule of Metaphor: Multi-Disciplinary Studies in the Creation of Meaning in Language* [1975], trans. R. Czerny, K. McLaughlin and J. Costello (London: Routledge, 1986), 6 (italics mine).

84 Paul Ricoeur, 'The Metaphorical Process as Cognition, Imagination, and Feeling', *Critical Inquiry* 5, no. 1 (1978): 143-159, 147-148.

85 Samuel Taylor Coleridge, *Biographia Literaria*, eds. J. Engell and W. Jackson Bate, *The Collected Works of Samuel Taylor Coleridge*, vol. 1 (Princeton: Princeton University Press, 1983), 6; John Keats, 'Letter of 21 December 1817 to his brothers George and Thomas', in *The Norton Anthology of English Literature*, vol. 2, eds. M. H. Abrams et al. (New York: W. W. W. Norton and Co., 1974), 705.

The third step in Ricoeur's scheme is the final move to the cognitive import of metaphor. This combination of the cognitive and the imaginative ties in with the division of knowledge in theoretical, or *épistèmè*, and practical, or *phronèsis*, in that it highlights the critical element of judicial *phronèsis*. The judge's imagination enables her to see what ties the singular situation of the case before her to the existing framework of law. At the same time, it asks her to determine which aspect of the singular situation calls for an adjustment in the application of the normative framework. *Phronèsis* and metaphoric insight thus enable the judge to bridge the gap between the generality of the legal rule and the particulars of the situation at hand. Rules and norms do not apply themselves. They are applied by humans, who in turn are responsible for avoiding reductive interpretations, both of the rule and the facts and circumstances of the case. Hence the importance of '*Rechtsgefühl*' as *sensus juridicus* also in relation to the topic of legal narrative, for, as Ricoeur puts it, 'One massive fact characteristic of the use of our languages [is]: *it is always possible to say the same thing in a different way*'.[86] Here, '*Rechtsgefühl*' connects to the right discrimination of the equitable in law in the individual case.[87]

5. Perspectival Reaction

It is precisely because the statutory norm is general that we need a perspectival reaction to which the Humanities, especially literature and philosophical hermeneutics, may help give form. In the *Nicomachean Ethics*, Aristotle argues that equity not only parallels written law but, where necessary, also prevails over it as a corrective. Thus, any error arising from the fact that any law is a general statement can be rectified by

> deciding as the lawgiver would himself decide if he were present on the occasion, and would have enacted if he had been cognizant of the

---

86 Paul Ricoeur, *Reflections on the Just*, trans. D. Pellauer (Chicago: University of Chicago Press, 2007), 116 (italics in the original).

87 Cf., Eduard von Hartmann, *Das sittliche Bewusstsein, eine Entwickelung seiner mannigfaltigen Gestalten in ihrem Zusammenhange* (Leipzig: Hermann Haacke Verlagshandlung, 1886), 231, that the feeling of and for the just that lives in human conciousness is the equitable conviction of justice ('das Gerechte wie es im menschlichen Bewusstsein ... als Überzeugung vom Gerechten lebt'), i.e., individualised and contextualised.

case in question. ... This is the essential nature of the equitable: it is a rectification of law where law is defective because of its generality.[88]

Equitable man is above all a man of empathic judgement, who shows consideration to others – also in the sense of forgiveness – 'that consideration which judges rightly what is equitable, judging *rightly* meaning what is *truly* equitable'.[89] Thus, Aristotle ties both the understanding of a case and the act of correct judgement to *phronèsis*. The doing of equity also depends on the particular circumstances of each occasion and each case – the προσ τον καίρον noted above – as it combines the virtue of legal justice and the moral virtue that is the product of ethos. If we combine this with Ricoeur's claim that 'Interpretation of the facts of what happened [is] in the final analysis of a narrative order',[90] the elements of *sensus juridicus*, taken together, suggest that equity's knowledge is also narrative in its attention to the particular aspects of the case, which are necessarily connected to the stories of the parties involved, not least of all, because judging requires hearing the other side in full. The idea of equity is also homogeneous with equality in the sense that Aristotle distinguished in Book 5 of the *Nicomachean Ethics*. There, he claimed that 'justice can only exist between those whose mutual relations are regulated by law, and law exists among those between whom there is a possibility of injustice, for the administration of the law means the discrimination of what is just and what is unjust'.[91] As noted above in section I.2, legal consciousness in the sense I am broadly conceiving it in this essay presupposes law, both codified and more generally as Ulpian's 'ars aequi et boni', the art of what is good, just and equitable. As a general notion of justness and fairness as fair dealing and doing to others as we would have them do to us, equity is also connected to the judge's conscience and consciousness of what is just, particularly if we look upon it from the point of view of the judge, who is responsible for bringing about justice. There is a rich and long tradition from Aristotle via St. Germain, Grotius and Kant to more recent authors such as Geoffrey Samuel and Gary Watt, on whether equity should to be viewed as part of law.[92] St. Germain, for example, argues that

---

88 Aristotle, *supra* note 74, at [1926] 2003) V.x.7-8, 1137b30-33, 317.

89 Aristotle, *supra* note 74, at VI.xi.1, 1143a24, 361 (italics in the original).

90 Ricoeur, *supra* note 86, at 69.

91 Aristotle, *supra* note 74, at V.vi.4, 291.

92 See G. Samuel, 'Equity and Legal Reasoning', *Pólemos* 11, no. 1 (2017): 41-53; G. Watt, *Equity Stirring: The Story of Justice Beyond Law* (Oxford and Portland/OR: Hart Publishing, 2009) for a common law view on equity.

the interrelation of conscience and equity is such that if you observe and keep equity in every general rule of the law, 'thy conscience shall never be extincted', because 'conscience [is] the law of our understanding'.[93] And while to Kant conscience and the equitable are part of one's inner forum rather than of the law, he defines the dictum of equity thus, 'The strictest right is the greatest wrong (*summum jus, summa injuria*) the remedies for which injustice cannot be brought before a court of law, but only before a court of conscience',[94] thus conceding that sometimes justice perhaps requires '*Rechtsgefühl*'.

IV. For Conscience's Sake

1. Popular Justice

Allow me to bring the strands of my argument together by returning to the second distinction made in section II between an individual and a societal '*Rechtsgefühl*', now in a different manner.

---

93 Christopher St. Germain, *The Doctor and Student, or, dialogues between a doctor of divinity and a student of the laws of England containing the grounds of those laws together with questions and cases concerning the equity thereof*, [1518], Lonang Institute, 2006 electronic edition of the 1874 edition revised and corrected by William Muchall, https://lonang.com/library/reference/stgermain-doctor-and-student/, last accessed 15 April 2019, Dialogue 1, chapters 15 and 16 'Of conscience' and 'What is equity' ('a right wiseness that considereth all the particular circumstances of the deed ... And such an equity must always be observed in every law of man, and in every general rule thereof: and that he knew well that said thus, Law covet to be ruled by equity. And the wise man saith, Be not overmuch right wise; for the extreme right wiseness is extreme wrong').

94 Kant's observations on equity can be found in an appendix to the first part of *The Metaphysics of Morals* (originally published in Königsberg in 1797 as the *Metaphysische Anfangsgründe der Rechtslehre von Immanuel Kant*). This first part is translated as the 'Introduction to the Elements of Justice' (*Metaphysical Elements of Justice*, second edition, trans. John Ladd [Indianapolis and Cambridge: Hackett Publishing Company, Inc., 1999]) or as the 'Introduction to the doctrine of rights' (*The Metaphysics of Morals*, trans. Mary Gregor, intr. by Roger J. Sullivan [Cambridge: Cambridge University Press, 1996]), or as the 'Introduction to the science of right' (*The Metaphysics of Morals*, trans. William Hastie, kant_morals.PDF (antilogicalism.com), last accessed 14 March 2021), and these differences in translation also show the complexity of the semantic problem of the concept of both law and equity.

When, as is often the case in today's world, the media, including social media, take up a legal issue, the *Volksgeist* can have severely negative effects in terms of actual justice when its feeling for law leads to a trial by media. This happened in October 2010 in Belgium, for instance, when a jury in the Court d'Assises convicted a woman of murder and sentenced her to thirty years imprisonment, presumably on the basis of the unpleasant impression she made during the trial which was prominently featured in the media, and despite the lack of directly incriminating evidence.[95] If the medium is indeed the message, our attention must be given to the combined effects of the medium's form and its narrative content. Narratives may be geared towards the development of empathy as much as towards an increase of antipathy. In other words, the judge who keeps in mind the Roman law maxim 'Give me the facts and I will give you the law' may find herself under serious pressure when she is bombarded by alternative facts and has to find her way through a morass of innuendo. If it comes to the point that her personal life becomes the object of media attention, this may cause professional dissonances as well, with negative consequences, for example, the judge's recusal for the wrong reason.

This brings me to a second perspective on popular justice in yet another sense: the decisions made by audiences of Ferdinand von Schirach's play *Terror*, in which the audience participates as the jury that has to decide on the question of whether or not the pilot Lars Koch is guilty of having killed the 164 persons on board an airplane that was hijacked by a terrorist and was on its way to crash into a sold-out football stadium.[96] How did it come about, and what does it mean that the audiences generally vote 60%:40% or more for an acquittal? Differences between national legal

---

95 Court of Cassation, Belgium, 3 May 2011, N292 – 3.5.11, available at https://justi tie.belgium.be/sites/default/files/downloads/AC%202011%2005.pdf, last accessed 1 March 2019. The defendant denied all of the charges. The facts were seemingly simple. The victim and the defendant had been having a love affair with the same man; they both belonged to the same parachute club; the victim's parachute had not opened when she jumped from a height of 4 kilometers; and the defendant was deemed to be knowledgeable about how to sabotage a parachute and how to enter the parachute club without being detected. The decision was not quashed by the Belgian Court of Cassation.

96 Ferdinand von Schirach, *Terror*, trans. David Tushingham (London: Faber and Faber, 2017); originally Ferdinand von Schirach, *Terror, ein Theaterstück und "Machen Sie unbedingt weiter"*, eine Rede (Munich: btb, 2016). See also Jeanne Gaakeer, "'Wrest once the law to your authority. To do a great right, do a little wrong?'" in *Law and the Humanities: Cultural Perspectives*, eds. Sidia Fiorato et al. (Berlin: De Gruyter, 2019), 477-498.

systems and jurisdictions have not seemed to influence European voting patterns. As noted by Mark Brown, in the United Kingdom 'A website for the play charts the number of guilty and not guilty verdicts across the 46 theatres in seven countries that have staged the show. In 1,063 trials, 91.9% of verdicts have been not guilty. Of the 287, 236 jurors who have cast a vote 60.7% voted not guilty.'[97] At the Berlin performance, the ratio was 255 to 207 for an acquittal.[98] The Dutch audience's vote, when the film adaption was broadcast on *National Geographic*, on 11 September 2017, was an astounding 95% for acquittal. Note that the way in which the film was broadcast was highly specific: the viewing was interlaced with commentaries of an air force general, a critic and an attorney, amongst others, each with their own form of legal consciousness.[99] So what does this tell us, as jurists, about our own legal cultures that from the point of view of positive (criminal) law, only the Japanese audience got it right?[100] Did the majority's '*Rechtsgefühl*' lead to a just decision, however utilitarian it is and however incorrect from a legal perspective? Or, did the majority vote arise out of the incorrect instructions given by the judge and the argumentative strategies of both the prosecutor and the attorney so that rhetorical and narrative affects won the case?[101] To me, the voting pattern for acquittal suggests that we should never forget that, 'in the telling of any story, it is possible to emphasize one particular aspect over another so that that aspect looms out of all proportion to the context'.[102] Nor should we forget that emotions are often unmanageable, and that popular justice usually does not sit well with the fundamental norms behind accepted legal principles if they are to be upheld under difficult circumstances. As

---

97 Mark Brown, 'Lyric Hammersmith's courtroom drama Terror will let audience be jury', *The Guardian online*, https://www.theguardian.com/stage/2017/mar/07/lyric-hammersmith-terror-courtroom-drama-ferdinand-von-schirach, last modified 7 March 2017, last accessed 28 August 2017.

98 Peter Kümmel, 'Ferdinand von Schirach, 255 gegen 207', *Die Zeit online*, last modified 10 October 2015, last accessed 10 May 2017, http://www.zeit.de/2015/41/ferdinand-von-schirach-terror-deutsches-theater. See also Thomas Möbius, *Ferdinand von Schirach, Terror* (Hollfeld: Bange Verlag, 2017), 105.

99 See 'Kijkers National Geographic vinden Lars Koch onschuldig', *Broadcastmagazin.nl*, last modified 11 September 2017, last accessed 15 September 2017, http://www.broadcastmagazine.nl/televisie/kijkers-national-geographic-vinden-lars-koch-onschuldig/.

100 Brown, *supra* note 97.

101 Cf. Greta Olson, 'The Turn to Passion: Has Law and Literature become Law and Affect?', *Law & Literature* 28, no. 3 (2016): 335-353.

102 Charlotte Rogan, *The Lifeboat* (London: Virago, 2012), 222-223. Cf., Ricoeur, *supra* the text accompanying note 86.

an aside: that legal professionals are not at all exempt from what von Schirach holds before us with his play *Terror* has been amply illustrated by the case of *Gäfgen v. Germany* before the European Court of Human Rights in Strasbourg.[103] The case inspired von Schirach to the degree that it also dealt with the border between legally justified and unjustified action. The majority decision expressed the formally correct legal norm that during the trial Gäfgen repeated his confession of having killed the boy he had kidnapped, one which had been made earlier under the threat of torture by the police. Yet, according to the dissenters, the majority decision diminished its value precisely by deciding that under these circumstances nothing had been wrong with Gäfgen's confession and trial. The dissenters held that

> there is an equally vital, compelling, and competing public interest in the preservation of the values of civilized societies founded upon the rule of law. ... Though the situation in this case was critical it is precisely in times of crisis that absolute values must remain uncompromised.[104]

As von Schirach notes, the situation in the Gäfgen case was one resembling the plot of a Greek tragedy: as a state official, the policeman was prohibited from acting as he wanted to as a human being – namely, threatening torture in order to hopefully save the boy's life – precisely because he has to uphold the law.[105]

2. Unpopular Decisions

This brings me to the topic of judicial conscience per se and also back to the Rümelins, father and son. To Gustav Rümelin, 'Conscience and a sense of law share the idea of the good as their common goal ... they pluck at the heart to realise the good'.[106] In the sense that Max Rümelin includes

---

103　European Court of Human Rights, *Case of Gäfgen v. Germany*, Application no. 22978/05, Grand Chamber, 1 June 2010, rectified 3 June 2010.

104　*Supra* note 103, *Gäfgen*, dissenting opinion, par. 12-13.

105　Ferdinand von Schirach, *Die Würde ist antastbar, Essays* [2014], (Munich: Piper Verlag, 2016), 109-116. In von Schirach's novel *Tabu*, the torture of the protagonist Sebastian von Eschberg is based on the defendant Gäfgen.

106　Gustav Rümelin, *supra* note 15, at 13, 'Gewissen und Rechtsgefühl haben die Idee des Guten zu ihrem gemeinsamen Inhalt und Ziel ... sie sind die Forderungen an das Gemüt, das Gute zu verwirklichen' (my translation).

a 'natural-law jurisprudence of emotion'[107] in the idea of '*Rechtsgefühl*', I see a connection to Radbruch. In his observation that 'The three aspects of the idea of law [i.e., justice, expediency, legal certainty as delineated in Section 9] are of equal value, and in case of conflict there is no decision between them but by individual conscience', Radbruch adds the important observation that 'there may be "shameful laws" which conscience refuses to obey'.[108] In other words, the conceptual borders between judicial conscience, legal consciousness and individual conscience may well become blurred in individual cases.

This is not to argue, however, that we should renew the theoretical debate on whether 'Rechtsgefühl' should be considered as part of law or outside it, or whether Max Rümelin and von Jhering should be contrasted with Radbruch or not.[109] Rather, it is to point out the simple fact that for a law to be set aside as 'supra-statutory law', one needs someone to interpret that law and that someone is the judge, if not the legislator who later changes that law. That is why *sensus juridicus* in the sense delineated here matters, not least of all because Radbruch insists that the goal of 'law, including positive law, cannot be otherwise defined than as a system and an institution whose very meaning is to serve justice'.[110] And, as Ian Ward observes, in his essay on 'Justice and Equity in International Relations', Radbruch invokes Aristotle's concept of equity as a kind of supra-norm of 'universal morality'.[111] From the perspective of legal practice this is important, given that Radbruch's view on law as a cultural phenomenon

---

107 Max Rümelin, *supra* note 49, at 50, 'naturrechtlichen Gefühlsjurisprudenz'. Cf., Leopold August Warnkönig, *Rechtsphilosophie als Naturlehre des Rechts* (Freiburg im Breisgau: Wagner, 1839), 6, 'Nichts könne positives Recht seyn als was es zu seyn verdiene'. Available at https://archive.org/details/bub_gb_fcwGAAAAcAAJ/page/n17, last accessed 26 April 2019.

108 Radbruch, *supra* note 65, at Section 10, 118.

109 For example, Behrends in von Jhering, *supra* note 23, at 97-98.

110 Gustav Radbruch, 'Statutory Lawlessness and Supra-Statutory Law', trans. Bonnie Litschewski-Paulson and Stanley Paulson, *Oxford Journal of Legal Studies* 26, no. 1 (2006): 1-11, 7. It should, however, also be noted that Radbruch radically changed his view on law and justice after the consequences of Nazi law became clear to him. Radbruch started out as a legal positivist and the original 1914 edition of his *Rechtsphilosophie* is testament to that: 'Wir verachten den Pfarrer, der gegen seine Überzeugung predigt, aber wir verehren den Richter, der sich durch sein widerstrebendes Rechtsgefühl in seiner Gesetzestreue nicht beirren lässt', on the view that the (codified) law obtains its value precisely because it is the sediment of what is thought to be just, Radbruch, *supra* note 65, at 178.

111 Ian Ward, *Law, Philosophy and National Socialism: Heidegger, Schmitt and Radbruch in Context* (Berne: Peter Lang, 1992), 186.

was inspired by actual cases occurring after World War II, involving necessary attempts to solve dilemmas of whether or not to apply legal norms retroactively, and that assignment pertained directly to the validity of law itself. To reiterate, Radbruch's jurisprudential position is a humanistic, intermediate one between the value-absolutism of natural law and the value-relativism of legal positivism. As we all know, this has been widely acknowledged by the judiciary as the Radbruch Formula.[112] Other than the Roman jurists, discussed in section I.2, we no longer hold the view that some precepts are innate to all human beings, we can then agree that some norms of human conduct are good at all times.

What does this suggest for judicial practice? Two more examples serve to illustrate the continued importance of my topic. The judge eats his meals in solitude, wrote Piero Calamandrei, and his only table companion is his independence.[113] That judicial integrity may come at a high price is made clear by the aftermath of a decision of the Court of Appeal in Leeuwarden, the Netherlands, in 1943 during the German occupation. A panel of three justices tried the case of a defendant accused of theft. In those days, the occupier had made the penitentiary regime increasingly harder. The conditions in the camp Erika in the city of Ommen, where those convicted of petty crimes by the Leeuwarden Court were sent, were so bad that they meant an increase in the usual penalty. Bodily harm was inflicted by the guards, and starvation, endless drills, and heavy physical labour caused many inmates to die, and those who did survive were physically wrecked. The judicial panel in this case decided that the expected outcome of applying such a form of imprisonment was not only an undesirable increase of the penalty, but that it was against the principles of humanity and the spirit of the law. So, they sentenced the defendant to the time he had already spent in pre-trial detention, because, as they wrote by way of justification of their decision, 'for their consciences' they could not apply the then current norm.[114] This was their solution to the

---

112 Cf., Döderlein, *supra* note 45, at 289. Döderlein offers the literary examples of Bernhard Schlink's *Der Vorleser* and Juli Zeh's *Corpus Delicti*. For the latter, see also Gaakeer, *Judging from Experience, supra* note 5, at chapter 13, for an analysis of the novel in relation to modern technology and privacy.

113 Piero Calamandrei, *Eulogy of Judges*, trans. John Clarke Adams, Princeton, Princeton University Press, 1946 (orig. *Elogio dei giudici, scritto da un avvocato*, 1936), par.121.

114 *Nederlandse Jurisprudentie* 1951, no. 643, Court of Appeal Leeuwarden, 25 February 1943.

moral-formal dilemma that they faced and the cognitive dissonance that they experienced.

Writing this judicial decision was not the task of producing a narrative of compromise, for while the deliberations in chambers, secret as these remain, took a very long time, the outcome was unanimous. The case remained unpublished until 1951, when it became a tribute to the judicial panel and its president Viehoff, who with one of the other two justices had been immediately removed from office 'owing to gross neglect of their official duties'. When the newspapers published the news of the justices having been interrogated about their decision, the inmates of the camp where dissident intellectuals were interned made a bunk bed ready for them. Both justices went into hiding immediately after the interrogations. They had their suitcases ready at home, as one of their children later divulged.[115]

That judicial integrity may come at an even higher price is exemplified in a story by the German author Ernst Wiechert, *Der Richter*.[116] Its protagonist experiences cognitive dissonance between his institutional role and his conscience. The story is set in the days before the Second World War. During a court session when the protagonist, a judge in a lower court, is interrogating a witness, the town's old berry gatherer Veronika suddenly enters the courtroom and tells him, 'He lies in the stone quarry ... and the light shines in his open eyes ... he is cold already'.[117] When the judge asks her who lies there, she replies that it is Joseph Huber. The judge reassures her that he will do what is necessary, and she then casually remarks that in earlier times the judge's son and Huber had been great friends. The judge breaks off the court session and makes a phone call to the public prosecutor. The judge goes to the quarry. When the body is removed from the scene, the judge finds an envelope with a name on it in the field of berries. When later that evening his son Christean comes home, the judge sees a blackberry leaf on his arm. The judge muses that he too came down the blackberry slope that afternoon. Then he tells his son that he has found the envelope. Christean admits to the deed: a new era has started, and

---

115   For the details surrounding the decision I draw on Herman L.C. Hermans, *Om des Gewetens Wille, de geschiedenis van een arrest in oorlogstijd* (Leeuwarden: Friese Pers Boekerij, 2003).

116   Ernst Wiechert (1887-1950), *Der Richter* (München: K. Desch, 1948). To my knowledge no English translation exists. A French translation of the story can be found in Ernst Wiechert, *Histoire d'un adolescent*, trans. C. Santelli (Paris: Mercure de France, 1962).

117   Wiechert, *supra* note 116, at 3, my translation.

the dead man was a traitor to his country. The judge responds, 'So you thought a closed mouth is a silent mouth. But now you know that it is not silent, dear son. It has opened'.[118] When the judge says that there are only two persons who can tell the truth, Christean takes responsibility and goes to the police.

The next day, however, it turns out that the police have refused to take Christean's deposition or to accept the envelope, because he supposedly deserved a reward rather than punishment for his deed. Then the judge sends his son to town to the public prosecutor, but again Christean returns. The judge tells Christean they will go to the last court, meaning the victim's parents to whom Christean confesses the deed. The victim's father speaks softly too when he addresses the judge and tells him there is no heart more heavily burdened than the judge's own. I take this to be a reference to the double burden that the judge carries, to turn in his own son and to come to a decision about his own position. Three days later, the war breaks out, and Christean heads to the front. The judge writes his letter of resignation. It ends, 'Where there is need for a judge, there must needs be law. And where there is a law, justice must be done. But where there is no justice, there is no room for law and neither for a judge.'[119] When the context in which the judge has to uphold the law becomes repugnant to him or her, the ultimate consequence of such dissonance is to resign.

To end on a sobering note: it is indeed as Paul Scholten argued that

> The judge is expected to act. He has to have the courage to bear the responsibility: in the end I say a or b, not a and b. The judge who hovers in doubt and can't arrive at the act of taking a decision, isn't fit to be a judge.[120]

To Scholten the fact that we 'finally end up with the conscience of the judge' is not problematic, for 'it is better to accept that which is defective and subjective, than to gape at an appearance of objectivity and certainty, which is nothing more than show and doesn't hold out against criticism'.[121] By way of a conclusion, I reiterate what von Jhering wrote: 'Our

---

118 Wiechert, *supra* note 116, at 8, my translation.
119 Wiechert, *supra* note 116, at 16, my translation.
120 Scholten, *supra* note 64, at par. 28. Cf., Ehrlich, *supra* the text accompanying note 44.
121 Scholten, *supra* note 64, at par. 28. Cf., Ulrich Matz, *Rechtsgefühl und ideales Wertreich* (Munich: Beck, 1966), 19-20, for the acknowledgment, 'dass die Erkenntnis des überpositiven Rechts in den emotionalen Bereich verlegt wird' and this

sense of justice ... depends on the real facts and circumstances that have been realised throughout history'.[122] Yet at the same time the unsimple fact is that in democratic societies under the rule of law, laws depend on real judges to interpret them, on their *sensus juridicus,* and on their guts. To think that it is otherwise would be a dangerous fiction.

---

leads to a 'Gefühlsjurisprudenz' that combined with the accepted traditional, 'rational' legal methodology gives primacy to judicial conscience and legal consciousness as decisive elements of the act of judging.

122 Von Jhering, *supra* the text accompanying note 25.

Rechtsgefühle. Die Relevanz des Affektiven für die Rechtsentwicklung[*]
– in Jherings *Kampf um's Recht* und im demokratischen Verfassungsstaat

Gabriele Britz

Die aktuelle wissenschaftliche Debatte um den Zusammenhang von Recht und Gefühl[1] hat in Rudolf von Jhering einen frühen Vordenker, der sich in *Der Kampf um's Recht*[2] auf eigene Weise und zu ganz eigenen Zwecken ausführlich dem Rechtsgefühl widmete: Jherings Abhandlung lässt sich als faszinierender Versuch lesen, die Idee des Rechtsgefühls zum Zwecke der (rechtspolitischen) Einforderung legislativer Rechtsentwicklung einzusetzen. Wird der Text vor seinem vordemokratischen zeitlichen Hintergrund gelesen, ergeben sich mögliche Erträge für die heute zu führenden Debatten um Recht und Gefühl gerade in dieser historischen Differenz des staatsrechtlichen und -tatsächlichen Kontexts.

Rechtsgefühl ist ein umfassendes Phänomen. Wo Recht ist, sind Menschen – als Rechtsbetroffene, als Rechtsetzende, als Rechtsanwendende, oder als Menschen, die Recht kommentieren oder erforschen; wo aber Menschen sind, sind stets auch Gefühle (I.). Jhering entfaltet sein Plädoyer für Rechtsentwicklung auf der Grundlage opulenter Annahmen über das Rechtsgefühl der rechtsunterworfenen Person. In dramatischen Bildern wird die individuelle und überindividuelle Lebensnotwendigkeit eines subjektiven Rechtsgefühls und des daraus erwachsenden sittlich-idealen Rechtsgefühls beschrieben. Über die empirischen und normativen Implikationen ließe sich diskutieren und streiten. Im Folgenden soll das Augenmerk jedoch vor allem auf das gerichtet werden, was in der hier

---

[*] Verschriftlichte Keynote zur gleichnamigen Tagung des Instituts für Anglistik und des Rudolf-von-Jhering-Instituts für Rechtswissenschaftliche Grundlagenforschung der Justus-Liebig-Universität Gießen am 13. Juni 2019. Der Vortragsstil wurde beibehalten.

[1] S. *Greta Olson*. The Turn to Passion: Has Law and Literature become Law and Affect? Law & Literature 28 (2016), S. 335 ff.

[2] *Rudolf von Jhering*. Der Kampf um's Recht. Abdruck der Originalausgabe von 1872 im Rudolf Haufe Verlag 1992.

gewählten Lesart des Textes den Flucht- und Zielpunkt der Jhering'schen Darlegungen bildet: der (empirisch-)argumentativen Absicherung der Forderung nach grundlegender Reform des Rechts (II.). Dieser methodische Zugriff ist vor dem konstitutionellen Hintergrund seiner Zeit zu sehen, regt aber durchaus zur Frage an, ob Rechtsgefühl auch heute sinnvoll als Begründung für die Forderung von Rechtsentwicklung dienen kann. Unzufriedenheit mit der geltenden Rechtslage als „Unrechtsgefühl" zu artikulieren, bleibt Verlockung, trifft im demokratischen Verfassungsstaat jedoch auf andere Vorzeichen, die es in Rechnung zu stellen gilt (III.).

I. Zusammenhänge von Recht und Gefühl

Einige praktische Zusammenhänge von Recht und Gefühl mögen die Allgegenwärtigkeit von Rechtsgefühl exemplarisch illustrieren. Dabei wird der fünfte und letzte der betrachteten Zusammenhänge jener sein, für den sich Jhering in seinem *Kampf um's Recht* interessiert.

1. Recht *erzeugt* Gefühle. Das können ablehnende Gefühle sein. Extrem negative Gefühle breiter Teile der Bevölkerung hat etwa in den späten 60er Jahren des letzten Jahrhunderts die sogenannte Notstandsverfassung[3] erzeugt. Auf der anderen politischen Seite hat etwa die Entscheidung des Bundesverfassungsgerichts zur Anwendung der Meinungsfreiheit auf die Aussage „Soldaten sind Mörder"[4] in Teilen der Gesellschaft regelrechte Aversionen ausgelöst, was nicht nur dazu beigetragen hat, dass der polizeiliche Schutz für betroffene Richter zeitweilig erhöht wurde, sondern auch ein Grund dafür war, dass im Bundesverfassungsgericht zur kommunikativen Begleitung der Gerichtsentscheidungen dauerhaft eine Pressestelle eingerichtet wurde. Eine positive Art des Gefühls scheint hingegen beispielsweise der Beschluss zur sogenannten dritten Option beim Geschlechtseintrag[5] bei Betroffenen ausgelöst zu haben, denen sich hierdurch wohl ein Gefühl des Anerkanntseins vermittelt hat. Auch die bloße Formulierung von Recht kann Gefühle erzeugen: Als „Gute-Kita-Gesetz"[6] und als „Ge-

---

3 Siebzehntes Gesetz zur Ergänzung des Grundgesetzes (24. Juni 1968, BGBl. I 709). Enthalten sind Regelungen zur Einschränkung des Grundgesetzes in Notsituationen der BRD (z.B. im Verteidigungsfall).

4 BVerfGE 93, 266 ff.

5 BVerfGE 147, 1 ff.

6 Gesetz zur Weiterentwicklung der Qualität und zur Teilhabe in der Kindertagesbetreuung (19. Dezember 2018, BGBl. I 2696).

ordnete-Rückkehr-Gesetz"[7] bezeichnete Gesetze zielten schon mit diesen Namen auf die Erzeugung guter Gefühle. Und schließlich hat Art. 2 Abs. 1 GG seine Formulierung („Jeder hat das Recht auf die freie Entfaltung seiner Persönlichkeit") nicht zuletzt wegen des feierlichen Klangs erhalten. Es ging um „das Würdevolle im Klang", das man in die Grundrechte hineinlegen wolle[8].

2. Recht *berücksichtigt* Gefühle. Beispielsweise ist der in vielen rechtlichen Zusammenhängen anzutreffende Schutz familiärer Bindungen auch als Rücksicht auf emotionale Lagen zu begreifen[9]. Im Datenschutzrecht ist Rücksichtnahme auf ein „Gefühl dauernden Überwachtwerdens"[10] einer der Urgründe für weitreichende Schutzregelungen. Auf die Stirn geschrieben ist die Rücksicht auf Gefühlslagen schuldrechtlichen Ansprüchen des Privatrechts wegen immaterieller Beeinträchtigungen wie etwa dem auch für seelisches Leid zustehenden Schmerzensgeld und dem Schadensersatzanspruch wegen entgangener Urlaubsfreude.

3. Unter Umständen *vermittelt sich* Recht den Rechtsanwendenden auch über Gefühle. Ob etwa eine gerichtliche Fehlentscheidung schon als nach Art. 3 Abs. 1 GG verbotene „Willkür"[11] zu bezeichnen ist, ob ein Unglücksfall bereits „katastrophische"[12] Dimensionen hat und deshalb – relevant für den Streitkräfteeinsatz im Inneren – als besonders schwerer Unglücksfall im Sinne von Art. 35 Abs. 2 Satz 2, Abs. 3 Satz 1 GG gilt oder ob die schlechte Behandlung eines Menschen durch den Staat bereits die „Menschenwürde" (Art. 1 Abs. 1 GG) verletzt, lässt sich schwer messerscharf anhand objektiver Kriterien abgrenzen. Alle drei Rechtsbegriffe appellieren auch an die Intuition der Rechtsanwendenden. Ihr Maßstab vermittelt sich wohl auch dadurch, dass sie bei den Rechtsanwendenden ein Gefühl von und für Willkür, Katastrophe und Würde erzeugen.

4. *Rechtsprofis haben* Gefühle. Professionelle Juristinnen und Juristen können persönliche emotionale Bindungen und Interessen haben. Weil diese nicht sicher vollständig unterdrückt werden können, objektiver Rechtsfin-

---

7 Zweites Gesetz zur besseren Durchsetzung der Ausreisepflicht (15. August 2019, BGBl. I 1294).
8 Entstehungsgeschichte des Grundgesetzes. JöR Band 1. 2. Auflage 2010, S. 61.
9 Besonders deutlich BVerfGE 136, 382, 388 f. Rn. 22 f.
10 S. etwa BVerfGE 125, 260, 335 m.w.N.
11 Zur Willkürgrenze (Art. 3 Abs. 1 GG) statt vieler BVerfGE 42, 64, 72 f.
12 BVerfGE 132, 1, 17 Rn. 43.

dung aber entgegenstehen könnten, enthalten alle Verfahrensordnungen Ausschluss- und Befangenheitsregeln[13]. Außerdem artikulieren Richterinnen und Richter bei der täglichen praktischen Rechtssuche „Störgefühle" und „Bauchgefühle". Als methodischer Zwischenschritt mögen diese euphemistisch als Judiz bezeichneten Phänomene hilfreich sein. Letztlich dürften die Regeln rechtsstaatlicher Entscheidungsfindung aber nur dann gewahrt sein, wenn diese Gefühle auf ihre rationalen Gehalte befragt und unter Heranziehung von Normtexten, Judikaten und begleitender Literatur argumentativ erhärtet oder eben auch verworfen werden.

5. Auch *juristische Laien haben* Rechtsgefühle und Gerechtigkeitsgefühle, die unterschiedlichste Kontexte betreffen können und die das Recht auf verschiedene Art und Weise in Rechnung stellt und verarbeitet. Das Rechtsgefühl juristischer Laien steht im Mittelpunkt von Jherings *Der Kampf um's Recht*. Er erzählt von den zwei Arten der Rechtsgefühle juristischer Laien und gewinnt daraus Argumente für seine Forderung nach grundlegender Fortentwicklung des Rechts. Rechtsgefühl und Rechtsentwicklung sind nicht nur Thema der heutigen Tagung, sondern bilden auch das zentrale Gespann in Jherings Abhandlung.

II. Rechtsgefühl als Argument für Rechtsentwicklung (Jhering)

Jherings Abhandlung zielt am Ende auf eine umfassende Rechtsentwicklung. Seine Forderung nach Rechtsentwicklung begründet er in einem Dreischritt des Rechtsgefühls. Rechtsgefühl wird erstens als physische Kraft beschrieben, die auf Durchsetzung von Recht drängt (1) und damit zweitens auch das Recht an sich und so zugleich das Bestehen des Staates nach innen und nach außen sichert (2). Damit Recht diese Rechtsgefühle dauerhaft erzeugen und so zu Stabilität beitragen kann, muss es aber drittens bestimmten Voraussetzungen genügen, hinter denen die Rechtswirklichkeit in Jherings Augen grob zurückblieb und damit defizitär war (3). So ist das Rechtsgefühl ein empirisch gekleidetes, aber doch weitgehend gedankliches Konstrukt zur Begründung von Rechtsentwicklungsbedarf. Jhering flaggt seine Begründung als praktische Zweckmäßigkeitsargumentation aus, die gerade aus ihrem (angeblich) empirischen Bezugs-

---

13 Exemplarisch für die Mitglieder des Bundesverfassungsgerichts §§ 18, 19 BVerfGG.

punkt (dem tatsächlichen Rechtsgefühl und dem körperlich empfundenen Schmerz von Rechtskränkung) ihre Überzeugungskraft nehmen will.

1. Rechtsgefühl aus persönlicher Kränkung

Jherings Begründungsgang beginnt beim Rechtsgefühl des Individuums; und zwar beim Gefühl in Bezug auf die eigene rechtliche Position im Verhältnis zu anderen Personen (Privatrecht). Weil die Verletzung privater Rechte von der betroffenen Person als Kränkung erlebt wird, ist der Gerichtsprozess „die Behauptung der Person selber und ihres Rechtsgefühls" (S. 25 f.). Dabei geht es nicht notwendig um die Durchsetzung objektiv wertvoller Positionen, sondern um die Wahrung der Persönlichkeit an sich: „Eine innere Stimme sagt ihm, dass er nicht zurücktreten darf, dass es sich nicht um das werthlose Object, sondern um sein Rechtsgefühl, seine Selbstachtung, seine Persönlichkeit handelt – kurz, der Process gestaltet sich für ihn aus einer blossen Interessenfrage zu einer Charakterfrage" (S. 26). Recht tritt im Moment der Verletzung als Gefühl und Schmerz erfahrbar ins Bewusstsein. Die erlebte Kränkung lässt den Kampf um's Recht entflammen, weil nun Genugtuung gesucht wird und gesucht werden muss. Empirisches und Normatives mischen sich in der Beschreibung dieser Situation.

2. Ideales Rechtsgefühl

Neben dieses ichbezogene Kränkungsgefühl angesichts „persönlichen Unrechts" tritt ein sittliches („ideales") Rechtsgefühl. Insoweit geht es nicht mehr um den einzelnen Menschen, sondern um die Behauptung des Rechts als Pflicht gegenüber dem Gemeinwesen (S. 51). „Indem er *sein* Recht behauptet, hält er *das* Recht aufrecht" (S. 54). Das ist „Mitwirkung an der Verwirklichung der Rechtsidee" (S. 58). „Welch hohe Bedeutung gewinnt damit der Kampf des Subjekts um sein Recht! ... Jeder der beim Anblick der Übermacht oder des Übermuthes des Unrechts Entrüstung, sittlichen Zorn empfindet, besitzt ihn [den idealen Sinn des Rechts], denn während das Gefühl, welches die Rechtskränkung hervorruft, der Verletzung der eigenen Person entstammt, hat jenes Gefühl seinen Grund in der Macht der sittlichen Idee über das menschliche Gemüth, ist es der Protest, der sittlichen kräftigen Natur gegen den Frevel am Recht, das schönste und erhabenste Zeugniss, welches das Rechtsgefühl von sich selber ablegen kann ..." (S. 59 f.).

Benötigt wird „dieser Idealismus des Rechtssinnes im Menschen der den Frevel und Hohn gegen die Idee des Rechts tiefer empfindet als das persönliche Unrecht, und für den eben dieser Schmerz die sittliche Nöthigung enthält, für die gefährdete Rechtsidee einzutreten, kurz jene Naturen, denen eine innere Stimme [den] Satz verkündet ...: Der Dienst für das Recht um des Rechtes halber ohne eigenes Interesse ist sittliche Pflicht" (S. 61).

Illustriert wird dies an der literarischen Gestalt des Michael Kohlhaas (Heinrich von Kleist): „Ein Mann, rechtschaffen, streng rechtlich, voller Liebe für seine Familie, von kindlich frommem Sinn wird zu einem Attila, der mit Feuer und Schwert die Orte vernichtet, in die sein Gegner sich geflüchtet hat. Und wodurch wird er es? Gerade durch die Eigenschaft, die ihn sittlich so hoch über seine Gegner stellt...: durch seine hohe Achtung vor dem Recht, seinen Glauben an die Heiligkeit desselben, die Thatkraft seines ächten, gesunden Rechtsgefühls. Und gerade darauf beruht die tief erschütternde Tragik seines Schicksals, dass eben das, was den Vorzug und den Adel seiner Natur ausmacht: der ideale Schwung seines Rechtsgefühls, seine heroische, Alles vergessende und Alles opfernde Dahingabe an die Idee des Rechts im Contact mit der elenden damaligen Welt, ... der Pflichtvergessenheit und Feigheit der Richter zu seinem Verderben ausschlägt" (S. 68).

3. Fluchtpunkt: Rechtskritik

Über das Schicksal des verratenen Michael Kohlhaas gelingt Jhering der entscheidende Schritt in die Rechtskritik: „... im Stich gelassen von der Macht, die es schützen sollte, ... [erhebt] das nationale Rechtsgefühl ... seine Anklage und seinen Protest gegen derartige Rechtszustände" (S. 69 f.). „Dieser Idealismus des gesunden Rechtsgefühls ... weiss nicht bloss, dass er in *seinem* Recht *das* Recht, sondern auch, dass er in *dem* Recht *sein* Recht vertheidigt. – Für einen Staat, der geachtet dastehen will nach Aussen, fest und unerschüttert im Innern, gibt es kein kostbareres Gut, das er zu hüten und zu pflegen hat, als das nationale Rechtsgefühl. ... In dem gesunden, kräftigen Rechtsgefühl jedes Einzelnen besitzt der Staat die sicherste Garantie seines eigenen Bestehens nach Innen wie nach Aussen; das Rechtsgefühl ist die Wurzel des ganzen Baumes; taugt die Wurzel nicht, verdorrt sie in Gestein und ödem Sand, so ist alles Andere Blendwerk – wenn der Sturm kommt, wird der ganze Baum entwurzelt. Aber der Stamm und die

Krone haben den Vorzug, dass man sie sieht, während die Wurzeln im Boden stecken und sich dem Blicke entziehen. Der zersetzende Einfluss, den ungerechte Gesetze und schlechte Rechtseinrichtungen auf die moralische Kraft des Volks ausüben, spielt unter der Erde, in jenen Regionen, die so mancher Politiker nicht seiner Betrachtung werth hält, indem es ihm bloss auf die stattliche Krone ankommt; von dem Gift, das aus der Wurzel in die Krone steigt, hat er keine Ahnung. Aber der Despotismus weiss, wo er ansetzen muss, um den Baum zu Fall zu bringen; er lässt die Krone zunächst unangetastet, aber er zerstört die Wurzeln. Mit Eingriffen in das Privatrecht, mit der Rechtlosigkeit des Individuums hat jeder Despotismus begonnen; hat er hier seine Arbeit vollendet, so stürzt der Stamm von selbst" (S. 74 ff.).

Es schließen sich praktische Empfehlungen an (S. 77 f.): „Die Kraft des Volkes ist gleichbedeutend mit der Kraft seines Rechtsgefühls – Pflege des nationalen Rechtsgefühls ist Pflege der Gesundheit und Kraft des Staats. Diese Pflege ist aber selbstverständlich nichts Doktrinäres: Schule und Unterricht, sondern sie besteht in der praktischen Durchführung der Grundsätze der Gerechtigkeit in allen Lebensverhältnissen. Festigkeit und Klarheit, Bestimmtheit des materiellen Rechts, Beseitigung aller Sätze in allen Sphären des Rechts, an denen ein gesundes Rechtsgefühl Anstoss nehmen muss, nicht bloss des Privatrechts, sondern der Polizei, der Verwaltung, der Finanzgesetzgebung; Unabhängigkeit der Gerichte, möglichste Vervollkommnung der processualischen Einrichtungen – das ist ein sichererer Weg zur Hebung der Kraft des Staats als die höchste Steigerung des Militärbudgets. Jede willkürliche oder ungerechte Bestimmung, welche die Staatsgewalt erlässt oder aufrecht erhält, ist eine Schädigung des nationalen Rechtsgefühls und damit der nationalen Kraft selbst, eine Versündigung gegen die Idee des Rechts, die auf den Staat selbst zurückschlägt, und die er oft theuer mit Zinseszinsen bezahlen muss …! Ich selber bin freilich der Ansicht, dass der Staat nicht bloss wegen solcher Zweckmässigkeitsrücksichten diese Sünden vermeiden soll, ich betrachte es vielmehr als seine höchste und heiligste Pflicht, diese Idee ihrer selbst willen zu verwirklichen, aber das ist ja doctrinäre Phantasterei, und ich will es dem praktischen Politiker und Staatsmann nicht verdenken, wenn er eine solche Zumutung achselzuckend abweist. Aber eben darum haben wir ihm gegenüber die praktische Seite der Frage hervorgekehrt, für die er das volle Verständnis hat – die Idee und das Interesse des Staats gehen hier Hand in Hand. Einem schlechten Recht ist auf Dauer kein noch so gesundes Rechtsgefühl gewachsen, es erlahmt, stumpft sich ab, verkümmert. Denn das Wesen des Rechts ist, wie schon öfter bemerkt, die That, – was der

Flamme die freie Luft, ist dem Rechtsgefühl die Freiheit der That, ihm die-
selbe verwehren oder verkümmern, heisst es ersticken."

Es folgt dann noch auf vielen Seiten eine furiose Generalabrechnung
mit dem geltenden Privatrecht und Strafrecht (insbesondere dem Recht
der Notwehr), das vom Volk nicht verstanden werde und das Volk nicht
verstehe, insbesondere nicht dem gesunden Rechtsgefühl Rechnung trage.
Obwohl Jhering dies scheinbar beiläufig anhängt, scheint doch alles gerade darauf zu zielen: „Ich könnte damit meinen Vortrag schließen, denn
mein Thema ist erschöpft. Ich hoffe aber, dass Sie es mir verstatten werden, wenn ich Ihre Aufmerksamkeit noch für eine Frage in Anspruch nehme, die mit dem Gegenstand meines Vortrages eng zusammenhängt, es ist
nämlich die: in wie weit unser heutiges Recht, über das ich mir allein ge-
traue ein Urtheil abzugeben, den von mir so eben entwickelten Anforderungen entspricht. Ich nehme keinen Anstand, diese Frage mit aller Ent-
schiedenheit zu verneinen. Dasselbe bleibt hinter den berechtigten Ansprüchen eines gesunden Rechtsgefühls weit zurück ..." (S. 79 f.).

Das empirisch angelegte Rechtsgefühl als Triebkraft eigenen Prozessie-
rens wird zur Voraussetzung des stabilen Staates – weil es hierfür der die
Rechtswahrung einfordernden Praxis der Individuen bedürfe. Der Staat
ersticke diese Triebkraft aber, wenn er nicht das passende Recht biete.
Erkennbar dient das als empirische Größe präsentierte Rechtsgefühl des
Volks als Grund und Legitimation für die Forderung nach einer grundlegenden Reform des geschriebenen Rechts.

III. Rechtsgefühl als Argument für Rechtsentwicklung heute?

Verletztes Rechtsgefühl dient Jhering im dritten und letzten Schritt also
als Quelle und Triebkraft von Rechtsentwicklung. Es soll nun allein dieser
letzte Gedankenschritt auf die heutige Zeit gewandt und auf seine Taug-
lichkeit unter den geltenden verfassungsrechtlichen Rahmenbedingungen
hin betrachtet werden. Taugt Rechtsgefühl heute als Argument für Rechtsentwicklung?

1. Rechtsgefühl als Argument für legislative Rechtsentwicklung?

Die im vordemokratischen Obrigkeitsstaat entwickelten Thesen zum Zusammenhang von Rechtsgefühl und Rechtsentwicklung können nicht unmittelbar an der heutigen Situation auf ihre Plausibilität überprüft wer-

den, in der Recht seine Legitimation normativ allein von den Gewaltunterworfenen her nehmen kann („Alle Staatsgewalt geht vom Volke aus", Art. 20 Abs. 2 Satz 1 GG) und entsprechende Verfahren verfassungsrechtlich eingerichtet sind, damit Gesetzgebung tatsächlich gegenüber „dem Volk" verantwortet wird. Forderungen nach Rechtsänderung finden unter diesen Bedingungen andere Möglichkeiten der Begründung und naturgemäß andere Wege der Durchsetzung als in einer vordemokratischen Ordnung. Weil der Mechanismus demokratischer Gesetzgebung zur Verfügung steht, muss nicht mit („heilig" gesprochenem) Rechtsgefühl begründet und legitimiert werden, sondern genügt politischer Wille, der überzeugen und Mehrheiten finden muss, sich dann aber – abgesehen von höherrangigen Bindungen etwa aus den Grund- und Menschenrechten – ohne weiteren Legitimationsbedarf in Rechtsentwicklung durch Gesetzgebung niederschlagen kann.

Inwiefern können aber auch unter dieser Prämisse Rechts- und Unrechtsgefühle bei der demokratischen Gesetzgebung genutzt und berücksichtigt und Forderungen an Gesetzgebung mit Rechts- und Unrechtsgefühlen begründet und unterstrichen werden? Was ist etwa davon zu halten, wenn heute Rechtsentwicklungsbedarf mit Rechtsgefühl begründet wird; wenn argumentiert wird, dass geltendes Recht hinter dem Rechtsgefühl der Bevölkerung zurückbleibe und deshalb weiterentwickelt werden müsse? Hierzu seien thesenartig einige Beobachtungen formuliert.

Die Betonung von Rechts- und Unrechtsgefühl als Argument für Rechtsänderung ist zunächst ein Vorgang des Labelings: Statt bloß vom „politischen Wunsch" nach einer bestimmten Rechtsänderung zu sprechen, ist eben vom Rechtsgefühl die Rede. Das hat Konsequenzen.

Die Ausweisung eines politischen Wunsches als *Rechts*gefühl nimmt dem Anliegen tendenziell an Verhandelbarkeit, weil ihm mit dem Rechtsattribut bereits ein Geltungsanspruch anhaftet. Das Anliegen steht dann vergleichsweise endgültig und unverfügbar da. Solche Abgeschlossenheit erschwert politisch reifende Willensbildung und Kompromiss.

Die Ausweisung des Reformanliegens als Rechtsanliegen kennzeichnet zudem die bestehende rechtliche Situation als rechtlich defizitär und ignoriert die notwendig politische Herkunft und die gerade darin zu findende Legitimation einer bisherigen Rechtslage. Konkrete Rechtslagen sind nicht Vorgefundenes, das vom Standpunkt der Reformisten am gewissermaßen externen Maßstab des Rechts zu kritisieren wäre, sondern Resultate politischer Prozesse der Willensbildung, die (sieht man zunächst einmal von den unverhandelbaren verfassungsrechtlichen Maßgaben ab) allein in eben diesen Prozessen weiterverhandelt werden müssen.

Die sprachliche Ersetzung von politischem Wollen durch Rechtsgefühl könnte das politische Wollen unnötig bemakeln. Jhering hat seinen im heutigen Sinne politischen Wunsch nach Rechtsänderung kaschiert und stattdessen mit Recht argumentiert, um seine Position zwingender erscheinen zu lassen. Unter den Bedingungen des demokratischen Verfassungsstaates gelten jedoch andere Prämissen. Politisches Wollen ist legitim und hat seine spezifischen Durchsetzungswege. Das geltende Recht ist dem politischen Wollen im Wesentlichen verfügbar. Es steht weitgehend zur Disposition (Grenzen ergeben sich aber aus der Verfassung). Es muss dafür nicht gezeigt werden, dass die bisherige Rechtslage falsch war und richtigem Rechtsgefühl widerspreche. Es genügt, dass neues Recht gewollt ist und sich der entsprechende Wunsch in den dafür vorgesehenen Verfahren durchsetzt. Politischer Wille muss also überzeugen und um Zustimmung werben.

Dabei muss politisches Wollen nicht einmal rational sein. Es kann nicht vollständig begründbare Präferenzen einschließen und das darf es auch[14], wenn sich denn Mehrheiten dafür gewinnen lassen – allerdings nur unter der Prämisse, dass es verfassungsrechtliche Maßgaben, insbesondere den Minderheitenschutz, achtet. Die Legitimität nicht weiter begründbaren politischen Wollens verlangt zudem ein gewisses Maß an Erkennbarkeit seiner Wollensgetriebenheit. Gerade indem solches Wollen als *Rechts*gefühl beschrieben würde, ginge potenziell ein nötiges Stück Rechtfertigungs- und Werbungslast verloren.

Selbstverständlich kann politischer Wille seinerseits auf Gerechtigkeitsvorstellungen gründen. Solange politisch nicht nur um Regelungen zur individuellen Nutzenmaximierung gerungen wird, werden Reformbemühungen ihren Ursprung sogar häufig in bestimmten Gerechtigkeitsvorstellungen haben. Das Potenzial von Gerechtigkeit ist durch die geltende Verfassung nicht ausgeschöpft. Es kann und darf Gerechtigkeitsvorstellungen über jene, die im Grundgesetz niedergelegt sind, hinaus geben. Jenseits der verfassungsrechtlichen Positivierungen muss um Gerechtigkeitsvorstellungen jedoch gerungen werden. Eine politische Forderung wird eben nicht automatisch dadurch stärker, dass sie als Gerechtigkeitspostulat formuliert ist.

---

14 S. etwa zur veränderten gesetzlichen Bewertung der Hinnehmbarkeit von Risiken der Kernenergienutzung BVerfGE 143, 246, 347: „Das Ziel des Gesetzgebers, das mit der Kernenergienutzung unvermeidbar in Kauf zu nehmende Restrisiko möglichst schnell und möglichst weitgehend zu beseitigen, ist – auch wenn es allein auf einer politischen Neubewertung der Bereitschaft zur Hinnahme dieses Restrisikos beruhen sollte – von Verfassungs wegen nicht zu beanstanden".

Schließlich könnte die Umstellung von „politischem Wunsch" auf „Rechtsgefühl" Spannungslagen mit der Verfassung erzeugen: Die Gestaltungsmöglichkeiten von Politik und Rechtsetzung finden in den verfassungsrechtlichen Grundrechtsgarantien Schranken. Hier stößt auch der Mehrheitswille an Grenzen. Das ist unter der Geltung des Grundgesetzes im Grunde eingespielt und akzeptiert. Wird politischer Wunsch nun aber als Rechtsgefühl ausgegeben, steht plötzlich Rechtsgefühl gegen Verfassungsgarantie. Wird das politische Wollen zum Anliegen aus Rechtsgefühl und Gerechtigkeit, könnte das rechtsgefühlig aufgeladene politische Wollen langfristig die Suprematie des Verfassungsrechts gefährden.

2. Rechtsgefühl als Orientierung gerichtlicher Rechtsentwicklung?

Während also einiges gegen die Sinnhaftigkeit des Unterfangens spricht, Gesetzesreformbestrebungen durch entsprechende Rechtsgefühle zu untermauern, kann Rechtsgefühl bei der Fortentwicklung des Rechts durch Fachgerichte wohl generell größere Bedeutung zukommen. Bei der Fortentwicklung des Rechts durch die Gerichte geht es nicht um die politische Veränderung von Recht, sondern um die Interpretation geltenden Rechts im Rahmen gerichtlicher Entscheidungsfindung. Hier hat das Rechtsgefühl der Betroffenen Relevanz – wobei Rechtsgefühl hier enger verstanden wird: als deren Vorstellung darüber, was das geltende Recht eigentlich konkret besagt.

Gerichtliche Fortentwicklung des Rechts muss sich grundsätzlich daran messen lassen, ob vermittelbar ist, dass sie zum legislativ gesetzten Recht passt. Es gehört zur alltäglichen richterlichen Selbstkontrolle, zu überlegen, inwiefern eine ins Auge gefasste Entscheidung mit dem Rechtsgefühl der Betroffenen und der Interessierten vereinbar ist. Das schließt die Erwägung ein, ob die Entscheidung so begründet werden kann, dass sie potenziell entgegenstehende Rechtsgefühle überwinden (nicht: überwältigen) kann. Kurz gesagt: Wenn sich eine Rechtsinterpretation nicht einigermaßen plausibel erklären lässt, ist sie vom geltenden Recht eher nicht gedeckt. Das (antizipierte) Rechtsgefühl der Betroffenen kann hier durchaus einen gedanklichen Kontrollmaßstab bilden.

Allerdings ist Rechtsgefühl auch hier nicht zu verabsolutieren. Schon seine empirische Feststellung fällt schwer. Vor allem aber muss sich Recht gelegentlich doch über feststehende Rechtsgefühle hinwegsetzen: Wenn etwa eine bestehende Regelung klar anderen Gehalt hat als landläufig angenommen wird oder wenn unhintergehbare Verfassungsgebote bestehen, muss entgegenstehendes Rechtsgefühl weichen. Auch wenn das Rechtsgefühl vieler offenbar anderes besagte: Selbst ein terroristischer Gefährder durfte nicht abgeschoben werden, wenn die verfahrensrechtlichen Voraussetzungen dafür fehlten[15], selbst die NPD konnte trotz Verfassungsfeindlichkeit nicht durch das Bundesverfassungsgericht verboten werden[16] und ohne gesetzliche Grundlage konnte auch der betrogene Ehemann von der untreuen Frau nicht zum Zwecke des Unterhaltsregresses die Preisgabe des Namens des wahren Erzeugers eines Kuckuckskindes erzwingen[17].

IV. Zusammenfassende Thesen

1. Rechtsgefühl ist ein allgegenwärtiges und mannigfaltiges Phänomen.
2. In Jherings *Kampf um's Recht* dient der teils empirisch, teils normativ gefasste Zusammenhang zwischen Rechtsgefühl und nationalem Staatswohl letztlich vor allem zur argumentativen Herleitung der Notwendigkeit, das geltende Recht fortzuentwickeln, weil demokratische Gesetzgebung als Mittel und Legitimation von Rechtsentwicklung noch nicht zur Verfügung stand.
3. Im demokratischen Staat kann die Forderung nach legislativer Rechtsentwicklung als politische Forderung formuliert und auf entsprechenden Wegen zu realisieren versucht werden. Eine Bezeichnung des politischen Wollens als *Rechts*gefühl verdeckt den politischen Charakter eines legislativen Änderungswunschs, woran auf Dauer sowohl politische Willensbildung als auch die Idee des Rechts Schaden nehmen könnten. Für die gerichtliche Fortentwicklung des Rechts kann Rechtsgefühl hingegen Orientierung bieten.

---

15 Fall Sami A., VG Gelsenkirchen, Beschluss vom 12. Juli 2018 (Az. 7 a L 1200/18.A).
16 BVerfGE 144, 20 ff.
17 BVerfGE 138, 377, 390 ff. Rn. 35 ff.

Feelings about Law/Justice:
The Relevance of Affect for the Development of Law[*]
– in Jhering's *Struggle for Law* and in Constitutional Democracies

Gabriele Britz

The current discourse about the relationship of law and affect can be traced back to Rudolf von Jhering, who extensively addressed feelings about law/justice[1] in his own way and for his own purposes in his book *The Struggle for Law* (*Der Kampf um's Recht*).[2] Jhering's work can be read as a fascinating attempt to utilize the idea of feelings about law/justice in terms of (legal political) demands for legislative developments. When read against its pre-democratic historical background, a possible benefit of Jhering's text for today's discourses about law and affect can be found in the differing constitutional context.

Feelings about law/justice are broad phenomena. Where there is law, there are people – in the form of their being affected by law, their legislating law, their applying law, or as people who comment on and research the law. Yet where there are people, there is always affect, as well (I.). Jhering develops his plea for the development of law on the basis of wide-ranging assumptions about the feelings about law/justice of those individuals who are subjected to law. The individual and meta-individual vital importance of subjective feelings about law/justice and the ethical-ide-

---

[*] This is a translation of the keynote address at the conference "Feelings about Law/Justice: The Relevance of Affect for the Development of Law" that was held at the English Department and the Rudolf von Jhering Institute for Fundamental Legal Research at Justus Liebig University Giessen on 13 June 2019. The presentation style has been maintained in the translation into English by Laura Borchert, with additions by Stefanie Rück.
1 See Greta Olson, *The Turn to Passion: Has Law and Literature become Law and Affect? Law & Literature* 28 (2016), pp. 335 ff. [Note by the editors: As noted by Greta Olson in her essay in this volume, "Recht" denotes both "law" and "justice" in German.].
2 Rudolf von Jhering, *Der Kampf um's Recht* (Freiburg im Breisgau: Haufe, 1992 [1872]), trans. in *The Struggle for Law*, trans. John J. Lalor (Chicago: Callaghan and Company, 1915), 5th ed.

al feelings about law, which follow out of the former, are illustrated by way of dramatic images. The empirical and normative implications are up for debate. In what follows, attention will be focused on Jhering's vanishing point (according to this reading of the text): the (empirical) argumentative validation of demanding a thorough reform of the law (II.). This methodological access has to be seen against the constitutional background of its time; however, it evokes questions of whether feelings about law/justice could still be put forth today as legitimate reasons for demanding developments in law. Framing a sense of discontentment with prevailing legal norms as "a feeling of injustice" may look appealing, yet in constitutional democracies, this practice will be met with other factors that have to be taken into account (III.).

I. Connections between Law and Affect

In order to exemplify the omnipresence of feelings about law/justice, some practical connections between law and affect will be illustrated in the following. In doing so, the fifth and last connection which is described here will be the one that Jhering was most interested in in his struggle for law.

1. Law *begets* feelings. These may be hostile, refusing, negative feelings. For example, the so-called 'Notstandsverfassung' (the *crisis constitution*)[3] evoked extremely negative feelings in the late 1960s in large parts of the population. On the other side of the political spectrum, the German Federal Constitutional Court's decision to treat the statement "Soldiers are Murderers" ("*Soldaten sind Mörder*")[4] as an instance of freedom of speech caused large parts of society to react with downright aversion. This decision led not only to a need for temporarily heightened police protection for the ruling jus-

---

3 17. Gesetz zur Ergänzung des Grundgesetzes (17th amendment of the Basic Law) (24 June 1968, BGBl. I 709). Included are regulations on restrictions of the Basic Law in emergency situations of the, e.g., in case of the need for defense. [Note by translator: This amendment was particularly contested because it broadened the state's right to intervene in emergency situations, thus leading to restrictions of individual rights such as the right to privacy of correspondence, as stated in Art. 10 GG. Given the experiences of the NS regime, both the governing and opposing parties, and particularly the FDP (Free Democratic Party), strongly protested against this strengthening of state powers.].

4 BVerfGE 93, 266 ff.

tices, but also to the establishment of a permanent press office that supports the Federal Constitutional Court's communications regarding its judgements. However, the order to legally recognize the so-called third gender option[5] in official documents seems to have elicited a positive feeling for those affected by the decision, since they appear to feel more validated by this order. Even the mere naming of a law can beget feelings: The naming of the "good-nursery-law" (Gute-Kita-Gesetz)[6] and the "orderly return law" (Geordnete-Rückkehr-Gesetz)[7] specifically aimed to evoke positive feelings. Finally, the formulation of Art. 2 (1) GG[8] ("Jeder hat das Recht auf die freie Entfaltung seiner Persönlichkeit"; "Every person shall have the right of free development of their personality") was chosen not least for the ceremonial tone of these words. It was "a dignified tone" with which one wanted to endow the fundamental rights.[9]

2. Law *considers* feelings. For instance, the protection of family ties, which can be found in multiple legal contexts, can also be understood as deference to emotional states.[10] In the German data protection law, a consideration of "feelings of being permanently monitored" ("Gefühl des dauernden Überwachtwerdens")[11] is the basic reason behind far-reaching protections in that area. This deference to feelings becomes especially apparent in claims under the law of obligation: In the German private law system, the practice of claiming immaterial damages such as compensations for emotional suffering and damage claims due to the loss of enjoyment during one's vacation evidently considers emotional states.

---

5 BVerfGE 147, 1 ff.
6 *Gesetz zur Weiterentwicklung der Qualität und zur Teilhabe in der Kindertagesbetreuung* (Law on the further development of quality and participation in child day care) (19 December 2018, BGBl. I 2696). [Note by translator: This law was meant to improve the quality of preschool education and day care by increasing the ratio of caretakers to children amongst other things.].
7 *Zweites Gesetz zur besseren Durchsetzung der Ausreisepflicht* (Second law for better enforcement of the obligation to leave the country) (15 August 2019, BGBl. I 1294). [Note by translator: This law was meant to restructure the deportation process by, for instance, not notifying immigrants about their planned deportation after a certain deadline.].
8 [Note by translator: The *Grundgesetz für die Bundesrepublik Deutschland* is abbreviated as GG (German Basic Law for the Federal Republic of Germany). The *Grundgesetz* is the German constitution and was drafted after World War II. It has been in force since 1949.].
9 *Entstehungsgeschichte des Grundgesetzes*, JöR Band 1, 2nd ed., 2010, p. 61.
10 See especially BVerfGE 136, 382, 388 f. Marginal note 22 f.
11 E.g., BVerfGE 125, 260, 335 m.w.N.

3. In some circumstances, law may also *be conveyed* to those applying the law via feelings. Whether, for example, a judicially false judgment qualifies as "arbitrariness"[12], which is prohibited under Art. 3 (1) GG, or whether an accident can already be perceived as "catastrophic"[13] and therefore – which is relevant for the deployment of armed forces within the country – is to be regarded as a particularly serious accident in the sense of Art. 35 GG, or whether the bad treatment of a person by the state already violates this person's "human dignity" (Art. 1 GG), is difficult to determine precisely on the basis of objective criteria. All of these three legal concepts also call upon the intuition of those applying the law. The standards applied here are probably also conveyed by the fact that they create feelings of and for arbitrariness, catastrophe and dignity in those applying the law.

4. *Legal professionals have* feelings. Professional jurists can have personal emotional relationships and interests. Since these feelings, which may not be repressed completely, can interfere with an objective finding of justice, all rules of court incorporate regulations regarding exclusion and bias.[14] Further, justices and judges articulate "disruptive feelings" and "gut feelings" on their practical daily quest for justice. As a methodologically intermediate step, these phenomena, which are euphemistically called *"Judiz,"* may be helpful. Ultimately, the rules of decision-making under the rule of law can only be adhered to when these kinds of feelings are rationally questioned and corroborated or dismissed using normative texts, precedents, and supporting literature.

5. *Legal laypersons* also have feelings about law and justice, which can refer to multiple contexts and to which law responds in different ways. Legal laypersons' feelings about law is Jhering's main focus in *The Struggle for Law*. Jhering discusses two kinds of legal laypersons' feelings about law and extracts from them arguments for his demands for a fundamental (re)development of the law. Feelings about law and the (re)development of

---

12　See *Willkürgrenze* (Arbitrariness limit) (Art. 3 (1) GG) instead of many BVerfGE 42, 64, 72 f. [Note by translator: The *Grundgesetz*'s equal protection provision is found in Art. 3 GG and states that there shall be no arbitrary unequal treatment of individuals.].

13　BVerfGE 132, 1, 17 Marginal note 43. [Note by translator: Art. 35 of the *Grundgesetz* cites natural disasters and grave accidents as instances of emergencies that warrant the deployment of armed forces.].

14　Exemplary for the members of the *Bundesverfassungsgericht* §§ 18, 19 BVerfGG.

the law are not only the foci of this conference, they are also the central motifs in Jhering's book.

II. Feelings about Law as Arguments for a (Re)Development of the Law (Jhering)

In the book's conclusion, Jhering aims at a thorough (re)development of the law. He explains his demands for this (re)development using a three-step analysis of feelings about law: Feelings about law are firstly to be understood as a physical force which pushes towards an enforcement of law (1); secondly, this force works to secure the law as such and thus guarantees the existence of the nation-state both internally and externally (2). Thirdly, for law to be able to create these feelings about justice in the long run and thus to contribute to stability, it must meet certain criteria which the legal reality, according to Jhering, did not satisfy and thus became deficient (3). That is why feelings about law may come across as empirical, yet they are mostly conceptual constructs calling for a (re)development of law. Jhering presents his reasoning as practical and convenient, and his argument tries to take its persuasive power precisely from its (supposedly) empirical point of reference (i.e., from the actual feelings about law and the affectively experienced suffering stemming from the violation of law).

1. Feelings about Law Due to Personal Affront

Jhering's line of argumentation starts with an individual's feelings about law, i.e., with the feeling of one's own legal position in relation to other people (private law). Since the violation of one's private rights is experienced as an affront by the affected person, the court proceedings are "the person's assertion of himself and of his feeling of right" (28). Here, it is not necessarily a matter of enforcing objectively valuable positions, it is rather a question of safeguarding one's personality as such: "An inner voice tells him that he should not retreat, that it is not the worthless object that is at stake but his own personality, his feeling of legal right, his self-respect – in short, the suit at law ceases to appear to him in the guise of a mere question of interest and becomes a question of character" (29). Law enters consciousness affectively and painfully in the moment of injury. The experienced affront ignites the fight for justice because now compensation is sought and has to be sought. In this description, empirical and normative factors mix.

2. Ideal Feelings about Law

Apart from this self-centered feeling of having been insulted in light of "personal injustice", there is an ethical ("ideal") feeling about justice and law. In this sense, the main focus is no longer the individual but asserting the law as a duty to the community (55; 69). "In defending his legal rights he asserts and defends the whole body of law" (74). This is one's "contribution towards the realization of the idea of law" (n. pag.)[15]. "What an immense importance does the struggle of the individual for his rights thus obtain! ... Every man who sees the law violated and feels indignation at the sight, possesses it. While, in fact, an egotistical motive is mixed up with the painful feeling caused by a personal wrong, this indignation is produced exclusively by the power of morality over the human heart. It is the energy of our moral nature protesting against the violation of the law; it is the most beautiful and the highest testimony which the feeling of legal right can bear to itself" (79 ff.). One needs "this ideal sentiment of legal right, possessed by the person by whom the wounding of the feeling of legal right is felt more sensitively than an attack upon him personally, and who disinterestedly sacrifices himself in the interest of oppressed right as if there were question only of his own rights, is the privilege of highly gifted natures" (n. pag.)[16].

The literary figure of Michael Kohlhaas (Heinrich von Kleist) serves to illustrate this point:

> Here is an honest and good man, filled with love for his family, with a simple, religious disposition, who becomes an Attila and destroys with fire and sword the cities in which his enemy has taken refuge. And how is this transformation effected? By the very quality which lifts him morally high above all his enemies ...: by his high esteem for the law, his faith in its sacredness, the energy of his genuine, healthy feeling of

---

15 Rudolf von Jhering, *Der Kampf um's Recht. Druckfassung des Vortrags* (Wien: Verlag der G.J. Manz'schen Buchhandlung [1872]), lecture from 11 March 1872, available online: https://www.hs-augsburg.de/~harsch/germanica/Chronologie/19Jh/Jhering/jhe_kamd.html (accessed 8 November 2021).

16 Ibid.; Jhering's opinion in the printed version of his lecture differs slightly from the one in his book.

legal right. The tragedy of his fate lies in this that his ruin was brought about by the superiority and nobility of his nature, his lofty feeling of legal right, and his heroic devotion to the idea of law, which made him oblivious to all else and ready to sacrifice everything for it, in contact with the miserable world of the time in which the arrogance of the great and the powerful was equalled only by the venality and cowardice of the judges. (91 f.).

3. Vanishing Point: Criticizing the Law

By referring to Michael Kohlhaas's fate, Jhering manages to tap into criticizing the law:

> ... left in the lurch by the power which should protect it, ... the national feeling of legal right raises its protest against such a condition of things" (94). "This idealism of the healthy feeling ... knows not only that in defending its own legal rights it defends the law, but that in defending the law it defends its own legal rights. ... For the state which desires to be respected abroad, and to be firm and unshaken internally, there is no more precious good which it has to guard and foster than the national feeling of legal right. ... In the healthy, vigorous feeling of legal right of the individual, the state possesses the most fruitful source of its own strength, the surest guaranty, from within and from without, of its own existence. The feeling of legal right is the root of the whole tree. If the root be good for nothing, if it withers in the rocks and in the sand, all the rest is but an illusion; the storm comes and plucks it up by the roots. But the trunk and the top have the advantage that they are seen, while the roots are hidden in the ground and veiled from sight. The disastrous influence which unjust laws and bad legal institutions exercise on the moral power of the nation acts under ground, in those regions which so many amateur statesmen do not consider worthy of their attention; they are concerned only with the stately top; of the poison which rises to the top from the root they have no idea whatever. But despotism knows where it must strike to fell the tree; it leaves the top untouched at first, but destroys the roots. Every despotism has begun with attacks on private law, with the violation of the legal rights of the individual; when its work is done the tree falls of itself. (102 ff.).

Then, Jhering equips his readers with some practical pieces of advice:

> The power of a people is synonymous with the strength of their feeling of legal right. The cultivation of the national feeling of legal right is care for the health and strength of the state. By this cultivation and care, I do not, of course, understand schooling and instruction, but the practical carrying out of all the principles of justice in all the relations of life. ... The fixedness, clearness, certainty of positive law, the doing away with all those principles at which a healthy feeling of legal right, might take offense in any sphere of the law, not only of private law, but in the police power, the administrative, financial, legislative, the independence of the courts, the greatest possible perfection of legal procedure – this is a surer way to increase the power of the state than the greatest possible increase of the military budget. Every provision which the people feel to be unjust, and every institution which they detest, is an injury to the national feeling of legal right and to the national strength, a sin against the idea of law, the burthen of which falls on the state itself, and for which it has not infrequently to pay dearly. ... I am not, indeed, of the opinion that the state should avoid these sins from reasons of expediency simply. Rather do I consider it the most sacred duty of the state to realize this idea for its own sake; but this may be doctrinarian idealism, and I have no word of blame for the practical politician and statesman who refuses such a demand with a shrug of the shoulders. And just on this account have I exposed the practical side of the question to view, the side which he fully understands; for the idea of law and the interest of the state go, here, hand in hand. There is no feeling of legal right, no matter how healthy it may be, which can, in the long run, resist the influence of bad laws; it grows blunted, withers and decays. For the essence of legal right is, as I have frequently remarked already, action. What the air is to the flame, freedom of action is to the feeling of legal right. Refuse it this freedom, and the feeling dies. (106 ff.)

What follows is a blazing attack on private and criminal law (particularly the right to defend oneself), which the people do not understand and which does not understand the people, particularly not their 'healthy' sense of law. Although Jhering mentions this aspect rather on a side note, his whole argumentation seems to aim at this point: "I might stop here, for my subject is exhausted. The reader, however, will allow me to claim his attention for another question closely related to my subject, the question how far our present law, or to speak more accurately, the Roman law of to-day as it obtains here, on which alone I can venture to express a judgment, comes up to the requirements described in the preceding pages. I do not hesitate to say that it does not, in any way, come up to them. It is far behind the rightful claims of a healthy feeling of legal right ..." (109).

Empirical feelings about law as force behind one's motivation to go to court become the prerequisites of a resilient nation-state – because such a state needs the individuals' praxes of claiming what they perceive as justice and as their rights. A state, however, suffocates this powerful force when it fails to offer adequate laws. Feelings about law, presented as empirical factors, evidently serve as reason and legitimation for demanding a reform of codified law.

III. *Feelings about Law as Arguments for a (Re)Development of Law Today?*

In his third and last argumentative step, Jhering cites affronts against feelings about law as source and motivation behind reforming the law. This argumentative step shall now be applied to today's situation under consideration of current constitutional frameworks. Do feelings about law nowadays qualify as valid arguments for law's (re)development?

1. *Feelings about Law as Arguments for a Legislative (Re)Development of Law?*

Whether the hypotheses about the relationship between feelings about law and law's (re)development, which were developed in a pre-democratic authoritarian state, are plausible, cannot be analysed directly on the basis of the current situation, in which law can only legitimate itself normatively through those subjected to power ("All state power is derived from the people," Art. 20 GG). Corresponding procedures have been established constitutionally so that legislation can actually be held accountable by "the people." Given these circumstances, demands for reforming the law find other ways of legitimation and, by their very nature, other ways of implementation than in pre-democratic orders. Since there is democratic legislation, one does not need ("canonized") feelings about law to substantiate and legitimize their position; it is sufficient to turn to political will, which needs to be convincing and to find a majority, yet does not need any further legitimation – apart from superior legal ties e.g., to fundamental or human rights – to be reflected in law's developments through legislation.

But to what degree can feelings about justice and injustice be considered and used under this premise? And in how far can demands for legislating be legitimized and emphasized with feelings about justice and injustice? What are we to think of justifying the need of reforming the law by referring to feelings about law; what are we to think of claims that existing law does not come up to people's feelings about law and should therefore be developed further? These questions are now being approached in the form of propositions.

Emphasizing feelings about justice and injustice as arguments for changes in law is first of all a process of labelling: Instead of referring to a particular change in law as a "political wish", one speaks of feelings about law. This has consequences.

Labelling a political wish as a feeling about *law* tends to erase this demand's negotiability since locating it in the legal domain already adds a validity claim to it. The claim then appears comparatively fixed and inaccessible. Such closure makes a gradual political decision-making process and compromise difficult.

Labelling the demand for reform as a legal issue also marks the existing legal situation as legally deficient and ignores its necessary political origin with its legitimation of the current legal situation. Concrete legal situations are not something that is already present and which may be criticized from a reformist's point of view by law's somewhat external standard, but they are rather the results of political processes of decision-making, which (apart from the non-negotiable constitutional provisions) must be further negotiated in these processes alone.

The linguistic replacement of political volition with feelings about law could unnecessarily stain the former. Jhering concealed his, in today's sense of the word, political desire for reforming the law, and instead used law to make his position more compelling. However, under a democratic constitutional state's conditions, different premises apply. Political volition is legitimate and has its specific ways of enforcement. Existing law is essentially available to political volition, and widely up for debate (although limits are set by the constitution, especially legitimate expectations and certain minimum and minority guarantees). One does not need to prove that the previous legal situation was wrong and contradictory to the right feelings about law. It is sufficient for new law to be desired and that the corresponding desire prevails in the provided procedures. Political will must thus be convincing and it must seek approval.

Political volition does not even need to be rational. It may include not completely justifiable preferences, and this is permissible[17] if supported by a majority – albeit under the premise that constitutional provisions are upheld, especially regarding minority protection. The legitimacy of not completely justifiable political will further demands that it is to a certain extent visibly driven by volition. Yet, precisely by describing such volition as feelings about *law*, a necessary part of the burden to justify and to advertise would potentially be lost.

Of course, political will can be grounded upon visions of justice. As long as the political discourse is not dominated by regulations of individual utility maximization, endeavours to reform will oftentimes be grounded in certain visions of justice. Justice's potential is not exhausted by our existing constitution. There can and may be visions about justice beyond those laid down in the *Grundgesetz*. Apart from constitutional positivations, however, one has to struggle for visions of justice. Political demands do not automatically become stronger when postulated as matters of justice.

Finally, switching from "political wishes" to "feelings about law" could create constitutional tensions. The possibilities for shaping political and legislative spheres are limited by the constitution's guarantees of fundamental rights. Here, the majority's will reaches its limits. Under the *Grundgesetz*, this is basically well established and accepted. However, as soon as a political wish is presented as feelings about law, feelings about law suddenly clash with constitutional guarantees. Whenever political volition becomes a matter of feelings about law and justice, this political volition which feeds on such feelings could endanger constitutional law's supremacy in the long run.

2. *Feelings about Law as Orientation Towards Judicial Development of Law?*

While there is a lot to be said against the reasonableness of trying to substantiate legal reform endeavours with corresponding feelings about law, such feelings can generally gain greater importance in the context of reforming the law via specialized courts. This process of reforming is not

---

17 For changed legislation on the legal assessment of the acceptability of risks of nuclear energy use see e.g., BVerfGE 143, 246, 347: "The legislator's intention to eliminate any unavoidable residual risk associated with the use of nuclear energy quickly and broadly, – even when it is grounded solely on the political reassessment of the willingness to accept this residual risk – is not objectionable constitutionally."

about a political transformation of the law but about interpreting existing law in the context of judicial decision-making. Here, the feelings about law of those affected are relevant – although feelings about law are understood more narrowly at this point: as the ideas of those affected about what existing law actually and concretely implies.

In principle, judicial reform of the law has to be measured against its compatibility with legislatively codified law. Part of the everyday judicial process of self-regulation is considering in how far a decision is compatible with the feelings about law of those affected and interested. This includes considering whether a decision can be justified in a way that it is able to overcome (not: overwhelm) potentially conflicting feelings about law. In other words: If an interpretation of law cannot be explained plausibly, it is most likely not covered by existing law. The (anticipated) feelings about law of those affected are certainly able to form a mental control standard.

However, feelings about law cannot be made absolute here either. It is even difficult to determine these feelings empirically. But most importantly, law has to occasionally disregard existing feelings about law: For instance, if an existing regulation clearly has a different content than generally perceived, or if there are uncircumventable constitutional imperatives, contradicting feelings about law have to yield. Even if the feelings about law of many others seemingly disagree: Even a person that is likely to threaten public safety could not be deported if the procedural requirements are missing[18]; even the NPD ('*Nationaldemokratische Partei Deutschlands*')[19] could not be prohibited by the *Bundesverfassungsgericht* although it is considered anti-constitutional[20]; without legal basis, even a husband who got cheated on could not force his unfaithful wife to reveal his cuckoo child's biological father in order to evade alimony[21].

---

18 Case Sami A., VG Gelsenkirchen, resolution from 12 July 2018 (Az. 7 a L 1200/18.A).

19 [Note by translator: The so-called National Democratic Party of Germany is an extreme right-wing political party.].

20 BVerfGE 144, 20 ff. [Note by translator: This decision is remarkable when compared to other German laws that target extreme right-wing parties. For instance, § 86 of the German Criminal Code (*Strafgesetzbuch*) prohibits the dissemination of "propaganda material 1. of a political party that has been declared unconstitutional" (§ 86, 1, no. 1). This includes, for example, displaying the flag of the Third Reich and displaying swastikas publically (§ 86a, 2).].

21 BVerfGE 138, 377, 390 ff. Marginal note 35 ff.

IV. Concluding Theses

1. Feelings about law are omnipresent and diverse phenomena.
2. In Jhering's *Struggle for Law*, the relationship between feelings about law and national welfare, which is partly conceived empirically and partly normatively, serves most of all as an argumentative reasoning for a necessary reform of the law because democratic legislation was not yet available as means and legitimation of legal reform.
3. In a democratic state, the demand for legislative reform of the law can be formulated as a political demand and one can try to realize this demand accordingly. Labelling political volition as feelings about *law* obscures the political character of the legislative wish for change, resulting in potential damage to both the political process of decision-making and the very idea of law in the long run. However, feelings about law are able to provide guidance for judicial reform of the law.

"The Empire of Laws and Not of Men": Gesetzesherrschaft als Gefühlsvermeidung? Rechtstheoretische Rückfragen*

Franz Reimer

I. Einleitung

Die Gegenüberstellung der Herrschaft von Gesetzen und derjenigen von Menschen ist alt, aber persistent. Sie hat nach wie vor sentenzartigen Charakter und dient als politisches Argument, insofern Gesetzesherrschaft mit erwünschter Rationalität, Menschenherrschaft mit unerwünschter Emotionalität assoziiert wird („Es gelten bei uns Regeln. Und diese Regeln können nicht durch Emotionen ersetzt werden. Das ist das Wesen des Rechtsstaates."[1]). Aber auch wissenschaftliche Beschreibungen des Rechtsstaats nutzen die Gegenüberstellung. So heißt es, der moderne Rechtsstaat ersetze „Unterdrückung und Willkür durch eine Staatsgewalt, in der das Gesetz und nicht Personen herrschen."[2] Der folgende Beitrag fragt, ob bzw. inwieweit vor dem Hintergrund der hergebrachten Gegenüberstellung unsere heutigen Überzeugungen von Rechtsstaatlichkeit die Ersetzung menschlicher Entscheidungen durch gesetzliche Determinierung oder gar Algorithmen fordern und ob sich damit eine sinnvolle Zurückdrängung von Gefühlen verbindet. Dazu möchte ich Herkunft und Funktionen der Gegenüberstellung skizzieren (II.), an die genetische Abhängigkeit der Gesetze von Menschen (III.) und an die Komplementarität gesetzlicher und menschlicher Entscheidungen erinnern (IV.). Abschließend soll die Frage gestellt werden, ob an die Stelle der Herrschaft von Gesetzen und Menschen künftig diejenige von Algorithmen treten kann und soll (V.). Leitend ist hierbei ein rechtstheoretisches Erkenntnisinteresse an Rechtsge-

---

* Dem Andenken Barbara Gaugers gewidmet.
1 Bundeskanzlerin Dr. *Angela Merkel* MdB, 47. Sitzung des 19. Deutschen Bundestages. 11.9.2018. Zit. n.: Das Parlament Nr. 38-39 v. 17.9.2018. Debattendokumentation, S. 10.
2 *Paul Kirchhof*. Rechtsstaat. In: Staatslexikon der Görres-Gesellschaft. 8. Aufl., Bd. 4. 2020, Sp. 1235.

fühlen (diese vorerst in einem weiten, unspezifischen Sinne verstanden[3]), wobei ich Rechtstheorie als Sockel für Juristische Methodenlehre und Rechtsetzungslehre fasse.

II. Die Gegenüberstellung von Gesetzen und Menschen: Herkunft und Funktionen

1. Das Ideal

Den Rechtsstaat denken wir häufig als *rule of law*, oder, schärfer formuliert, als *the empire of laws and not of men*[4] oder als *government of laws and not of men*[5], als „Herrschaft des Rechts statt menschlicher Willkür"[6]. Die Entwicklungs- und Wirkungsgeschichte dieses Motivs ist lang[7] und kann hier nur schlaglichtartig rekapituliert werden. In der Antike begegneten sowohl die Personifikation des νόμος zum König[8] wie auch umgekehrt die Reifizierung des Herrschers zum νόμος ἔμψυχος (belebten Gesetz)[9].

---

3 Nämlich als rechtsbezogene Gefühle, wobei „Gefühl" vorerst wiederum als Oberbegriff über alle affektiven Phänomene genutzt wird; die z.T. gebräuchliche Abgrenzung gegenüber „Emotion" als episodischem und nach außen gerichtetem Gefühl (vgl. bspw. *Hilge Landweer/Dirk Koppelberg*. Der verkannte Zusammenhang von Recht und Emotion. In: dies. [Hrsg.]. Recht und Emotion I: Verkannte Zusammenhänge. 2016, S. 13 f.; *David Nink*. Justiz und Algorithmen. Über die Schwächen menschlicher Entscheidungsfindung und die Möglichkeiten neuer Technologien in der Rechtsprechung. 2021, S. 40 f.) spielt an dieser Stelle keine Rolle. Instruktive Unterscheidung von vier Bedeutungen des Begriffs „Rechtsgefühl" bei *Landweer/Koppelburg*. a.a.O., S. 25.

4 *James Harrington*. The Commonwealth of Oceana (1656). 1771, S. 35 (Cambridge University Press. 1992, S. 8): "Relation being had unto these two times, government (to define it *de jure* or according to ancient prudence) is an art whereby a civil society of men is instituted and preserved upon the foundation of common right or interest, or (to follow Aristotle and Livy) it is the empire of laws and not of men."

5 Part the First, Art. XXX der Constitution of the Commonwealth of Massachusetts (1780).

6 *Kirchhof* (Fn. 2).

7 Näher *Klaus Thomalla*. „Herrschaft des Gesetzes, nicht des Menschen". Zur Ideengeschichte eines staatsphilosophischen Topos. 2019; ferner *Red.*, Nomokratie. In: Joachim Ritter/Karlfried Gründer (Hrsg.). Historisches Wörterbuch der Philosophie, Bd. 6. 1984, Sp. 889 ff., DOI: 10.24894/HWPh.2776.

8 *Pindar*. fr. 169.

9 *Diotogenes*. Hier zit. n. *Peter Siewert*. Nomos. In: Hubert Cancik/Helmuth Schneider (Hrsg.). Der Neue Pauly, Bd. 8. 2003/2012, Sp. 982 (983 f.).

Erst der Gedanke an politisch-gesellschaftliche Gestaltungsmöglichkeiten dürfte aber die prägnante Gegenüberstellung (bei der menschliche Satzung und Mensch dann im Plural stehen) provoziert haben. Sie setzt die Deutung der Gesetze als funktionale Äquivalente menschlicher Herrscher (genauer: als überlegener Alternative zu ihnen) und damit die konkrete Personifikation der staatlichen Normen voraus, wie sie nachdrücklich in Platons Dialog „Kriton" begegnet[10]: Im Gespräch zwischen Sokrates und seinem Freund Kriton, der ihn zur Flucht vor der bereits verhängten Todesstrafe überreden will, erscheinen die Gesetze in Sokrates' Gegenrede zunächst als Erzeuger und Erzieher des einzelnen Polisbürgers, als Träger von *ratio* und *peitho* (Überzeugungskraft), als Garanten von Gerechtigkeit, d.h. Ordnung und Beständigkeit. Am Ende sind sie aber auch Gegenpol zu den Unrecht tuenden Menschen: „Du gehst als einer, der Unrecht erleidet, wenn du jetzt gehst – Unrecht nicht durch unsere Gesetze, sondern durch Menschen."[11] So tritt zur berühmten, die Geschichte der Rechtsphilosophie durchziehenden Physis-Nomos-Antithese an dieser Stelle eine Ánthropos-Nomos-Antithese. Allerdings stehen Gesetze und Menschen hier nicht in einem Alternativverhältnis, sondern in Komplementarität: Es entscheiden Gesetze *und* Menschen, nämlich schlechte Menschen anhand guter Gesetze, nicht Menschen anstelle von Gesetzen oder Gesetze anstelle von Menschen, wie es die neuzeitliche Formel vom *empire of laws and not of men* suggeriert. In der sokratischen Entscheidung für Gesetzesgehorsam und gegen das Drängen des Freundes kann man freilich selbst eine Huldigung an die unverbrüchliche Herrschaft des Gesetzes anstelle menschlichen Wankelmuts sehen; insofern waltet bei Sokrates rationales Tugendverständnis und „emotionale Kälte"[12].

Aber auch die Sichtweise, nach der Gesetze *anstelle* von Menschen entscheiden, lässt sich bereits bei Platon finden. Im Dialog „Politikos"[13] dient als Ausgangspunkt die Behauptung, dass es zwar am besten sei, wenn ein vernünftiger Monarch entscheide, weil Gesetze aufgrund ihrer Allgemeinheit starr seien[14]; das Gesetz gleiche daher „einem arroganten und

---

10 50a 7 ff. – Eindrückliche Nachzeichnung des Gesprächs (in Gegenwartssprache) bei *Barbara Gauger*. Der Nachlass des Sokrates. 2012, S. 87 ff.
11 54b 9 f.; eigene Übersetzung.
12 *Gauger* (Fn. 10), S. 94.
13 Politikos, 293c 5 ff.; Nomoi, 875a ff.
14 294a 9 ff.

ignoranten Mann"[15]. Dennoch sei es aus praktischen Gründen notwendig, Gesetze zu erlassen: Kein Herrscher könne ausreichend Einzelweisungen erteilen, überall und immer präsent sein[16]. Insofern ihn daher das Gesetz ersetzt, ist von der „substitutive[n] Funktion des Gesetzes" gesprochen worden[17]. Sie ist auch deshalb wichtig, weil gegen Alleinherrscher (unabhängig von ihrer Qualität) stets Argwohn und Misstrauen bestehe[18]. Zu den rechtsbezogenen Gefühlen (d.h. zu den Rechtsgefühlen im weitesten Sinne) kann man daher auch Vertrauen in die Diskriminierungsfreiheit des allgemeinen Gesetzes und umgekehrt Misstrauen gegenüber nichtgesetzlicher Herrschaft zählen. In den „Nomoi" wird die Notwendigkeit der Gesetze mit der Degeneration selbst des besten Herrschers begründet[19]. „Für den Republikaner der Neuzeit ist das Gesetz der Triumph über die fürstliche Willkürherrschaft. Für Platon ist es ein Surrogat für die eigentlich erwünschte Herrschaft der Einsichtigen und Tüchtigen."[20]

Aristoteles betont in der „Politik" bei der Frage nach dem vorzugswürdigen Herrscher die Leidenschaften, die mit der Herrschaft des Menschen im Gegensatz zur Herrschaft des Gesetzes verbunden seien[21]. „Wer [...] dem Gesetz die Regierung zuweist, der weist sie [...] allein Gott und der Vernunft zu, wer aber dem Menschen, der fügt auch noch das Tier hinzu. Denn die Begierde ist etwas derartiges und der Zorn verleitet die Regierenden, auch wenn es die besten Männer sind. Und so ist denn das Gesetz als Vernunft ohne Wünsche zu bezeichnen."[22] Aristoteles resümiert, „daß die oberste Staatsgewalt den Gesetzen zukommen muß, vorausgesetzt, daß diese wohlgeordnet sind, der Regierende aber, mag er einer sein oder mehrere, nur über das Gewalt haben soll, was die Gesetze nicht genau zu bestimmen vermögen, weil nicht leicht über alles sich zutreffende allgemeine Regeln geben lassen."[23] Hiernach ersetzt, soweit möglich, das Ge-

---

15 294c 1, Übersetzung: *André Laks*. Form und Inhalt des platonischen Gesetzes. In: Wolfgang Bock (Hrsg.). Gesetz und Gesetzlichkeit in den Wissenschaften. 2006, S. 11 (15).

16 294d ff.

17 *Laks* (Fn. 15), S. 14.

18 300d 1-4, hierzu *Laks* (Fn. 15), S. 14 f.

19 875b 1 ff.

20 *Henning Ottmann*. Platons Mischverfassungslehre. In: Politisches Denken, Jahrbuch 2008, S. 33 (38).

21 Politik, 1281a 35 f.

22 1287a 29 ff., Übersetzung: Franz Susemihl, Bearbeitung von Nelly Tsouyopoulos und Ernesto Grassi (1965), neu herausgegeben von Ursula Wolf, 3. Aufl. 2009, S. 170.

23 1282b 2 ff., Übersetzung wie oben (Fn. 22), S. 153.

setz die Menschen als Herrscher[24]. Grund ist die Leidenschaftslosigkeit des Gesetzes, oder sind, umgekehrt formuliert, die Leidenschaften (πάθη), die Begierde (ἐπιθυμία), der Zorn (θυμός) und die Wünsche (ὀρέξεις) des Menschen. Neben die praktisch-substitutive Funktion des Gesetzes tritt daher die prinzipielle oder protektive Funktion als Schutz vor Launenhaftigkeit und Willkür. Das Gesetz entfaltet hier seine Wirkung als Institution[25].

Das neuzeitliche Plädoyer für eine Herrschaft der Gesetze anstelle derjenigen der Menschen (erst das 18. Jahrhundert prägt für diese – vermeintliche – Herrschaftsform den Begriff „Nomokratie"[26]) dient primär dieser Ausfilterung von Willkür und Wankelmut und soll formale Rechtsgleichheit und Rechtssicherheit gewährleisten. Hierzu trägt entscheidend bei, dass Gesetze die Adressaten, aber (bis zu einem etwaigen *actus contrarius*) auch den Staat selbst binden: „Der Rechtsstaat hat die ‚Herrschaft der Gesetze' auf seine Fahnen geschrieben. Das bedeutet die Gebundenheit staatlichen Handelns an ein festgelegtes, zweiseitig verbindliches Recht."[27]

Ferner trägt zur rationalitätssichernden Distanz der Gesetze vom Einzelfall auch ihr Charakter als abstrakt-generelle Regelungen bei. Das Leitbild der Gesetze ist seit der Antike das allgemeine Gesetz: Es enthält eine in sachlicher Hinsicht nicht konkrete, sondern abstrakte, und in personeller Hinsicht nicht individuelle, sondern generelle Regelung. Durch diese doppelte (oder auch mehrfache[28]) Allgemeinheit behandelt das abstrakt-generelle Gesetz die subsumierbaren Fälle gleich.

Schließlich erhebt das Gesetz im formellen Sinne (d.h. das Parlamentsgesetz) wegen des rationalitätssichernden Verfahrens, in dem es zustande kommt, den Anspruch der Rationalität[29], was nicht ausschließt, dass sein Zustandekommen durch Emotionen motiviert und geprägt ist (s.u. III.). Seine Anwendung soll zwar nicht durch Subsumtionsautomaten oder den

---

24 Näher und diff. *Thomalla* (Fn. 7), S. 62 ff.
25 Vgl. den Hinweis von *Ada Neschke-Hentschke*. Recht und Gerechtigkeit. In: Barbara Zehnpfennig (Hrsg.). Die „Politik" des Aristoteles. 2012, S. 106 (115), „dass Aristoteles […] die Herrschaft des Gesetzes, also die *Institution*, in Übereinstimmung mit Platon, zur besten Garantie guter Herrschaft erklärt."
26 *Red.* (Fn. 7), Sp. 889: „gelehrte Neuprägung der zweiten Hälfte des 18. Jh."
27 *Ernst-Wolfgang Böckenförde*. Verfassungsgerichtsbarkeit: Strukturfragen, Organisation, Legitimation. NJW 1999, S. 9 (10).
28 *Gregor Kirchhof*. Die Allgemeinheit des Gesetzes. Über einen notwendigen Garanten der Gleichheit und der Demokratie. S. 160 ff., unterscheidet sprachliche, temporale, territoriale, personale, gegenständliche, finale und instrumentelle Allgemeinheit.
29 *Franz Reimer*. Das Parlamentsgesetz als Steuerungsmittel und Kontrollmaßstab. In: GVwR I, 3. Aufl. 2022, § 11 Rn. 7 m.w.N.

Richter als Mund des Gesetzes erfolgen, aber doch gereinigt von der Subjektivität des einzelnen Mitglieds des Rechtsstabs. Dies ist eine verfassungsrechtliche Vorgabe, die sich aus der Trennung von Amt und Person qua Republikprinzip (Art. 20 Abs. 1 GG), aus der Bindung an Gesetz und Recht (Art. 20 Abs. 3 GG) und aus der ausschließlichen Unterworfenheit der Richter unter das Gesetz (Art. 97 Abs. 1 GG) herleiten lässt. In diesem Sinne lässt sich sagen „Das Rechtsanwendungs- und Rechtsdurchsetzungsmodell des Grundgesetzes ist affektavers."[30] Rechtsgefühle sind im Rechtsstaat für die Angehörigen des Rechtsstabs suspekt.

2. Einwände

Es gibt freilich nicht nur abstrakt-generelle Gesetze, sondern auch zahlreiche konkrete Gesetze – und dies ist nicht nur als ein rechtstatsächlicher, sondern auch als ein verfassungsrechtlicher Befund gemeint: Die bundesrepublikanische Rechtsordnung akzeptiert im Grundsatz auch Einzelpersonen- und Einzelfallgesetze[31], etwa Planungsgesetze („Legalplanung") und Enteignungsgesetze („Legalenteignung"). Das abstrakt-generelle Gesetz ist „Prototyp"[32], aber keineswegs einzige zulässige Form des Gesetzes. Die Rede von der „Herrschaft der Gesetze" aber wird im Falle eines enteignenden oder eines Planungsgesetzes schal; das Gesetz ist hier in besonders deutlicher Weise politisches Instrument, nicht Ordnungsrahmen für das Handeln aller als Gleicher.

Aber auch innerhalb der Kategorie abstrakt-genereller Rechtsnormen, also der Gesetze im prototypischen Sinne, ist die Rede von der „Herrschaft der Gesetze" seit langem als idealistisch, ja naiv gebrandmarkt worden. Thomas Hobbes hielt es für einen Irrtum der aristotelischen Politik,

> „daß in einem wohlgeordneten Staat nicht Menschen, sondern Gesetze herrschen sollten. Welcher Mensch, der seine natürlichen Sinne beisammen hat [...], hält sich nicht von denjenigen beherrscht, die er fürchtet und von denen er annimmt, daß sie ihn töten oder ihm schaden können, wenn er nicht gehorcht? Oder wer glaubt, das Gesetz

---

30 *Wilhelm Wolf.* Rechtsgefühle in der Justiz zwischen Rechtssoziologie und Methodenlehre. Vortrag v. 14.6.2019, These 1.

31 Vgl. Art. 14 Abs. 3 Satz 2 Alt. 1 GG und *arg. e* Art. 19 Abs. 1 S. 1 GG, näher und krit. zu dessen Behandlung durch die Rspr. *Kirchhof* (Fn. 28), S. 174 ff.

32 Hierzu *Alexander Hollerbach.* Norm/II. Rechtsnorm. In: Staatslexikon der Görres-Gesellschaft. 7. Aufl., Bd. 4, 1988, Sp. 67.

könne ihm schaden, das heißt Worte und Papier, ohne die Hände und Schwerter von Menschen?"[33]

Dieser Einwand ist allerdings recht oberflächlich, denn natürlich können Gesetze selbst nicht handeln. Überzeugender stellt *James Harrington* der juristisch-idealistischen[34] eine realistische Lesart sozialer Herrschaft gegenüber:

> „And government (to define it de facto or according unto modern prudence) is an art whereby some man, or some few men, subject a city or a nation, and rule it according unto his or their private interest; which, because the laws in such cases are made according to the interest of a man or of some few families, may be said to be the empire of men and not of laws."[35]

Gesetze gibt es also auch in einem solchen „empire of men", aber sie sind nicht selber Herrscher, sondern Instrumente in der Hand der Mächtigen; ihre Herrschaft ist nur scheinbar, weil sie die Interessen Einzelner oder einzelner Familien eskamotieren und exekutieren.

Und im 20. Jahrhundert hat Franz Neumann darauf hingewiesen, dass „die Beschwörung der Gesetzesherrschaft es überflüssig macht, die tatsächlich Herrschenden in der Gesellschaft direkt zu benennen."[36] Mit anderen Worten kann die Formel „Herrschaft der Gesetze" zur Bemäntelung personaler Gewaltverhältnisse dienen[37], weil Herrschaft der Gesetze nicht ohne Menschen denkbar ist: Gesetze benötigen – was sogleich für Rechtsetzung (III.) wie für Rechtsanwendung (IV.) näher auszuführen ist – bislang in jedem ihrer Lebensabschnitte Menschen.

---

33 Leviathan IV, 46; Übersetzung: Walter Euchner, hrsg. von Iring Fetscher, 5. Aufl. 1992, S. 521. Hierzu (mit anderer Akzentuierung) *Thomalla* (Fn. 7), S. 165 f.
34 S. o. Fn. 4.
35 *Harrington* (Fn. 4), S. 9. Dass Gesetze das Produkt von Menschen sind, wird bereits bei *Demosthenes* (24. Rede / Gegen Timokrates, 75 f.) deutlich herausgearbeitet.
36 *Franz Neumann.* Die Herrschaft des Gesetzes (The Governance of the Rule of Law, 1936). 1980, S. 300.
37 *Locus classicus* für die Antike dürfte der auf Perikles gemünzte Satz sein: ἐγίγνετό τε λόγῳ μὲν δημοκρατία, ἔργῳ δὲ ὑπὸ τοῦ πρώτου ἀνδρὸς ἀρχή: „dem Namen nach eine Demokratie, der Sache nach die Herrschaft des ersten Mannes" (Thukydides, 2, 65, 10, eigene Übers.).

III. Rechtsetzung: Priorität von Menschen gegenüber Gesetzen

1. Gesetzgebung als Menschenwerk

Gesetze[38] kommen nicht aus dem Nichts, sondern sind – im Guten wie im Schlechten, im positiven wie im pejorativen Sinne – Menschenwerk. Dies gilt zunächst ganz oberflächlich für den Entstehungsprozess: Bundesgesetze (um sie als Beispiel zu nehmen) verdanken sich meist einem Regierungsentwurf, d.h. dem Beschluss eines Kollegialorgans; aber hinter einem solchen Entwurf stehen häufig: im Ausgangspunkt eine Einigung zwischen Spitzenpolitikern einer Koalition, die sich in einem Koalitionsvertrag niederschlägt; die Abrede der Mitglieder eines Koalitionsausschusses; das Eckpunktepapier zuständiger Kabinettsmitglieder; ein Entwurf von Fachleuten aus dem federführenden Ministerium oder in deren Auftrag (im Falle des Gesetzgebungsoutsourcing) ein Entwurf einzelner Anwältinnen oder auch ein Entwurf profilierter Politiker aus der Mitte des Bundestages. Einzelne Politikerinnen können über die gesamte Dauer des formellen parlamentarischen Verfahrens großen Einfluss ausüben (und für Einflüsse Dritter offen sein). Am Ende des Verfahrens kann die Bundespräsidentin oder der Bundespräsident bei Überzeugung von der Verfassungswidrigkeit (nicht also bei bloßem „Störgefühl") die Ausfertigung des Gesetzes verweigern. An dieser Skizze wird zweierlei deutlich: Erstens, dass Gesetze zwar in einer komplizierten Maschinerie mit zahllosen Beteiligten zustande kommen, aber – wegen der starken innerparlamentarischen Arbeitsteilung, des Ankereffekts und der Machtgefälle – häufig unter prägendem Einfluss einzelner Beteiligter. Zweitens, dass Gesetze zwar Politik in Recht transformieren, damit aber (als „in Rechtsform gegossene Politik"[39]) auch Politik bleiben: In ihnen können sich die Interessen durchsetzungsstarker Einzelner oder Gruppen niederschlagen; die Effizienz der Interessendurchsetzung steigert sich dann durch das Instrument der abstrakt-generellen Anordnung und Verschriftlichung.

Kurz: Gesetze sind Menschenwerk, und das heißt in der Demokratie zwar formal: Mehrheitswerk, bei materialer (politologischer oder verfassungssoziologischer Betrachtung) sind sie aber häufig durchaus Produkte einiger weniger. Sie verdanken ihre Legitimation dem demokratischen Meinungsbildungsprozess. Die Gegenprobe macht dies deutlich: Ein ma-

---

38 Hier und im Folgenden zur Abkürzung verengt auf die aktuell wichtigste Kategorie, Gesetze im formellen Sinne (Parlamentsgesetze).

39 *Christian Waldhoff*. Das Gesetz zwischen Recht und Politik. ZfP 2019, S. 98 (99).

schinell erstelltes Gesetz hätte in unserer Rechtsgemeinschaft weder Legitimation noch Legitimität.

2. *Rationalität als Erfordernis der Gesetzgebung?*

Dass Gesetzgebung Menschenwerk (und in der Demokratie Mehrheitswerk) ist und dabei in hohem Maße dem Einfluss Einzelner unterliegt, entbindet nicht von der Frage, in welcher Weise und in welchem Umfang sie „rational" sein soll oder (von Verfassungs wegen) sein muss. Es handelt sich hierbei, näher betrachtet, um ein ganzes Fragenbündel, das verfassungsrechtlich in Einzelfragen zu Zuständigkeiten, Verfahren, Form (bspw. gesetzgeberische Begründungspflichten), aber auch zu Gesetzesinhalten (etwa zur Verhältnismäßigkeit von Gesetzen) aufzuspalten ist. An dieser Stelle muss der Hinweis genügen, dass Rationalität (wie auch immer definiert) als solche keine Anforderung des Bundes- oder Landesverfassungsrechts für Gesetze darstellt[40], und dass dies aus demokratischen Gründen auch kein Zufall ist. Vielmehr würden Rationalitätskriterien dem demokratisch unmittelbar legitimierten Gesetzgeber in weitem Umfang politische Gestaltungsmöglichkeiten nehmen (und damit zugleich der Verfassungsgerichtsbarkeit Macht zuweisen). Als in Rechtsform gegossene Politik dürfen sich Gesetze – Einhaltung grundrechtlicher Grenzen vorausgesetzt – Gefühlen oder Emotionen verdanken, Emotionen verkörpern und selbst auch emotional formuliert sein. So verfiele ein verfassungsänderndes Gesetz, das ein allgemeines Verschleierungs- oder Verhüllungsverbot enthält[41], nicht dadurch der Verfassungswidrigkeit, dass es von Ressentiments oder Unbehagen getragen wäre.

3. *Thematisierung von Gefühlen in der Gesetzgebung*

Es verwundert nicht, dass die Rechtsetzungslehre als Disziplin und auch die Rechtsetzungslehren als Handreichungen innerhalb dieser Disziplin

---

40 Näher *Reimer* (Fn. 29), § 11 Rn. 8.
41 Wie Art. 10a Absatz 1 der Schweizerischen BV (Volksinitiative vom 15. September 2017 und Volksabstimmung vom 7. März 2021): „Niemand darf sein Gesicht im öffentlichen Raum und an Orten verhüllen, die öffentlich zugänglich sind oder an denen grundsätzlich von jedermann beanspruchbare Dienstleistungen angeboten werden; das Verbot gilt nicht für Sakralstätten."

wenig bis gar nicht von Rechtsgefühlen sprechen[42]. Recht versteht sich als autonome und rationale Ordnung, und zwar auch als Ordnung, die rational, nicht emotional wirkt, die auf Einsicht und vernunftgeleitete Akzeptanz setzt, nicht auf Furcht, Stolz, Hoffnung o.ä. Infolgedessen spricht der Gesetzgeber selten – immer seltener[43] – vom „Rechtsgefühl". Ob darin eine Eskamotierung, eine Invisibilisierung des Phänomens einer von prägnanten Rechtsgefühlen getragenen Gesetzgebung liegt, ließe sich durch eine interdisziplinäre Untersuchung beantworten. Auffallend allerdings ist die vielkritisierte und jüngst wieder häufiger auftretende Emotionalisierung von Gesetzestiteln[44]. Auffallend ist ferner, dass die deutschen

---

42 So schweigt – verständlicherweise – das auf redaktionelle Fragen konzentrierte „Handbuch der Rechtsförmlichkeit" des BMJ (3. Aufl. 2008) zu diesem Thema; aber auch die Lehrbücher wie *Georg Müller/Felix Uhlmann*. Elemente einer Rechtssetzungslehre. 3. Aufl., Zürich/Basel/Genf 2013, oder *Winfried Kluth/Günter Krings* (Hrsg.). Gesetzgebung. 2014, sind vergleichsweise technisch orientiert; ausgewiesen bei Müller/Uhlmann hins. der Kriterien Sachgerechtigkeit und Fairness: „Die Rechtssetzungslehre tut sich mit dieser ‚materiellen' Frage schwer" (S. 55).

43 „Rechtsgefühl" und „Rechtsempfinden" sind, soweit ersichtlich, keine Rechtssatzbegriffe im geltenden Bundesrecht; im hessischen Landesrecht wird einmal an entlegener Stelle auf „Rechtsempfinden" Bezug genommen (Zf. 9.2.1. der Anlage 5 zur Hessischen Weiterbildungs- und Prüfungsordnung für die Pflege und Entbindungspflege v. 6.12.2010: „Spezifisches Pflegewissen im Maßregelvollzug: a) Auseinandersetzung mit gesellschaftlichen Normen, dem individuellen Rechtsempfinden und dem öffentlichen Bild"). In der Rechtsetzung und im parlamentarischen Diskurs auf Bundesebene nimmt die Verwendung der beiden Vokabeln insgesamt ab. Verzeichnet die Datenbank des Deutschen Bundestages für die 1. Wahlperiode (1949-1953) noch 33 Treffer (davon 5 in Drucksachen, die übrigen in Plenarprotokollen), so für die 14. WP noch 8 (2/6), für die 15. WP einen (0/1), für die 16. WP zwei (1/1), für die 17. WP einen (1/0), für die 18. WP keinen und für die 19. WP zwei Treffer (0/2, siehe Zitat Fn. 61). Ein weniger eindeutiges Bild ergibt sich für das Lemma „Rechtsempfinden": in der 1. WP 28 Treffer, in der 14. WP 13 Treffer , in der 15. WP 8 Treffer, in der 16. WP ebenfalls 8 Treffer, in der 17. WP allerdings 16 Treffer, in der 18. WP 8 Treffer und in der 19. WP 22 Treffer . Unter den Drucksachen handelt es sich nur zum Teil um Gesetzesbegründungen, zu einem Gutteil auch um Anfragen und deren Beantwortung.

44 Zwar heißt das „Gute-Kita-Gesetz" eigentlich „Gesetz zur Weiterentwicklung der Qualität und zur Teilhabe in der Kindertagesbetreuung", aber schon hierin mag man einen emotionalen Euphemismus sehen; und das „Starke-Familien-Gesetz", d.h. das „Gesetz zur zielgenauen Stärkung von Familien und ihren Kindern durch die Neugestaltung des Kinderzuschlags und die Verbesserung der Leistungen für Bildung und Teilhabe" vom 29. April 2019, BGBl. I S. 530 (ein Artikelgesetz mit neun Artikeln) hat der Gesetzgeber mit dem Kurztitel „Starke-Familien-Gesetz" und der Abkürzung „StaFamG" versehen, es heißt also auch offiziell so.

Gesetzgeber wieder häufiger Präambeln nutzen, also Vorsprüche, die nur eine mittelbare normative Funktion, dafür aber unmittelbare appellative, edukative oder Leitbildfunktion haben[45] – was in der NS-Zeit und in der DDR üblich, in der Bundesrepublik aber weitgehend unüblich war[46].

In ihrem Inhalt, ihren Regelungen geben Gesetze meist Nüchternheit, Generalität, Abstraktion, Distanz zum Einzelfall vor; aber gerade darum dürfen sie – wie wir seit Platon[47] und Aristoteles wissen[48] – Ausnahmen zulassen, sich erweichen lassen; das lässt sich als Einfallstor für Gefühle deuten: „Unsere Gesetze selbst, diese kaltblütigen Pedanten, lassen sich rühren und halten ihre Strafe zurück."[49] Häufig werden die zivilrechtlichen Generalklauseln (wie §§ 138, 242, 826 BGB etc.) als Möglichkeit gedeutet, außerrechtlichen Wertungen Bedeutung in der Rechtsordnung Raum zu verschaffen[50]; so wird als Maßstab für die Sittenwidrigkeit (i.S.v. §§ 138, 826 BGB) nach wie vor das „Anstandsgefühl aller billig und gerecht Denkenden"[51] herangezogen[52]. Ob und in welchem Sinne dieses „Anstandsgefühl" wirklich ein Gefühl ist, erscheint fraglich. Bei Lichte betrachtet handelt es sich um eine zugleich kognitive und volitive Haltung,

---

45 Zu einer Theorie der Präambel vgl. neben *Platon*. Nomoi. 719e 7 ff. insbes. *Marie Theres Fögen*. Das Lied vom Gesetz. 2006, S. 9 ff.; knapp: *Winfried Kluth*. In: ders./ Krings (Fn. 42), § 1 Rn. 102.

46 Ein frühes Gegenbeispiel war die Präambel des Lastenausgleichsgesetzes (v. 14.8.1952, BGBl. I S. 446 [447]). Neuere Präambeln finden sich auf Bundesebene im Berlin/Bonn-Gesetz (Gesetz zur Umsetzung des Beschlusses des Deutschen Bundestages vom 20. Juni 1991 zur Vollendung der Einheit Deutschlands v. 26.4.1994, BGBl. I S. 918), auf Länderebene in Hessen bspw. im Gesetz über die Metropolregion Frankfurt/Rhein-Main
(MetropolG) v. 8.3.2011 (GVBl. I S. 153), im Psychisch-Kranken-Hilfe-Gesetz (PsychKHG) v. 4.5.2017 (GVBl. S. 66), im Hessischen Verfassungsschutzgesetz v. 25.6.2018 (GVBl. S. 302), in Bayern im Bayerischen Integrationsgesetz (BayIntG) v. 13.12.2016 (GVBl. S. 335), wo die Präambel als Indiz einer bedrohlichen Moralisierung des Rechts gelesen werden kann.

47 Politikos, 294a f.

48 Nikomachische Ethik V (zur Bedeutung der ἐπιείκεια als Ausgleich der Allgemeinheit des νόμος).

49 So Werther im Gespräch mit Albert: *Johann Wolfgang Goethe*. Die Leiden des jungen Werther, Erstes Buch, Brief v. 12. August [1771], hier zit. n. der Ausgabe der Reclam-Universalbibliothek Nr. 67, Stuttgart 1986, S. 54.

50 Näher und diff. *Marietta Auer*. Materialisierung, Flexibilisierung, Richterfreiheit. Generalklauseln im Spiegel der Antinomien des Privatrechtsdenkens. 2005.

51 RGZ 48, 114 (124) offenbar im Anschluss an Mot. II 727; Synonym ist für das Reichsgericht das „herrschende Volksbewusstsein".

52 Dies reflektierend und im Grundsatz rechtfertigend *Armbrüster*, in: MüKo-BGB, 18. Aufl. 2018, § 138 Rn. 14 f.

nämlich eine Wahrnehmung und Bejahung bestimmter (und Missbilligung anderer) gesellschaftlicher Verhaltensstandards.

4. Rationalität und Emotionalität: Gegenbegriffe?

Zugleich deutet sich (auch) hier an, dass Rationalität und Emotionalität eine suggestive, aber irreführende Gegenüberstellung sind[53]: Die Begriffe greifen so weit aus, dass sie als sich gegenseitig ausschließend und gemeinsam erschöpfend erscheinen[54], tatsächlich aber (wie gleich anhand des Einfühlungsvermögens, der Empathie zu zeigen sein wird: IV.3) wichtige Nuancen menschlichen Verhaltens bzw. menschlicher Welteinstellung einebnen. Schon was Empathie, Scham, Sehnsucht nach Gerechtigkeit, Ekel, Rachedurst, Einschüchterung, Dankbarkeit und andere Regungen, die sich als rechtsbezogene Gefühle bezeichnen ließen, verbindet und was sie unterscheidet, ist alles andere als klar; es bedarf eher differenzierender Untersuchung als der Bekräftigung durch ein nivellierendes Etikett. Wenn „Gefühl" als Auffangkategorie für alles verwendet wird, was nicht rational zwingend (bewiesen oder beweisbar) ist, verliert der Begriff seine Analyse- und Beschreibungskraft. So können Gefühle im weiten Sinne auch Intuitionen und Evidenzannahmen umfassen; sie werden möglicherweise leidenschaftslos, wenn auch vorurteilsbeladen gebildet. Solche Prämissen können aber ihren Aggregatzustand verändern, nämlich zu Gefühlen im engeren Sinne werden, etwa, wenn Evidenzen angegriffen oder auf andere Weise in Frage gestellt werden. Die Emotionalität kann in bestimmten Überzeugungen schlummern, gewissermaßen überwintern, und sie kann in bestimmten Situationen machtvoll erwachen. Aber die nicht-rationale Überzeugung ist damit nicht automatisch schon „Gefühl".

---

53 Zur möglichen Rationalität rechtsrelevanter Emotionen *Landweer/Koppelberg* (Fn. 3), S. 13 (45 f.) unter Bezugnahme auf *Ronald de Sousa*. The Rationality of Emotions. 1978.

54 Bspw. *Andreas Fischer-Lescano*. Radikale Rechtskritik. KJ 2014, 171 (177): „Das Recht hat sich der Emotionalität verschlossen. Bis heute definiert sich Recht als Verkörperung von Rationalität, Vernunft, Objektivität."

IV. Rechtsanwendung: Komplementarität von Gesetzen und Menschen

Wie bereits von Hobbes herausgestellt[55], bedürfen Gesetze zu ihrer Durchsetzung der Menschen. Aber nicht nur der letzte Schritt ihrer Verwirklichung ist auf menschliche Hilfe angewiesen. Vielmehr sind von wenigen Ausnahmen abgesehen *alle* Schritte der Rechtsverwirklichung im Einzelfall auf menschliche Vollzüge angewiesen und damit von den jeweils beteiligten Menschen und ihrer Konstitution abhängig.

1. Klärung und Bewertung der Interessen und des Sachverhalts

Schon die ersten Schritte vieler – wenn auch nicht aller – Rechtsanwendungsvorgänge, die Erfassung des jeweiligen Interesses und des Sachverhalts (zwei in der Juristischen Methodenlehre nach wie vor unterbelichtete Aspekte), sind genuin personale Vorgänge. Sie erfordern menschliche Kommunikation und Interpretation. Ob ein Kopftuch, wenn in einer Kita oder einer Schule von einer Erzieherin oder Lehrerin getragen, Unterdrückung indiziert, einschüchtert, ein freies Bekenntnis zu einer kulturellen Tradition oder zu einer nichtsäkularen Weltsicht, Ausdruck geistig-geistlicher Nonkonformität oder modischer Selbstbestimmung ist, lässt sich nicht mechanisch klären. Ob von einer gelben Warnweste mit dem Aufdruck „Sharia Police" in einer bestimmten Situation (etwa bei Nacht von mehreren Personen patrouillenartig in der Öffentlichkeit getragen) eine einschüchternde Wirkung ausgeht[56], so dass es sich um eine Uniform, ein Uniformteil oder ein gleichartiges Kleidungsstück im Sinne des versammlungsrechtlichen Uniformverbots (§ 3 Abs. 1 VersG) handeln kann[57], ist eine Frage, die wiederum nicht das Gesetz oder andere Rechtsnormen,

---

55 Oben Fn. 33.
56 Zu dieser Voraussetzung des § 3 Abs. 1 VersG Sächs. OVG, NVwZ-RR 2002, 435: Vom Uniformverbot werden „Kleidungsstücke nicht erfasst, wenn diese zwar eine gemeinsame politische Gesinnung zum Ausdruck bringen, jedoch keine Gewaltbereitschaft signalisieren. Denn in diesem Fall sind diese Bekleidungsstücke ein Element der durch die Versammlung beabsichtigten und durch Art. 5 Abs. 1 und Art. 8 GG gewährleisteten Kommunikation. Sind solche Bekleidungsstücke jedoch ein Symbol für eine Zurschaustellung von Gewaltbereitschaft und Einschüchterung Andersdenkender, dann sind sie keine der Kommunikation dienende Elemente, sondern Symbole, durch die der gewaltsame Abbruch von Kommunikation signalisiert wird."; ähnlich OLG Koblenz, NStZ-RR 2011, 187; BGH NJW 2018, 1893 (1894).
57 Bejahend *in casu* LG Wuppertal, Urt. v. 17.05.2019, Az. 26 KLs 20/18.

sondern nur die mit ihrer Anwendung beauftragten Menschen klären können. Insofern sind Herrschaft der Gesetze und Herrschaft der Menschen keine Alternativen, sondern nur gemeinsam möglich. Eine angemessene Antwort erfordert Klarheit über das von Rechts wegen erlaubte und das unerlaubte Maß an Einwirkung auf Betroffene, aber auch Vorstellungs- und Einfühlungsvermögen hinsichtlich der konkreten Situation – kein Gefühl (hierzu sogleich), aber doch eine gewisse emotionale Beweglichkeit und die Bereitschaft, von ihr zugunsten einer angemessenen Rechtsfindung Gebrauch zu machen.

2. Zusammenstellung, Auslegung und Subsumtion der relevanten Rechtsnormen

Auch die Identifikation und Aufarbeitung der relevanten Normen ist keine Frage mechanischer Syllogistik. Kommt im Beispiel der Scharia-Polizei als Straftatbestand auch eine versuchte Nötigung in Betracht, d.h. ist die Androhung des Übels einer sozialen (religiösen) Disziplinierung zu dem angestrebten Zweck als verwerflich anzusehen (§ 240 Abs. 2 StGB)? Oder um ein gravierenderes Delikt aufzugreifen: Wann und in welchem Ausmaß greift bei einem „Ehrenmord" ein *cultural defense*? Alle diese Wertungsfragen werden von Personen entschieden, d.h. Instanzen, die nicht in isolierter Rationalität arbeiten und dies auch nicht sollen. Die Entscheidung eines Falles durch die Richterin oder den Richter als ganzer Person, mit Leib und Seele, mit Herz und Verstand, ist möglicherweise kein defizitärer, sondern für die individuelle Akzeptanz und den gesellschaftlichen Rechtsfrieden essentiell wichtiger Entscheidungsmodus. Eine Herrschaft der Gesetze schließt Entscheidungen von Menschen unter Umständen nicht nur nicht aus, sondern erfordert sie gerade.

Das ist auch aus traditioneller, auf Homogenität der Rechtsanwendung zielender Perspektive solange kein Problem, wie die Entscheidungsfaktoren der die Gesetze anwendenden Menschen vergleichsweise homogen sind: durch einen gemeinsamen kulturell-weltanschaulichen Hintergrund, durch gemeinsame Wertvorstellungen, durch gemeinsame Sozialisation etc. Wenn demgegenüber die Wahrnehmung einer sozialen, religiös-weltanschaulichen, ethnischen, kulturellen Ausdifferenzierung und Pluralisierung der Gesellschaft zutrifft (was hier nicht zu klären ist), so kann dies die Brisanz des Befunds steigern, dass mit den Gesetzen immer auch Menschen herrschen. Je individualisierter, parzellierter und damit disparater die Anschauungen, Überzeugungen, Gefühle der Entscheider sind, desto wichtiger mag die Schulung eines professionalisierten Rechtsgefühls, des

„Judiz", erscheinen, also eine rigorose juristische Sozialisation, und die Vermittlung der Entscheidungsparameter und -ergebnisse an eine heterogen wahrnehmende und wertende Öffentlichkeit.

3. Abwägung und Entscheidung

Wenn Interessen der Beteiligten, Sachverhalt und anwendbare Normen im Rahmen des Möglichen und situativ Angemessenen geklärt sind, ist eine Entscheidung zu fällen. In aller Regel besteht hierbei nach den gesetzlichen Grundlagen ein Entscheidungsspielraum (etwa hinsichtlich des Strafmaßes; oder bei verwaltungsrechtlichen Entscheidungen – selbst wenn sie einmal gebundene Entscheidungen sind – durch Ermessen hinsichtlich der Nebenbestimmungen etc.).

Hierfür bedarf es je nach Situation der Empathie, des Einfühlungsvermögens. Der Schluss liegt nahe, hier sei wiederum die Sphäre des Gefühls, der Emotionalität, betroffen. Doch trügt der Schein, insofern Einfühlung gerade kein Gefühl im Sinne spontaner Emotionalität und Subjektivität ist, ja vielleicht gar nicht als Gefühl qualifiziert werden sollte[58]. Das ist von dem eminenten Staatsrechtler und Rechtstheoretiker *Martin Kriele* wie folgt beschrieben worden:

> „Was tun wir, wenn wir [...] entscheiden müssen? Wir versuchen Vorstellung, Abschätzung und Abwägung der Konsequenzen, die es hätte, wenn wir auf die eine oder andere Weise entscheiden würden: „Wohin führt das?" Das erfordert zunächst einmal ein Einfühlen in die Situation der Betroffenen, auch der künftig von der Entscheidung Betroffenen, also unter Berücksichtigung der präjudiziellen Zukunftswirkung. Dieses Einfühlen ist nicht Gefühl, ist nicht Subjektivität, sondern ein sich in die Lage derer Versetzen, die etwa durch die Entscheidungsmaxime betroffen werden, und ein Abwägen gegen die Konsequenzen, die auf der anderen Seite in Frage stehen. Das heißt, wir versetzen uns in die Lage der betroffenen Menschen. Indem wir das tun, bringen wir nicht unsere Subjektivität ins Spiel, sondern bemühen uns im Gegenteil, soviel wie möglich von unserer Subjektivität zu abstrahieren und betätigen gerade dadurch die Unparteilichkeit unseres juristischen Denkens."[59]

---

58 Sie ist es auch in keiner der vier unterschiedenen Bedeutungen (s. oben Fn. 3 a.E.).

59 *Martin Kriele*. Diskussionsbeitrag. VVDStRL 34, S. 122 (123).

Kurz: „Einfühlung ist nicht ‚Gefühl‘, sondern Einsicht. Genauer gesagt handelt es sich um einen Akt der inneren Identifikation."[60] Denn Einfühlung setzt gerade die Distanzierung von den eigenen Gefühlen voraus. Der Nachvollzug der Situation, Interessen, Gestimmtheit und Hintergrundanliegen eines Betroffenen, die innere Identifikation erfordert in dieser Perspektive das Absehen von der eigenen Subjektivität. In einer weniger konfrontativen Sichtweise ließe sich umgekehrt sagen, dass die Aufgabe den Einsatz der *ganzen* Person in allen ihren Facetten, besonders mit ihrer emotionalen Intelligenz, erfordert. Wenn in diesem Kontext überhaupt von Gefühlen gesprochen werden soll, dann jedenfalls in ihrer rezeptiven, nicht einer kreativen Dimension.

Vom „Einfühlungsvermögen" abgesehen, ist „Rechtsgefühl" in der öffentlichen Diskussion in Deutschland heute häufig durchaus negativ konnotiert, etwa als Gegenbegriff zu „Rechtslage", d.h. als Ausdruck individueller, instabiler, letztlich willkürlicher Maßstäbe[61]. In der akademischen Diskussion kommen Rechtsgefühle erst allmählich wieder zu ihrem Recht. Methodenlehren behandeln die Rolle von Gefühlen bei der Rechtsanwendung nur in Ansätzen[62]. Nur selten werden Gefühle oder Affekte so klar angesprochen wie in folgendem Passus:

> „Affekte sind, obwohl Affektkontrolle zur professionellen Sachlichkeit gehört, nicht ausgeschlossen: Betroffenheit darf sich in den gehörigen

---

60 *Martin Kriele*. Theorie der Rechtsgewinnung. 2. Aufl. 1976, S. 334 f.

61 So Prof. Dr. *Stephan Harbarth* MdB (jetzt Präsident des Bundesverfassungsgerichts), Rede im Deutschen Bundestag am 13.9.2018, PlProt. 19/49, S. 5173 D: „Der Staat erwartet vom Bürger zu Recht, dass er sich der Selbstjustiz und auch der Vorverurteilung enthält, auch dort, wo brutale Verbrechen geschehen und vielleicht gar ein Täter auf frischer Tat ertappt wird. Ebenso wie wir aushalten müssen, dass in gewissen Grenzen auch Menschen demonstrieren, deren politische Auffassung wir nicht teilen, muss jeder das Strafen unabhängigen Gerichten überlassen, und zwar nicht nach dem Rechtsgefühl, sondern nach der Rechtslage. Aber so wenig wie das Rechtsgefühl bei Urteilen eine Rolle spielt: Wir müssen wachsam sein, wenn dauerhaft die Akzeptanz in der Bevölkerung zu schwinden droht."

62 *Karl Larenz/Claus-Wilhelm Canaris*. Methodenlehre der Rechtswissenschaft. 3. Aufl., Berlin u.a. 1995, S. 168 f.; *Dirk Looschelders/Wolfgang Roth*, Juristische Methodik im Prozeß der Rechtsanwendung, Berlin 1996, S. 78 f.; *Franz Reimer*, Juristische Methodenlehre. Baden-Baden 2016, Rn. 60 f., 372, 415; *Thomas M. J. Möllers*. Juristische Methodenlehre. München 2017, § 1 Rn. 25; *Hans-Joachim Strauch*. Methodenlehre des gerichtlichen Erkenntnisverfahrens. Freiburg 2017, S. 41, 542.

Formeln äußern („Besonders verwerflich ist das Verhalten des Ange-klagten deshalb, weil...").[63]

Das Rechtssystem legt beim Rechtsstab also Wert auf eine Kanalisierung, eine Stilisierung, freundlicher formuliert: eine Disziplinierung der Gefüh-le. Dass Gefühle der Rechtsanwender im Rechtsstaat ein Risiko bedeuten, schließt nicht aus, dass sie auch positive Funktionen oder Effekte haben.

4. Mittel zur Einhegung der Subjektivität

Festhalten lässt sich: „Die alte republikanische Idee, daß Gesetze regieren sollen und nicht Menschen, reibt sich an der staatlichen Wirklichkeit: daß die Gesetze nicht aus sich selbst heraus herrschen, sondern dass sie der Menschen als Mittler bedürfen, die sie interpretieren und anwenden."[64] Diese Menschen stehen hinsichtlich der Interessenlage, des Sachverhalts und der rechtlichen Maßstäbe vor Deutungs- und Abwägungsaufgaben, die sie als ganze Personen fordern. Die immer präsente emotionale bzw. affektive Dimension der Person stellt ein starkes Movens dar, das in hergebrachter Sicht der Kanalisierung oder Disziplinierung bedarf. Diese wird nicht (oder nicht nur) durch ethische Appelle geleistet, sondern vornehmlich durch sachlich-institutionelle Vorkehrungen. Hierzu zählt grundlegend die Unterscheidung von Person und Amt: „Über das Medium des Amtes wandelt sich die Herrschaft des Menschen in die Herrschaft des Rechts."[65] Das Amt ist der „institutionelle Ausdruck der Gemeinwohl-idee": „Die rechtliche und ethische Inpflichtnahme des Amtswalters dient dazu, unabhängig von seinem subjektiven Willen, den objektivierten Wil-len der Allgemeinheit zu definieren und zu vermitteln. Das Amt verlangt von seinem Inhaber Askese: die Zurücknahme seiner Subjektivität, damit das Gesetz herrschen kann."[66] Zu den Mitteln, mit denen die Subjektivität der Rechtsanwender eingehegt wird, gehört ferner das Kollegialprinzip: Wichtige Entscheidungen werden in allen drei Gewalten auf der Basis ei-nes Diskurses durch Personenmehrheiten getroffen, die sich in ihrer Ratio-

---

63 Pointiert *Wolfgang Gast*. Juristische Rhetorik. 5. Aufl., Heidelberg 2015, Rn. 477.
64 *Josef Isensee*. Staat und Verfassung. HdBStR II, § 15 Rn. 172.
65 *Josef Isensee*. Transformation von Macht in Recht – das Amt. ZBR 2004, S. 3; hier zit. n. *Thomalla*. S. 377.
66 Zitate: *Isensee* (Fn. 64), § 15 Rn. 131.

nalität und Emotionalität gegenseitig ergänzen[67]. Und schließlich entfalten die zahlreichen im Rechtssystem vorgesehenen Kontrollmöglichkeiten (keineswegs nur der gerichtliche Instanzenzug!) eine qualitätssichernde, willkürhemmende Vorwirkung auf Entscheidungen.

5. *Zwischenergebnis*

„Herrschaft der Gesetze" bedeutet fast ausnahmslos auch „Herrschaft von Menschen". Natürliche Personen sind in der Rechtsetzung und in der Rechtsverwirklichung bislang nicht nur unentbehrlich, sondern von entscheidender Bedeutung für die tatsächlichen Wirkungen der Gesetze. Denn ein Gesetz ist in Abwandlung des berühmten, auf die Verfassung gemünzten Diktums von Cardozo letztlich, „what the judges say it is". Nach einem Jahrhundert Richtersoziologie kann man mit dem Hinweis auf die Personabhängigkeit der Tätigkeiten der Judikative nicht mehr auf Erstaunen stoßen. Nichts anderes ergibt sich, wenn man anstelle der personal-akteurszentrierten Frage die Frage nach der Bedeutung der Staatsgewalten stellt: Denn die Legislative ist in vielfacher Hinsicht auf die Exekutive angewiesen, der Herrschaft der Gesetze die „Mitherrschaft der Verwaltung"[68] zur Seite zu stellen, vor allem aber – im Übergang „vom parlamentarischen Gesetzgebungsstaat zum verfassungsvollziehenden Jurisdiktionsstaat"[69] – die Judikative, insbesondere die Verfassungsgerichtsbarkeit, und das heißt wiederum nichts anderes als: Verfassungsrichterinnen und Verfassungsrichter[70].

---

67 Betonung des Mehrheitsprinzips (für die Zweite Gewalt) dagegen bei *Thomas Groß*. Das Kollegialprinzip in der Verwaltungsorganisation. 1999, S. 49 f. u.ö.

68 *Horst Dreier*. Hierarchische Verwaltung im demokratischen Staat. Genese, aktuelle Bedeutung und funktionelle Grenzen eines Bauprinzips der Exekutive. 1991, S. 200 ff.

69 *Ernst-Wolfgang Böckenförde*. Gesetz und gesetzgebende Gewalt. 2. Aufl. 1981, S. 402; zum Problem *Andreas Voßkuhle*. In: von Mangoldt/Klein/Starck/Huber/ Voßkuhle (Hrsg.). GG, 7. Aufl. 2018, Art. 93 Rn. 35 m.w.N.

70 Eindringliche Betonung der Verantwortung der „Personen, die Verfassungsgerichtsbarkeit ausüben", bei *Ernst-Wolfgang Böckenförde*. Verfassungsgerichtsbarkeit. Strukturfragen, Organisation, Legitimation. In: *ders*. Staat, Nation, Europa, 1999. S. 157 (182).

V. *Rechtsgefühle in Zeiten der Algorithmen: The Empire of Machines and Not of Men?*

In jüngerer Zeit ist eine intensive Diskussion um Legal Tech und Rechtsgewinnung durch Algorithmen entbrannt[71]. „Legal Tech" wird dabei als „Schlagwort für einen grundlegenden Medienwechsel"[72] betrachtet und weiter aufgefächert: So bezeichnet „Legal Tech 2.0" die derzeit am weitesten verbreitete Entwicklungsstufe, die Automatisierung standardisierter und repetitiver Tätigkeiten, wohingegen „Legal Tech 3.0" die Einbeziehung Künstlicher Intelligenz in juristische Tätigkeiten meint[73]. Die Möglichkeiten der Künstlichen Intelligenz werden in Zukunft[74] die Rechtsanwendung (aus demokratischen Gründen weniger die Rechtsetzung) verändern. Wohin der Weg führt, ist sowohl in technologischer Hinsicht als auch mit Blick auf die Effekte offen: „Mehr Objektivität oder mehr Diskriminierung?"[75] In jedem Fall wird *Legal Tech* in den unterschiedlichen Bereichen in sehr unterschiedlichem Ausmaß zur Anwendung kommen: Es erscheint unwahrscheinlich, dass familienrechtliche Streitigkeiten – etwa über Sorgerechtsfragen – in gleicher Weise und gleichem Umfang werden automatisiert werden wie vermögensrechtliche Streitigkeiten, Konflikte zwischen natürlichen Personen ebenso wie solche zwischen juristischen Personen. Auch strafrechtliche Entscheidungen werden auf lange Sicht weiterhin händisch getroffen werden. Dazu zwingen die verfassungsrechtlichen Vorgaben; denn die rechtsprechende Gewalt ist nach Art. 92 HS 1 GG „den Richtern" anvertraut, also Personen, nicht Institutionen[76] (und

---

71 Bspw. *Christoph Rollberg.* Algorithmen in der Justiz. 2020; *Jean-Pierre Clavier* (Hrsg.). L'algorithmisation de la justice. 2020; *Martin Ebers/Susana Navas* (Hrsg.). Algorithms and Law. 2020; *Susanne Hähnchen/Paul T. Schrader/Frank Weiler/ Thomas Wischmeyer.* Legal Tech. Rechtsanwendung durch Menschen als Auslaufmodell?. JuS 2020, S. 625 ff.; *Nink* (Fn. 3) (u.v.a.m.).

72 *Hähnchen/Schrader/Weiler/Wischmeyer* (Fn. 71). JuS 2020, S. 625 (635).

73 *Hähnchen/Schrader/Weiler/Wischmeyer* (Fn. 71). JuS 2020, S. 625 (626).

74 Allerdings nicht kurzfristig und revolutionär, vgl. die Einschätzung eines Branchen- bzw. Verbandsvertreters: „Wir alle werden den Tag nicht erleben, an dem KI eine komplexe Rechtsberatung übernimmt" (*Holger Zscheyge.* Interviewäußerung. In: *Pia Lorenz.* Legal Tech nach dem Hype. „Wir erleben den Tag nicht, an dem KI eine komplexe Rechtsberatung übernimmt". Legal Tribune Online v. 9.3.2021, zugänglich über https://www.lto.de/recht/legal-tech/seite/3/).

75 *Rollberg* (Fn. 71), S. 38 unter Hinweis auf die Programmierungsbedürftigkeit der Algorithmen (S. 39 f.): „Bewusste und unbewusste Vorurteile können sich dadurch in ihrer Breitenwirkung potenzieren." (S. 40).

76 Näher *Rollberg* (Fn. 71), S. 88 f.

dies nach Art. 79 Abs. 3 GG auch verfassungsänderungsfest[77]). Für die menschliche anstelle einer maschinellen Entscheidung sprechen aber auch rechts- und verfassungspolitische Gründe: Denn wünschen wir uns, dass über die Bestrafung einer Person (jenseits von Bagatelldelikten), etwa in einem Ehrenmordfall, und zwar sowohl über das „Ob" der Strafbarkeit wie bejahendenfalls über das Strafmaß, im Wege des Legal Tech von Maschinen entschieden wird? Ist nicht zumindest Empathie (jedenfalls in existenzielle Belange berührenden Rechtskonflikten) eine Mindesterwartung an die Entscheidungsinstanzen[78]? Über Menschen jedenfalls sollen nur Menschen richten – dies sicher nach vorab bestimmten, egalitären und transparenten Maßstäben, den Gesetzen; aber eben nicht mechanisch, sondern in einem diesen Namen verdienenden Kommunikationsprozess und unter Ernstnahme der Menschenwürde aller beteiligten Individuen.

Dies beleuchtet zwei wichtige Aspekte: Erstens zielt Recht auf Seiten der Rechtsunterworfenen auch auf die Sicherung von Rechtsfrieden, auf Akzeptanz, auf (um das Modewort zu benutzen) Selbstwirksamkeit. Rechtsverwirklichung zielt nicht auf isolierte Gerechtigkeit um jeden Preis („fiat iustitia, pereat mundus"). Rechtsfrieden, Akzeptanz, Selbstwirksamkeit aber sind Ziele, die es erfordern, dass Entscheider die emotionalen Wirkungen von Entscheidungen nicht ausblenden.

Zweitens dienen Gefühle auf Seiten des Rechtsstabs als Motivations- und als Kontrollkriterien. Sie drängen auf eine intensivere Auseinandersetzung mit den Tatsachen und dem Recht; sie können zu einer erneuten Reflexion über anwendbare Normen, etwaige Gesetzeslücken, über die Verfassungs- und Europarechtmäßigkeit des einfachen Rechts u.ä. anhalten und damit zu einer Korrektur des vorläufigen Ergebnisses führen. Auch das eng verstandene Rechtsgefühl (im Singular) dient dann nicht als Entscheidungskriterium, wohl aber als Kontrollkriterium. In einer „Herr-

---

77 Insoweit wohl ohne Stellungnahme *Karl-Peter Sommermann*. In: von Mangoldt/ Klein/Starck/Huber/Voßkuhle (Hrsg.). GG. 7. Aufl. 2018, Bd. 2, Art. 20 Rn. 220: Verbot, „den Gerichten ihre Kernkompetenzen" zu entziehen.

78 So nachdrücklich *Jochen Zenthöfer*. Angst vor Algorithmen. FAZ v. 1.3.2021, S. 16; ferner *Nink* (Fn. 71), S. 227: „Mangels Empathie verbleibt Algorithmen auch eine Unfähigkeit, die (sozialen) Folgen einer Entscheidung im Leben des von ihr Betroffenen adäquat abzuschätzen."; anders wohl *Mario Martini*. Regulating Algorithms. How to Demystify the Alchemy of Code? In: Ebers/Navas (Fn. 71), S. 100 (107): "Algorithms have no ethical compass. Their approach is not to do justice to the individual. They lack empathy and social skills. Thus, an algorithmic process cannot generally be considered better or worse than a human decision maker. An algorithm must rather be programmed to the conditions under which it can exploit its advantages and avoid unethical decisions."

schaft der Gesetze", verstanden als „Herrschaft der Algorithmen" wäre für eine solche Selbstkorrektur im Einzelfall und möglicherweise auch für eine Rückspeisung unbefriedigender Rechtsanwendungsergebnisse an die Rechtsetzung kein Raum.

VI. Zusammenfassung und Ausblick

1. Die alte, aber erstaunlich lebendige Losung „Herrschaft der Gesetze, nicht der Menschen" hebt die Omnipräsenz, Transparenz, Stabilität und Willkürresistenz geschriebener Normen als entscheidender gesellschaftlicher Handlungsmaßstäbe hervor. Unterstellt man, dass es sich bei Gesetzen im hier gemeinten Sinne um abstrakt-generelle Anordnungen (nicht um Einzelfall- oder Einzelpersonengesetze) handelt, so haben sie auch den Vorteil der Generalität; in diesem Fall können sie das öffentliche Interesse im Sinne der „Bedingungen für die Erhaltung einer spontanen Ordnung" sichern, also die „Schaffung von Voraussetzungen, welche jedermanns Chance bei der Verfolgung seiner eigenen Ziele verbessern"[79]. Gesetze sind dann nicht Ausdruck von, sondern Schutz vor Interventionismus.

2. Die Formel von der „Herrschaft der Gesetze, nicht der Menschen" suggeriert aber den Ersatz von Personen durch Institutionen. Damit invisibilisiert sie durch die Gegenüberstellung gesetzlicher und menschlicher Herrschaft erstens, dass Gesetze stets Produkte von Menschen sind, und zwar auch in modernen arbeitsteiligen parlamentarischen Demokratien unter Umständen durchaus Produkte einiger weniger Menschen. Daran werden weder Globalisierung noch Digitalisierung noch Granularisierung in absehbarer Zeit etwas ändern. Zweitens verschleiert die Gegenüberstellung, dass Gesetzanwendung in allen wesentlichen Phasen und Aspekten auf spezifisch menschliche Kompetenzen angewiesen ist: beginnend bei der Erfassung von Interessenkonstellationen über die Klärung und Bewertung von Sachverhalten bis hin zum Umgang mit Spielräumen auf Rechtsfolgenseite.

3. Wie der Kontrast zu einer denkbaren künftigen Rechtsfindung durch Legal Tech (oder jedenfalls der naiven Vorstellung von ihr, in der Menschen keine Rolle mehr spielen) zeigt, ist der Einbezug von Menschen

---

79 *Friedrich A. von Hayek*, Recht. Gesetz und Freiheit. 2003, S. 152 mit explizitem Verweis auf *Harrington* (Fn. 4).

– Individuen mit all ihren Wahrnehmungs-, Einfühlungs-, Bewertungs-
und Entscheidungsfähigkeiten – kein defizitärer Modus der Rechtsverwirklichung, sondern deren Königsweg. Zu einer im doppelten Sinne menschlichen Gesellschaft gehört ebenso wie Erziehung durch Menschen und
Pflege durch Menschen die Rechtsverwirklichung durch Menschen; auch
sie ist ein personaler Kommunikationsvorgang. Rechtsverwirklichung sollte und wird ein Dialog, Trilog oder Polylog bleiben.

4. Dabei wäre es irreführend, das spezifisch Menschliche der Rechtsverwirklichung auf die Bedeutung von „Gefühlen" zurückzuführen. Denn
das Großaggregat „Gefühle" (und zumal die übliche, aber dysfunktionale
Gegenüberstellung von Rationalität und Emotionalität) ebnet die Vielfalt
menschlicher Potentiale, der Wahrnehmungen, Strebungen und Regungen, der Rezeptions-, Positions- und Produktionsmöglichkeiten ein. Die
starke Ausrichtung der rechtswissenschaftlichen Dogmatik und Methodenlehre auf Rationalität von Rechtsetzung und Rechtsanwendung speist sich
aus dem vermeintlichen Gegenüber zur Irrationalität und ist insoweit re-
duktionistisch.

5. Institutionen – auch die des Rechtsstaats – sind in Entstehung und
Wirken von Personen abhängig. Was zuweilen als Defizienz erscheinen
mag, ist in Wahrheit ihr bestimmender Zug und ihr größter Vorzug.

IV: The Impact of *Rechtsgefühle* on Politics

IV: Die Wirkung von Rechtsgefühlen auf die Politik

Besmirching Judges, Undermining Authority: Populists' Carnivalesque Play with Feelings of Law and Justice

Frans-Willem Korsten

> Every provision which the people feel to be unjust, and every institution which they detest, is an injury to the national feeling of legal right and to the national strength, a sin against the idea of law, the burthen of which falls on the state itself, and for which it has not infrequently to pay dearly.[1]

1. A Dutch Case of Populism: Legal Authorities Challenged

In 2014, and for the second time, a case was brought against the nationally and internationally best-known Dutch right-wing populist: Geert Wilders. The latter is now the longest-sitting member in the Dutch parliament for the *Partij voor de Vrijheid* (PVV; *Freedom Party*), and the sole member and leader of it.[2] The party was called into life in 2005 and has since been hovering in Dutch elections and polls at between 7 and 25 percent of all votes.[3] The case brought against Wilders was conducted in the law court The Hague. The sentence, which was announced on 9 December 2016, found Wilders guilty of '*groepsbelediging*': group defamation. The court did not impose any punishment, though.[4] Wilders appealed, and the case went

---

1 Rudolph von Jhering, *The Struggle for Law* [1879], trans. from the 5th edition in German by John J. Lalor, (New Jersey: The Union, 1997), 107.

2 To some it may be incompatible with a democracy that a party has only one member. Yet this is the case; see https://www.parlement.com/id/vhnnmt7m4rqi/partij_voor_de_vrijheid_pvv.

3 As of March 2021, shortly after the national elections, the PVV is the third largest party in the Netherlands, with 17 seats out of 150. In the years 2010-2012, the PVV was not officially part of the government but had participated in the coalition talks and agreed to make the government possible by helping it to a majority in parliament. This agreement was unilaterally stopped by the PVV. Since then, its participation in new coalitions has become unlikely. 'Politieke barometer'. *Ipsos*, n.d., https://www.ipsos.com/nl-nl/politieke-barometer.

4 See http://deeplink.rechtspraak.nl/uitspraak?id=ECLI:NL:RBDHA:2016:15014.

to the Court of Justice The Hague, at the second highest national level.[5] Its verdict found Wilders again guilty of group defamation on 4 September 2020. Once again, no punishment was imposed. In response, Wilders announced that he would appeal his case in the highest legal council of the Netherlands: the 'Hoge Raad' – the High Council. Its decision was made public on 6 July 2021. The High Council decided to leave the decision of the previous courts 'intact' and confirmed that Wilders was guilty but should not be punished.[6] Since its start in 2014, then, the affair was a matter of national concern for seven years.

In what follows, Wilders's case will be considered as a paradigmatic instance of how populists try to undermine the authority of the judiciary. My conclusion will be that this has severe consequences for the collective, or rather disparate *Rechtsgefühle* – the affective attachments to law and justice – of a populace. The case exemplifies much more than an attempt by the accused to avoid being declared guilty or facing punishment. It concerns a veritable struggle for what people feel to be just, both in a legal sense and in terms of a sense for justice. With regard to both, the case made me consider three semantic aspects of the German word *Kampf* that are only partly captured in the translation of Rudolf von Jhering's *Der Kampf ums Recht* (1872) as *The Struggle for Law*. These three aspects are: '*sportlicher Wettkampf*'; '*intensive Bemühungen um ein Ziel*'; and '*Situation, in der Meinungen, Bedürfnisse usw. aufeinandertreffen, die nicht zusammenpassen*'. That is to say: *Kampf* may indicate a game of sports; intense efforts to achieve a goal; or a situation in which interests come together that are incompatible. The three aspects of *Kampf* were all at stake in the case that was brought against Wilders. So let me briefly sketch what the case entailed in terms of the three aspects, to then focus on the three separately.

The case against Wilders found its origin in an event that occurred on election night of 19 March 2014. The elections were held nationwide but were municipal ones. For the first time in its history, the national PVV party had participated on the local level – in two cities. In the city of Almere it

---

5 The Netherlands has eleven courts of law, based in the capitals of the provinces; there are four higher level Courts of Justice: Amsterdam, The Hague, 's-Hertogenbosch, and Arnhem-Leeuwarden. As a result, The Hague has both a court of law and a Court of Justice. For an overview of the case, see the official website of the Ministry of Justice; https://www.rechtspraak.nl/Bekende-rechtszaken/Strafzaak-Wilders.

6 Case reference: ECLI:NL:GDHA:2020:1606; https://uitspraken.rechtspraak.nl/inziendocument?id=ECLI:NL:HR:2021:1036.

had won the most votes; in The Hague, the country's governmental center, the party came in second. In a victory speech to voters in The Hague, Wilders asked whether they would want fewer or more Dutch Moroccans in the Netherlands.[7] The audience started to shout 'less, less, less'. Wilders responded with a dry: 'Ok, that's what we are going to organize then'.[8] The event caused general outrage, nationally and internationally. Due to the rhetorical build-up of the speech, it was compared in some German journals and by the German press agency, the DPA, to the infamous *Sportpalastrede* by Nazi leader Joseph Goebbels, with its recurring question '*Wollt ihr den totalen Krieg?*' (Do you want total war?).[9] This comparison, in turn, led to indignation on Wilders's part.

At the time it was not yet possible to analyze the event as an instance of a more common tactic used by contemporary extreme political figures from the left and right. Cultural analyst Sara Polak defines this tactic in terms of a 'cartoon logic',[10] a logic that shifts the emphasis from politicians being the object of cartoons, to their using them. As Polak states, with regard to the case of Donald Trump:

> Trump, of course, is not literally a cartoon character, but he seems to inhabit a universe that is governed by its laws. The recurring suggestion is that nothing he does or says can really harm him, like the cartoon cat who cannot die. This is a cartoonesque hyperreality enabled by social media. Translated to the extradiegetic reality of political communication, this becomes a cartoon logic that short-circuits traditional content-driven and consensus-seeking political communication. Instead, the logic enables the enjoyment of cartoon violence, and this response is rhetorically excused by the suggestion that there is no

---

7 Around 409,000 Dutch are first- or second-generation Moroccan immigrants. This group constitutes the third largest ethnic community in the Netherlands, and constitutes 2.3% of the Dutch population. CBS 2020: https://longreads.cbs.nl/inte gratie-2020/bevolking/.

8 For the judicial background of the case, see Rb. Den Haag 9 December 2016, ECLI:NL:RBDHA:2016:15014, *NBSTRAF* 2017/8; http://deeplink.rechtspraak.nl/u itspraak?id=ECLI:NL:RBDHA:2016:15014.

9 See, for instance, 'Wilders hetzt gegen Marokkaner', *Die Zeit online*, 20 Apr. 2014, https://www.zeit.de/politik/ausland/2014-03/geert-wilders-niederlande-marokk aner; or 'Wilders hetzt Anhänger gegen Marokkaner auf', *Frankfurter Allgemeine Zeitung online*, 20 Mar. 2014, https://www.faz.net/aktuell/politik/ausland/europa/g eert-wilders-hetzt-anhaenger-gegen-marokkaner-auf-12855232.html.

10 Sara Polak, 'Posting the presidency: Cartoon politics in a social media landscape', *Media and Arts Review* 22, no. 4 (2018): 403-419, quote on 417.

real world impact – that it is all just a game, with the kind of teenage boy innocence that characterizes cartoons.[11]

Apparently, then, in following this logic political actors do not stick to the standards of seriousness that normally characterize politics. Instead, they use the much more fluid, satirical, clichéd but also combative logic of cartoons, in a game-like manner.

Whether Wilders was using cartoon logic or was simply being ironic (another tactic used by extreme right-wing politicians),[12] it was hard to assess whether he was being serious when he responded to his audience with the words: 'Ok, that's what we are going to organize then.' In this context, the comparison with Goebbels's speech from 1943 was out of order. At the time, Goebbels was a pivotal minister in the German Nazi regime and in the midst of a war that had become a total war. Whereas Goebbels was dead serious and was an acting minister, Wilders was provoking the center of power from the municipal margins. To many this was a nasty tactic, or a 'deplorable' one, as media scholar Viveca S. Greene terms this type of behavior.[13] It might have been a game, albeit one with serious consequences. Yet first and foremost, Wilders's answer constituted a willful testing of the limits of what was, and is, socially and politically and legally acceptable.

The societal responses to Wilders's remarks were immediate and proved that, indeed, a collective battle for law and justice was going on. Sixty-one charges were brought against Wilders, and forty of these charges were accepted. When the case was opened in the lower court in The Hague, the defense first challenged the sitting judge as not being independent enough. The Dutch term for this is '*wraking*', the German *Ablehnung*. For a legally informed audience, *wraking* is formally clear. For a more general audience, *wraking* connotes the Dutch word 'wraak', meaning 'revenge' – and this has affectively charged connotations. When the judge refused to be excused from the case, a separate legal body – the so-called '*wrakingskamer*' – had to assess the validity of the challenge. This chamber rejected

---

11 Polak, *supra* note 10, at 416.

12 For instance, Noam Gal, 'Ironic humor on social media as participatory boundary work', *New Media and Society* 21, no. 3 (2019): 729-749. For a pre-populist analysis of the contemporary use of irony in the rapidly changing landscape of social media, see Ted Gournelos and Viveca Greene, eds, *A Decade of Dark Humor: How Comedy, Irony, and Satire Shaped Post-9/11 America* (University of Mississippi Press: Jackson, MS, 2011).

13 Vivica S. Greene, '"Deplorable" Satire: Alt-Right Memes, White Genocide Tweets, and Redpilling Normies', *Studies in American Humor* 5, no.1 (2019): 31-69.

the challenge on 11 November 2016, and the judge delivered her verdict a month later. When the case then moved to the higher Court of Justice The Hague, the tactic by the defense was the same. This time the presiding judge was accused of having left-wing tendencies, because she had been the chair of a jury responsible for giving a prize to the student author of an MA thesis that was supposedly leftist. On this basis, the defense asked her to excuse herself. The refusal of the judge was broadcast on national television and this was the moment when a legally proper challenge acquired a carnivalesque aura due to an ambiguity in the Dutch phrasing by means of which the judge has to refuse to be excused. The German '*Ausschließung*', or the English 'to be excused' is '*verschoning*' in Dutch. So, whereas in English usage, a judge simply has to refuse to be excused, a Dutch judge has to say: 'Ik zal mij niet verschonen'. Whereas for any legal expert the formal meaning is clear, for a non-legally trained audience the phrase literally means: 'I will not put on fresh clothes', or more awkwardly still: 'I refuse to put on fresh underwear'. In this case, legally speaking, the challenge failed. Yet affectively speaking, it had its carnivalesque success.

The next move proved to be more controversial, legally speaking. The defense asked the court whether the prosecution had not been arbitrary in bringing Wilders to court. A phrase uttered by a left-wing politician (Alexander Pechtold) was presented as an analogous case; and this case, so the defense argued, had simply been dismissed by the prosecution. So why had the case against Wilders not been dismissed? The sitting judges did not consider the defense's request necessary for the defense's case; a criterion of necessity defined by law. The reasoning of the judges was that such a request should have been brought forward before the case had started, not during the trial. The defense did not like this, and the judges were challenged again. This time the Court of Justice in Amsterdam was used as a '*wrakingskamer*'. This court considered that the The Hague court's judges had failed to adequately motivate their decision not to recognize the defense's request; or, their motivation was defined as 'lacking'. Moreover, the Court of Justice in Amsterdam did not consider the defense's request a matter of a 'fishing expedition'. Consequently, the judges were taken off the case; a new set of judges was installed.

The decision of the Amsterdam court led to considerable legal controversy. One telling (and unusual) response by a former member of the High Council, Fred Hammerstein, held that the Amsterdam court had made two fundamental mistakes.[14] The Amsterdam court had argued that there could be relevant 'parallels' between the two politicians' cases. Hammerstein argued that the possible parallels were legally speaking superficial. Then, the defense had asked that the case be re-opened by hearing witnesses anew so that a comparison could be made between the two cases. The judges in the Court of Justice The Hague had refused this because the two cases were not identical, and because the case could not be re-opened from scratch. The Amsterdam court considered this a sign of the judges being biased, in Dutch: *'vooringenomenheid'*. The result was a flood of challenges to various cases in the Netherlands. This led the High Council to give a response on 25 September 2018 on the basis of a different case, though motivated directly by the Wilders case. The High Council decided that: 'It does not fit the *'wrakingskamer'* to judge on decisions or on the decision not to decide. This judgment is the prerogative [...] of the judge who is handling the case'.[15] The Amsterdam *'wrakingskamer'* had been reprimanded, then. This constituted a legal correction but not a correction of the collective feelings of justice that had already been influenced by the handling of the Wilders case. In Hammerstein's analysis, the Amsterdam court's decision had severely damaged 'trust in the judiciary'.

The Wilders case is paradigmatic for the three aspects of *Kampf* that I introduced above. Firstly, it shows how law and judges' authority can be made subject to battle, or a *Kampf*, as part of a game and a tactic. Perhaps the defense was not on a 'fishing expedition', perhaps it was; otherwise, the Court of Justice Amsterdam would not have needed to mention it. In any case, the defense followed rules that cohered with the game of law, while also attempting to test those very rules. Secondly, the moves on the sides of both parties were not easy. They involved an intense effort to achieve a goal, or multiple goals. Thirdly, several of these goals proved to be incompatible, and this propelled an antagonism between parties. For instance, whereas Wilders was accused of inciting Dutch people against

---

14 Fred Hammerstein, 'Hoe wraking het vertrouwen in de rechtspraak kan ondermijnen', 30 May 2018, *Verder denken, scherper zijn*, CPO website; https://www.ru.nl/cpo/verderdenken/columns/wraking-vertrouwen-rechtspraak-ondermijnen/.

15 In the original: 'Wrakingskamer komt geen oordeel toe over juistheid van (tussen)beslissing noch over verzuim te beslissen. Dat oordeel is voorbehouden aan rechter die in geval van aanwending van rechtsmiddel belast is met behandeling van zaak.' The case on which the High Council based its verdict can be found under ECLI:N:HR:2018:1413, the conclusion of the High Council under ECLI:NL:PHR:2018:736 https://uitspraken.rechtspraak.nl/inziendocument?id=ECLI:NL:HR:2018:1413.

Dutch Moroccans, he used the case to incite his constituency against the judiciary by depicting it as elitist, and by suggesting that, if he were to be convicted, the Dutch *Rechtstaat* would prove itself to be biased and dysfunctional.

So a struggle, or a *Kampf*, was clearly going on. Yet it was not the struggle that Jhering was talking about. To see this, let me first focus in more detail on the game aspect of *Kampf*.

2. Law as a Game: Carnival Politics and the Attempt to Carnivalize the Judiciary

In response to a case brought against Wilders in 2011, a national newspaper called Wilders's and his lawyers' actions in court a farce and a bad one at that.[16] Apparently, the newspaper failed to take seriously that the actions purposely constituted a farce. For, besides cartoon logic or the use of irony, another model that would be applicable to the case in question is that of 'carnival politics'. In a study of two carnivalesque events in the UK – The Notting Hill Carnival that has taken place yearly since 1965 and the one-time Carnival Against Capital in 1999 –, cultural analyst Esther Peeren came to define them as forms of 'carnival politics'. The purpose of such a form of politics is the acquisition of territory, in these cases: the streets. In analyzing the struggles that were involved, Peeren considered the events to be

> translations and displacements of the Bakhtinian carnival, effecting what Deleuze and Guattari call a deterritorialization: a movement of acceleration, rupture, change and multiple connectivities. Both events quite literally answer the injunction [...] to 'increase your territory by deterritorialization'.[17]

Forms of carnival are used, then, to infiltrate a space that is (considered to be) someone else's territory. First, this space is deterritorialized in a carni-

---

16 Willem Schoonen, 'Het is een farce, en nog een slechte ook' *Trouw*, 16 April 2011, https://www.trouw.nl/nieuws/het-is-een-klucht-en-nog-een-slechte-ook~bad9f82c/?referrer=https%3A%2F%2Fwww.google.com%2F.

17 Esther Peeren, 'Carnival Politics and the Territory of the Street', in *Constellations of the Transnational* – Thamyris/Intersecting: Place, Sex and Race vol.14, eds. Sudeep Dasgusta and Esther Peeren (Amsterdam: Brill, 2007), 69-82. The quote is from Gilles Deleuze and Félix Guattari, *A Thousand Plateaus: Capitalism and Schizophrenia* (Minneapolis: University of Minnesota Press, 1987), 12.

valesque manner, to then be reappropriated. The carnival is not a matter of a counterworld à la Bakhtin, here. To Bakhtin, the carnival is the opposite of official culture and is as such extra-political.[18] The two worlds are very strictly separated, also in terms of the time in which the carnival rules take precedence; the very manifestation of carnival is officially controlled and allowed. Yet in both of the events that Peeren focuses on, a more complex simultaneity of worlds was at stake, and the events were only in part subject to official regulation.

The notion of 'carnival politics' is a productive heuristic tool that can shed a light on the actions of contemporary populists. The issue is not, then, how carnival is used politically, but how populists use forms of carnival. First of all, their persistent attacks on so-called elites who rule the political realm, or on official media that supposedly controls the news, constitute the dynamics of the carnival's two-world system, in which the one forms the counterpart to the other. This tension could simply be marked as antagonistic, and as such serious. Yet although the attacks are indeed sometimes serious, they are often also carnivalesque in nature. Sometimes populist politicians themselves, like the Italian Beppo Grillo but also the Dutch Thierry Baudet, act in a carnivalesque way, for instance by dressing up, disguising themselves, or using memes, jokes, and forms of caricature. More often than not, their supporters act in this manner. In the Netherlands, the carnivalesque nature of this struggle is captured by one of the most influential right-wing news sites that calls itself *GeenStijl* – literally 'no style', or better: 'BadForm'. Its mission is captured by the motto: 'insinuating, unfounded and needlessly offensive'.[19] This may sound offensive in itself but it has venerable classical roots, as with the provocative and ruthlessly mocking figure of Momus, the most carnivalesque of classical gods.[20]

As Peeren argues, with 'carnival politics' there is a territory at stake. Here, populist policies are not just aimed at getting people out on the streets, whether these be real streets or the quasi-public realm of internet

---

18 Michail Bakhtin, *Rabelais and his World*, trans. Hélène Iswolsky (Bloomington: Indiana University Press, 1993), 6.

19 In Dutch: 'tendentieus, ongefundeerd en nodeloos kwetsend'; http://www.geens tijl.nl/. The site was first owned by official media companies but is now independent.

20 Frans-Willem Korsten, 'Historical prefigurations of vitriol: communities, constituencies and a plutocratic insurgency', in *Social Media: History, Affect, and Effects of Online Vitriol*, eds. Sara Polak and Daniel Trottier (Amsterdam: Amsterdam University Press, 2020), 87-108.

spaces, but to deterritorialize such spaces in order to enlarge their own territory. In the case of Wilders's remark about Dutch Moroccans, two territories were at stake simultaneously. With hindsight, these concerned the struggle about what can be said in public space politically, or as a matter of free speech – whether this be needlessly or ruthlessly offensive. It also concerned the struggle about who owns very real streets and public space in the city of The Hague, or any other city in the Netherlands. The struggle combined a more or less abstract constitutional and national issue with very concrete local ones. When the case was brought to court, another struggle consequently started that again used forms of carnival politics in the context of which the territory at stake was a symbolic territory: it concerned the authority of the judiciary.

The ability to challenge the law depends on the fact that law acts according to prescribed rules and rituals, or on the fact that legal cases intrinsically follow the logic of a game. The analogy was captured by cultural historian Johan Huizinga when he stated:

> The arena, the card-table, the magic circle, the temple, the stage, the screen, the tennis court, the court of justice, etc., are all in form and function play-grounds, i.e. forbidden spots, isolated, hedged round, hallowed, within which special rules obtain. All are temporary worlds within the ordinary world, dedicated to the performance of an act apart.[21]

Before we move on to consider what Huizinga is arguing for, let us first note that in Dutch there is no distinction between play and game. In Dutch, for instance, several games are captured under the heading of 'bordspel', a 'boardgame'; but a literal translation in English would have to be 'board*play*'. If two chess players meet, they are evidently defined as players, yet one always speaks of 'a game of chess'. Dutch *spel* is close, here, to German *Spiel*, but different from *Kampf*, from English *play*, French *jeu*, or Spanish *juego*. The latter two have their source in Latin *iocus*, which means joke, but also amusement and sport. *Play* has it origin in *pleien* or *plegan*, which means to 'move quickly', possibly also 'dance'. *Spel* and *Spiel* have their origin in words that indicate the making of music or the state of being elated. *Game* has its origin in Old English *gamenian*, which means to play, jest, joke. German *Kampf* connotes the Latin *campus*, meaning 'fight'

---

21 Johan Huizinga, *Homo Ludens: A Study of the Play-Element in Culture* (Boston: Beacon Press, 1955), 10.

or 'struggle', and this is analogous to what in Dutch accords best with game, namely *wedstrijd* – German *Wettkampf*.

In what follows, I partly build forth on, but also sharpen the distinction between play and game introduced by Roger Caillois in *Les jeux et les hommes* (1958), translated as *Man, Game and Play* (1961).[22] In my use of the two terms, *play* is marked by its non-obligatory nature; its separateness from daily reality; its open, unpredictable outcome; its unproductiveness; and its ability to create worlds on the basis of make-believe. *Game* is marked by its dependence on rules that, once people engage in a game, are obligatory; it can be regular part of daily reality (like soccer); it will have a restricted outcome (like winning or losing); it can be very productive (there is a lot of money to be made); and it may follow the logic of what is the case in reality (like when games are competitive).

In relation to Huizinga's quote, law is not a play, then, but a game. And in conformity with what I distinguished above, law, in its following a game logic, is distinctly a serious matter (as Huizinga also argued). Law, enacted in courts of justice that embody its 'magic circle', may even be experienced as hallowed. Yet law's very hallowedness or seriousness may be precisely what populists want to ridicule. Their appearing before a court is marginally considered, then, as a personal, ethical or even political problem, but first and foremost as an opportunity to provoke the authorities dealing with them, thus enhancing the bond with their constituencies. The tactic followed does not consist in ignoring the rules of the legal game, but in using them to the extreme, or in exploring how and to what extent they can be tinkered with. A primary aim of this tactic is to not be declared guilty; another one is to undermine the authority of judges so that in the event of a guilty verdict, this loses its force. Effectively, such undermining will result in a fragmentation of the collective *Rechtsgefühle* of people.[23]

There is a telling analogy, here, with a principle that made Jhering famous in the international legal field: the *culpa in contrahendo*. The pivot

---

22 Roger Caillois, *Man, Game and Play* (Champaign: University of Illinois Press, 2001).
23 One notable example is the US American extreme right wing ideologue Steve Bannon, for whom societal disorder and the recalibration of legal authority are needed to get to a new situation, under a new rule; see Bridge Initiative Team, 'Factsheet: Steve Bannon', *Bridge*, 16 Sept. 2016, https://bridge.georgetown.edu /research/factsheet-steve-bannon/. An opposite yet very similar process is going on with regard to the legal systems of Poland and Hungary, where in the name of order the balance of interests is swapped for the sake of a legal system that is supposed to listen to one party alone.

of the principle was that if parties engage in a contract, their mutual relation is ruled by *diligentia*, a matter of good faith, which implies that parties know they need to care for one another. Jhering's idea, provoked by real societal problems, was that this is not only the case when a contract was officially established, but also in the pre-contractual phase. This shift in focus meant that a formally legal issue needed to be considered in its social context.[24] Now, obviously, when someone is brought before a court, this is not a matter of contract, if only because one of the parties may not wish to be there. Yet socially speaking, or in the context of a society, the presumption is that both parties will act in good faith, as would hold with any kind of game. If judges, for instance, ridicule the accused, this is considered a rightful cause for challenge or objection. On the other side, in general, people who are brought before a court are expected to behave decently, or in good faith, as well. All this of course only holds true if the judiciary, from its side, also behaves in good faith – and in the many histories of social activism, of anarchy, or revolt, in the histories of racism or feminism, legal systems and their judiciary were often considered with reason to be biased, prejudiced, and not acting at all in good faith.

Now, in cases of legal bias, a carnivalesque response could be a playful option, with play indicating the attempt to get beyond the rules of the game, or to open them up.[25] The same potential holds for right-wing populists. Yet in their case, this potential is explored not so much because judges are biased, but because the actors playing want to do away with the rules of the game and with legal authority.

In this context, law's theatricality contains a certain danger, as was noticed by legal scholar Julie Stone Peters. Whereas the seventeenth-century lawyer Giovanni Battista de Luca defined the trial as a 'theatre of Justice and Truth', the necessary implication was that this theatre was a serious one. At all costs, so Stone Peters argues, the courtroom should prevent that it become the site of a circus or carnival.[26] Instead, law is, and should

---

24 Tim Hartman, *'Een schitterend jurist'* – *Invloed en beeldvorming van Rudolf von Jhering in het Nederlandse privaatrecht (1861-1921): rechtsleer en culpa in contrahendo* (Weert: Celsus, 2020), 61.

25 There is an argument to be made that play is involved in the creation of new legal theories or new laws. Jhering's introduction of *Interessenjurisprudenz* as an alternative to *Pandektenrecht* has been considered as such. For this see: Edward J. Eberle and Bernhard Grossfeld, 'Law and Poetry,' *Roger Williams University Law Review* 11, no. 2 (2006): 353-401; especially p. 353. The point requires separate elaboration.

26 Julie Stone Peters, 'Law as Performance: Historical Interpretation, Objects, Lexicons, and Other Methodological Problems', in *New Directions in Law and Lite-*

be, boring; also theatrically. It brought the jurist, critic and theatre-maker Klaas Tindemans to mark law's theatricality as an archaic phenomenon.[27] And indeed, whereas a legal case may offer surprises in terms of developments or verdicts, the procedures of law are all familiar, laid down and fixed. Considered thus, it would seem that the struggle for law does not concern procedures; the rules of the game are clear. Yet important aspects of the defense and of Wilders's use of the media were not about content but about the rules of the game. The game part of the tactic was to use them to their extreme; the play part of the tactic was to get outside of the serious, magic circle of the rules.

Law's rules have only gotten a stronger aura of being archaic due to a struggle between different media with their different rates of transmission, or speeds, and different desires and fears that propel them. In this context, the philosophically reassuring qualifier 'archaic' may easily shift into something that is felt to be 'out-dated'. As Tessa de Zeeuw analyzed it, the theatricality of law is distinctly in friction here with new, contemporary media.[28] To trace this, de Zeeuw compared the legal situation with the cultural theatrical one, which witnessed an important transformation in the last half of the previous century. The transformation was studied in Hans-Thies Lehmann's *Postdramatic Theatre*, in which he established the characteristically postmodern fascination of theatre makers with intermediality.[29] The 'postdramatic' indicated a break with especially the late 19th century and early 20th century form of theatre that worked on the basis of a strict separation of the audience from what was shown on stage; and what was shown on stage had a dramatic plot as its pivot. In postdramatic theatre, these two were reversed. Audiences came to be more and more involved with the action, and this action was no longer defined by a coherent plot. In the world of theatre, new media helped to tear apart the 'fourth wall' that had separated the audience and the action on stage, and helped to multiply or fragmentize the plot.

---

rature, eds. Elizabeth Anker and Bernadette Meyler (Oxford: Oxford University Press, 2017), 193-209, 196.

27 Klaas Tindemans, 'De theatraliteit van het recht', *Etcetera* 150 (2017): 39 https://e-t cetera.be/de-theatraliteit-van-het-recht/. In the original it says: *'archaïsch fenomeen'*.

28 The confrontation between law's classic, theatrical form and new modern media is central to Tessa de Zeeuw, *Postdramatic Legal Theatres: Space, Body, Media and Genre* (Leiden, thesis, 2021).

29 Hans Thies Lehmann, *Postdramatic Theatre*. Translated by Karen Jürs-Munby (London: Routledge, 2006). The importance of Lehmann's analysis was assessed in Elinor Fuchs, *'Postdramatic Theatre* by Hans-Thies Lehmann,' *TDR: The Drama Review* 52, no. 2 (2008): pp. 178-183.

In the context of legal theatricality, such intermediality may have a more devastating force than the aesthetically or politically functional disruption that Lehmann was studying. One archaic aspect of legal procedures has already been mentioned: their being boring, which connects to their being slow. When Wilders's case proceeded to the High Council, the law's dealings with this case since 2014 had come close to having lasted a decade long. Evidently, law works slowly, and rightfully so. Yet this aspect of law and legal procedures stands in sharp contrast with one of the most decisive, and already mentioned characteristics of social media: their speed. Whereas classic media such as newspapers or national broadcast corporations are interested in the news, obviously, their speed does not offer a serious provocation to the procedures of law, if only because the presence of these media in courtrooms is restricted by means of regulation. Yet social media, although they are not officially allowed to work in courtrooms, are present in courtrooms and around them, spiralling through them, before them, and after them. This does not mean they spiral erratically, though. Whereas newspapers, of whatever colour or political conviction, still cater to national or regional audiences, social media are more specific, in their getting the like-minded together in algorithmic bubbles. They also act more extensively in transcending national borders. As a result, constituencies have become much more flexible. They have also become more disparate. They are constantly affectively at work while being worked on. And they very much influence the ways in which people feel to be attached, or not, to law and justice.

Though the speed of social media has been researched in several areas, ranging from media studies to business, it has not yet been studied thoroughly in the legal context.[30] If this were to materialize, such study would have to address two forms of speed. Social media works by means of speed, as captured in the phrase 'going viral'. Yet the entire infrastructure itself that has made social media possible also developed with incredible speed. Here, media scholars José van Dijck, Thomas Poell, and Martijn de Waal noticed that 'many platforms have grown surprisingly influential before a real debate about public values and common goods could get

---

30 See, for instance, Josep Rialp-Criado, María-del-Carmen Alarcón-del-Amo, Alex Rialp, 'Speed of Use of Social Media as an Antecedent of Speed of Business Internationalization', *Journal of Global Information Management* 28, no.1 (2020): 142-166.

started'.[31] The rapid development of platform 'ecosystems',[32] most of them privately owned, was helped by the fact that they could all use the same computational architecture.[33] And due to this, the speedy proliferation and interconnection of these platforms have, as to date, not been met by robust legal tools that regulate these platforms, or that regulate the technologies allowing them to exert their power.[34] It may be called the paradox of platforms, then, that they have greatly enlarged the agency of people, and have left them vulnerable to far-reaching forms of manipulation.

In this context, it now appears that to some constituencies law's being slow, boring, and serious does not have the desired effect of underpinning its authority and showing that law can be trusted. For these constituencies, law is felt to be slow, boring and serious because it wants to spoil the game. The judiciary, according to this feeling, is not willing to conform to a media-propelled quasi self-evident truth, but has decided beforehand that it will come to its desired verdict at the cost of the accused, while taking its time. In response, some constituencies no longer take the game of law seriously and desire to start to play with it. This brings me to the second aspect of *Kampf*: the intense effort to achieve something. As will become clear, such intense efforts do not just concern older media and newer social media forms but involve a much vaster landscape of different media, or cultural techniques.

3. *Media that Connect Rechtsgefühle with Legal Authority; the Postal and the Erotic*

Legal authority, and by extension the authority of judges, is in its core a matter of affect. Even if people realize that judges are supposed to be authorities, they are only so, effectively, when they are *felt* to be authorities – and authorities can only manifest themselves if they have the true potency to affect others. The affective force of authority has decisive effects, in turn, on whether people feel that they are being dealt with justly. Those individuals who are sentenced by judges to whom they did not grant

---

31 José van Dijck, Thomas Poell and Martijn de Waal, *The Platform Society: Public Values in a Connective World* (Oxford: Oxford University Press, 2018), 3.
32 The choice of 'ecosystem' as a descriptor for the networks formed by platforms is the target of critique, for instance in running research by Rianne Riemens (Radboud University, Nijmegen).
33 Dijck, Poell and de Waal, *supra* note 31, at 15.
34 Dijck, Poell and de Waal, *supra* note 31, at 46.

any authority, will tend to feel that they were dealt with unjustly. There is a marked distinction, here, between law's power and law's force. Max Weber's distinction between power and authority implies that power can be taken and executed but that authority is granted, both by higher powers and by the ones subjected to it, as a matter of force.[35] As a consequence, there is a distinctly different affective dynamic at stake between the power of law and law's force, or, between the power that judges have and the authority granted to them that characterizes the force of their judgments.

Issues like these were perhaps not central to Jhering when he dealt with the struggle for law, at least not in the reception of his work.[36] Yet conceptually speaking they were, or are. This is why they made legal philosopher Neil Duxbury speak of Jhering's work in terms of a 'philosophy of authority'.[37] If this is a slightly too grand way of putting it, there is indeed a philosophy of authority lingering in Jhering's thoughts. As for authority, he clearly did not belong to those who propagate divine or mysterious underpinnings of law. Rather, his problem was how law can have an authoritative force on its own account in practice, throughout its existence. When the already mentioned Weber defined this kind of authority as a rational-legal one, he meant an authority based on established and collectively agreed-upon rules. In Jhering's logic, legal authority can never base itself simply on a system of rules, nor on a system that was supposedly agreed upon collectively. Legal authority is always in the making in practice, and has never full collective consent due to the different interests that people have.[38] As a consequence, legal authority can never be self-evident and will always contain an element of fragility. Or, as Duxbury put it, Jhering's ideas on authority are based on 'the essentially Hegelian idea that the continuing life of the law depends on that which has the potential

---

35 Max Weber, *Economy and Society*, ed. Guenther Roth and Claus Wittich (Berkeley: University of California Press, 1978); and 'Politics as Vocation' [1919], in *Weber's Rationalism and Modern Society*, ed. and trans. Tony Waters and Dagmar Waters (Basingstoke: Palgrave Macmillan, 2015), 129-198.

36 In recent years the issues were central to the work of Joseph Raz, who seems to have skipped the work of Jhering in this respect, but whose work can be considered in a similar vein, for instance with Joseph Raz, *The Authority of Law* (Oxford: Clarendon Press, 1979) and *Authority* (New York: New York University Press, 1990).

37 Neil Duxbury, 'Jhering's Philosophy of Authority', *Oxford Journal of Legal Studies* 27, no.1 (2007): 23-47.

38 On the value-relative nature of positive law, see Gaakeer in this volume, but also the work of the already mentioned Joseph Raz.

to negate it: namely, the human capacity for self-realization through self-assertion'.[39] Legal authority, that is, depends on a continuous struggle.

Although Jhering was mostly concerned with private law, he developed his arguments in the context of the *Sozialfrage* of a nineteenth-century Germany that witnessed massive inequalities due to its economic acceleration. In this context, economic, or private interest was a self-evident and pivotal concept. Yet the multiple meanings of interest, both then and now, ask us to consider Jhering's 'philosophy of authority' in a more general way. If we do so in the light of current circumstances and with regard to Wilders's case, it is clear that interests are again central, and private in not so much an economic as a political sense. When brought to court, contemporary populists may try to escape the rule of law. They may suggest that judges are biased, or they may want to mold a judiciary that into one that is subject to their demands. Yet, basically, they challenge the law on the basis of their private, political interests. The challenge is both serious, following the rules of the game, and it is playful, as a matter of carnival politics.

If a continuous struggle is needed in favor of law, this will both be motivated by feelings of justice, but will also influence the *Rechtsgefühle* of people. As the very notion of 'influence' suggests, the issue is the ontological status of the motivation. As Duxbury argues, there is a disturbing or confusing ambiguity in Jhering's dealing with collective feelings, even to the degree that Duxbury calls Jhering's conceptualisation 'questionable by any standards'.[40] Sometimes Jhering appears to say that feelings of justice find their origin in a response when one's actual rights are violated, yet in other cases, he refers to 'violations of what one feels to be right'.[41] In the latter case, what is actually the case may topple over what is in the eye of the beholder, so Duxbury protests. To him, this could lead to a 'gangster psychology'. This may be true, yet the point that Duxbury in turn ignores, is that affective attachments to the rule of law are not organic or self-evident, but are the result of hard work, or the intense efforts to achieve the desired goal – one of the meanings of *Kampf*. Feelings of justice are not simply there, that is, they need to be nourished, tested, and trained. And they can be influenced. This is another reason why 'struggle is the eternal labor of the law'.

With respect to this, although Jhering acknowledged the implications of this struggle, he did not pay attention to the media that are needed to

---

39 Duxbury, *supra* note 37, at 25.
40 Duxbury, *supra* note 37, at 46.
41 Duxbury, *supra* note 37, at 46.

make this labor effective. There is every reason to historicize his thoughts, here, because there are intrinsic connections between media and the affective bonds implied by *Rechtsgefühl*. The role of media in their ability to help organize the affective households of people made media philosophers and historians such as Sybille Krämer (to whom we will return below) or Bernhard Siegert speak of them as 'cultural techniques'.[42] With this, they did not just mean regular 'media'. Rather, as Siegert contended:

> Harold Innis and Marshall McLuhan already emphasized that the decision taken by communication studies, sociology and economics to speak of media only in terms of mass media is woefully insufficient. Any approach to communication that places media exclusively within the 'public sphere' (which is itself a fictional construct bequeathed to us by the Enlightenment) will systematically misconstrue the abyss of non-meaning in and from which media operate.[43]

With the 'abyss of non-meaning', Siegert refers to the fact that media are not just tools of communication, but also mediators of affective attachments. This does not mean that what we generally understand 'media' to do is no longer applicable, but this doing needs to be considered in an affective context. Newspapers, for instance, functioned decisively differently in the nineteenth century – at the time of Jhering's writings – or in the early twentieth century, or in the contemporary twenty-first century situation. Whereas Benedict Anderson showed that collective national feelings of community could not have existed without the work of newspapers in the nineteenth century, this is no longer the case.[44] Historically, newspapers connect to different spaces that in turn have acquired different functions themselves, whether these be coffee houses or private homes. The same medium does rather different things, then; or the question is more whether it is the same medium.

Secondly, the number of media that can be considered as 'cultural techniques' has become much broader. Examples that both Krämer and Siegert give, range from basic linguistic ones to computational techniques, to postal ones, and so forth. Siegert mentions the shift, for instance, from parchment to paper under the chancelleries of Emperor Frederick II of

---

42 Bernhard Siegert, 'Cultural Techniques: Or the End of the Intellectual Postwar Era in German Media Theory', *Theory, Culture & Society* 30, no. 6 (2013): 48–65.
43 Siegert, *supra* note 42, at 51.
44 Benedict Anderson, *Imagined Communities: Reflections on the Origin and Spread of Nationalism* [1983] (London: Verso, London, 1991).

Hohenstaufen; a shift that connoted a shift in power.[45] It may also concern the ways in which the telescope changed modes of seeing and sensing and, consequently, also of epistemologies and ontologies.[46] Or, it concerns the ways in which postal systems were not just tools of communication but came to redefine the relations between people *per se* and the world they lived in.[47] In summary, Siegert states that within a 'new media-theoretical and cultural studies paradigm, cultural techniques now also include means of time measurement, legal procedures, and the sacred'.[48] Siegert's mentioning of legal procedures is telling here, especially in the context of *Rechtsgefühl*. Considering legal procedures as media or cultural techniques makes explicit what intense efforts are needed to achieve the desired goal: a people's affective attachment to law.

In this more general frame, a consideration of populists' play with law and the judiciary in terms of social media only, would be a mistake. Rather, it concerns a confrontation between, or a coincidence of different forms of cultural techniques. The question is not just what kind of contemporary media, as cultural techniques, underpin or threaten the current authority of the judiciary, but also how in terms of jurisprudence the judiciary's affective force is constantly reinforced – or weakened – by the use of different cultural techniques. A distinction made by Krämer is pivotal, here, namely between what she called the postal or the erotic potential in media.[49] With the first she indicated their potential to bridge the distance between actors without annihilating the difference; with the second she indicated the potential in media to bring entities together by means of communication. The first is only possible due to the medium, and as a consequence emphasizes the existence of that medium. The second is more concerned with the effect of media and will, consequently, consider the medium as a marginal matter. The distinction may help us to see

---

45 Siegert, *supra* note 42, at 52. Siegert bases his argument, here, on Cornelia Vismann, *Files: Law and Media Technology*, trans. Geoffrey Winthrop Young (Stanford: Stanford University Press, 2008).

46 In this case Siegert is referencing Joseph Vogl, 'Becoming-Media: Galileo's Telescope', *Grey Room* 29 (2007): 14-25.

47 Here, Siegert is referencing himself: Bernhard Siegert, *Relays: Literature as an Epoch of the Postal System*, trans. K. Repp (Stanford: Stanford University Press, 1999).

48 Siegert, *supra* note 42, at 57.

49 Krämer's work came relatively late to an international, English speaking audience; see Sybille Krämer, *Medium, Messenger, Transmission: An Approach to Media Philosophy* (Amsterdam: Amsterdam University Press, 2015).

how several media, as cultural techniques, define contemporary ways of influencing people's affective attachments to law.

In all Dutch legal cases, the legal verdict is pronounced 'in the name of the King', which is also why in every court room there is a picture of the Dutch king or queen. Obviously, the term 'King' in this phrase does not refer to a natural person in the legal sense, but to an institution (which is why when a queen is head of state, the phrase remains the same). Now, if royalty is considered as a source of order and justice, pictures or paintings in courtrooms are important media and forms of representation. They operate as indices to the body and voice of the king as both make themselves present and heard via the judge. In this case the representations of the king clearly fall under the heading of what Krämer called the erotic. Their being a painting or photograph does not matter; what matters is what they communicate, as a result of which a form of community makes itself felt. Yet the question is whether these representations – or the reality of the body and voice of the king – work in the same way in current circumstances, when royalty has been taken up in the circulation of news and gossip via different media. Or, if in previous times the king was considered more or less generally a stable source of authority, royalty has nowadays become subject to the same mechanisms that any celebrity is subject to. As a consequence, the king's authoritative force is severely weakened. Media that report on royalty and celebrities need their daily feeds. Here the postal is dominant.

Then, as was explored by legal scholar Cornelia Vismann, legal rule was embodied first in archives, during the Roman era, but shifted towards rule by document in the sixth century, to turn back to archives again from the twelfth century onwards.[50] To Vismann, records and documents follow a different logic and, consequently, are at the heart of different cultural techniques.[51] Whereas documents are not stored but kept by the recipient (the passport would be a primary example),[52] records are kept by an authority in order to transcend time and space and to embody law's stability. Historically, the law had a considerable monopoly, here, in its capacity to make and use archives officially and authoritatively. Here, again, and despite the neutral force of archives, Krämer's 'erotic' is dominant. It is not the archive

---

50 Cornelia Vismann, *Files: Law and Media Technology*, translated by Geoffrey Winthrop Young, (Stanford University Press, 2008), especially chapters 3 and 4.

51 In the German original Vismann used *Urkunde* as a general term. The English equivalents are 'charter', 'deed' or 'certificate', but a general translation is 'document' (Vismann, *supra* note 50, at 175). The term 'logic' is mentioned on 71.

52 Vismann, *supra* note 50, at 72.

as a medium that is emphasized but what it makes possible in terms of establishing a community. The archive connotes what 'we' agreed upon. Yet with the advent of the internet, other, massive archives are at work that rather follow the logic of the postal. Affectively speaking, they exert the force of an archive as well, which is then a counter-archive, but one that leaves differences intact. For instance, whereas in the legal domain cases can be closed, or drafts will be cancelled, the internet provides people with an archive that does not work on the basis of legal cancellations. Rather it hosts a variety of documents that confirm or contradict one another, and that may keep on producing new confirmations and contradictions.

Thirdly, as we already discussed, legal procedures are still organised theatrically, which ensures that they work according to a fixed plan or plot, and that an audience may be present to check whether the game is played according to the rules. These rules are not the focal point, however; here the erotic is dominant again in that the medium is marginal to what is being communicated. Yet with the coming of modern media such as cinema and television, it would be foolish to underestimate people's affective attachments to law and justice, or their *Rechtsgefühle*, apart from the enormous impact that television and cinema have had on the representation and *feeling* for the legal system.[53] Many people will have a stronger sense and feeling for how the legal system works through televised or cinematographic forms of representation than through real cases, with the live, theatrical experiences these offer. At least one affective impact of this trend may be that real court cases are evaluated more and more in the light of their being some kind of a show. Here the postal is again dominant. Cinema and television have brought law closer than ever, but without lifting a pivotal difference.

In the light of the above, and if it is clear that feelings of justice do not just exist but are the result of intensive efforts to work on them, the question is what happens if contradictory forces are at work, or such a complex mixture of forces that feelings of justice become volatile instead of being the anchor in the struggle for law.

---

53 One study addressing this is Peter Goodrich and Christian Delage, eds., *The Scene of the Mass Crime: History, Film and International Tribunals* (London: Routledge, 2012).

4. From Value Relativism to Incompatibilities of Interest

In terms of the historical contextualization of Jhering's 'struggle for law', it is important to note that, next to the *Sozialfrage*, Jhering was developing his thoughts in a Germany that was rapidly growing towards becoming a coherent nation state, with the construction of modernized, codified, positive law as its necessary anchor point. When Jhering was considering the struggle for law, the frame that kept that struggle productively together was a nation-state that hosted or facilitated a variety of collectives and private entities that embodied considerable differences of interests and values, but did not threaten the communal frame that kept them together. There is a pivotal difference, here, between value relativism and legal plurality on the one hand, and value disparity and legal antagonism, on the other. In this context, the question is whether populists' tactical use of rules and procedures takes the rule of law to be an unquestionable frame, or whether this use holds and promises the potential of legal antagonism.

The struggles at stake appear to coincide with Chantal Mouffe's distinction between productive political agonism and the disruptive force of antagonism.[54] With the first, Mouffe indicated the forcefield of politics as a matter of relentless struggle. With the second she considered that in the domain of the political, incompatible positions may play a role, which can bring actors into a dynamic of antagonism. Translated to the domain of law, Jhering's struggle is a matter of productive agonism, and not of divisive antagonism. In fact, if law and justice are to be preserved, the struggle should never become an antagonistic one.

As for antagonism, in his analysis of extreme left-wing social media discourses in Israel, Noam Gal, an expert on visual culture, noticed their intensive efforts in terms of 'boundary work'.[55] This 'boundary work' concerns all of the more or less combative attempts to draw a boundary between one group and another. As Gal notes, irony has a dominant role in this work. This is in line with one of the most important studies on

---

54 Chantal Mouffe, *On the Political* (London: Routledge, 2005).
55 Gal, *supra* note 12; Gal was building forth here on the pioneering work of T.F. Gieryn, 'Boundary-work and the demarcation of science from non-science: strains and interests in professional ideologies on scientists', *American Sociological Review* 48, no. 6 (1983): 781–795. Later the term was used in socio-cultural contexts, with S. Friedman and G. Kuipers, 'The divisive power of humour: comedy, taste and symbolic boundaries', *Cultural Sociology* 7, no. 2 (2013): 179–195; Naom Gal, L. Shifman L. and Z. Kampf, '"It gets better": Internet memes and the construction of collective identity', *New Media & Society* 18, no. 8 (2016): 1698–1714.

irony by Linda Hutcheon, which notes that irony has an 'edge' that makes it intrinsically dependent on an in- or out-logic. When Hutcheon argues that 'the final responsibility for deciding whether irony actually happens in an utterance or not [...] rests, in the end, with the interpreter',[56] she does so in the context of a group dynamic that separates the ones who recognise the irony from those who do not. The resulting in- or out-logic has a benign and an aggressive edge. On the one hand, it may allow people to live within a system ironically, as when, for instance, they do not fully agree with a legal system or the judiciary and can address the ones embodying it ironically as 'your honour'. To those who understand the irony, the person addressed with an ironic 'your honour' is not considered to be honourable, really. So s/he is 'out', in a sense, but benignly so. Or, even though the use of irony ridicules authority, here, it still leaves it intact.

The more aggressive edge of irony resides in its potential to make others feel they are indeed 'out'. This could still fall under the heading of agonism or struggle, in that the irony only has shifted from benign to being felt to be painful. In the latter case the authority of judges is questioned, but not lifted. As Gal noted, however, the 'out'-part of irony can become antagonistic when groups or communities are drawn out of their context through the use of social media. If irony depends on an in- and out-logic, this in turn depends on group demarcations, or contexts, within which the irony is sensed. Yet the 'context collapse' studied in social media is the result of the fact that such media, like Twitter (to mention just one), 'flatten out multiple audiences'.[57] That is to say: audiences that would act separately within their own context (family, neighbours, friends, colleagues, acquaintances, religious communities), are now brought together on one platform that takes people out of recognizable contexts. If irony is used in this context, it may work rather the other way around. Whereas with Hutcheon the recognition of irony creates an 'in'-sphere with a benign or less benign attitude to someone who is considered to be 'out', the use of irony in what Gal defined as *collective* context collapse',[58] may have the effect of aggressively throwing others out, namely those who do not get the irony. With the phrase 'collective context collapse', Gal noted

---

56   As Linda Hutcheon pointed out, irony is not a textual attribute but something that happens in relation to an audience. See *Irony's Edge: The Theory and Politics of Irony* (London/New York: Routledge, 1995), 45.
57   Alice E. Marwick and Danah Boyd, 'I Tweet Honestly, I Tweet Passionately: Twitter Users, Context Collapse, and the Imagined Audience', *New Media Society* 13 no. 1 (2010): 1-20.
58   Gal, *supra* note 12, 731; emphasis in the original.

that contemporary social media do not just gather certain groups, but the collective of a populace. Within that collective, then, irony has become a marker of exclusion; and struggle makes way for antagonism.

To be sure, the potential in social media to flatten out multiple audiences is countered by their potential to gather the like-minded. In their study on platforms Van Dijck, Poell, and De Waal noticed the 'inextricable relation between online platforms and societal structures.'[59] Here, platforms may become vehicles for the like-minded who consider their own interests to supersede all others and no longer consider themselves or their own interests in light of a vast array of differences held together by a society. Yet this transforms the so-called collective context collapse into a collapse of collective context. There is no longer a shared horizon.

The collapse of a shared horizon may coincide with a shift from value-relativism to the relativism of values that is facilitated by social media bubbles and platforms and is used by powers who busy themselves with what Eyal Weizman called 'dark epistemologies'. With this phrase, Weizman made a pivotal distinction between familiar modes of deception, on the one hand, and 'ongoing attacks against the institutional authorities that buttress facts' on the other.[60] As for the familiar modes of deception, it is a given throughout history that political powers on all levels will try to manipulate the facts. One could argue that a manipulation of facts is by necessity operative in any legal case, if we include the positive meaning of manipulation as a 'skillful handling of'. Yet this is something else than what Weizman and others note, namely that currently some powers do not just manipulate but actually thwart facts in an 'attempt to cast doubt over the very possibility of there being a way to reliably establish them at all'.[61] The given that facts will always have a relative edge to them is radicalized, in this case, beyond its extreme, when a consciously produced and systemic doubt 'to reliably establish facts at all' is easily combined with the undoubted establishment of, and belief in one's private facts.

If the authority of judges depends on their capacity to stand above parties in an attempt to establish the facts, this capacity not only connotes, but in a sense depends on the existence of a collective context. In taking his case to the highest council of the Netherlands, the 'Hoge Raad', or 'High Council', Wilders appeared to suggest that he would trust the rule

---

59 Dijck, Poell and de Waal, *supra* note 31, at 2.
60 Eyal Weizman, 'An Impromptu Glossary, Open Verification', in *Propositions for Non-Fascist Living, Tentative and Urgent*, eds. Maria Hlavajova and Wietske Maas (Cambridge/MA: MIT Press, 2019), 141–164, 148.
61 Weizman, *supra* note 60, at 150.

of law as a matter of collective context, and that he respected the task of judges to establish the facts to the max of their ability and in good faith. Yet, as became clear through his remarks earlier in the development of the case, or during a session of the Dutch parliament on 17 September 2020, he will only trust the rule of law if it rules in his favor. If it does not, the Netherlands are, according to Wilders, no longer a *Rechtstaat*. In parliament he stated that, because courts had declared him guilty of group defamation, the Dutch *Rechtstaat* is 'broken and corrupt'.[62] Here he joins the chorus of populists in their 'ongoing attacks against the institutional authorities that buttress facts'. The struggle *for* law does not simply shift into a struggle *against* law, as a consequence. Rather, the potential of plurality in any system driven by differences of interest is attacked and short-circuited in a desire to make one interest rule. Differences of interest make way for incompatibilities of interest.

Here, one final and pivotal element of Jhering's analysis of the struggle for law needs to be addressed. To Jhering, the struggle for law was not simply propelled by private interests but by people who felt that they had been hurt and who considered it a threat to their character if they did not protest against this violation.[63] This point made legal scholars Carel Smith and Harm Kloosterhuis argue that the struggle for law concerns 'the poetry of character'. The term 'poetry' might be slightly misleading, for the character at stake is not a matter of aesthetics. Basically, character is a matter of ethics, here. Jhering's variant of the Anglo-Saxon 'reasonable man' concerned upright persons who did not attack the possibility of establishing facts but who instead wanted to set things straight legally, acting in good faith. Yet when feelings of justice become a material for populists to play with, in a skein of cultural techniques, algorithmic bubbles, and sometimes straightforward manipulations but also dark epistemologies, acting in good faith may no longer be a generally operative principle. In such circumstances, the rule of law is threatened, and so is society at large.

---

62 In the original phrasing: 'failliet and corrupt'; see PVVpers, 'Geert Wilders: "De rechtsstaat is failliet en corrupt premier Rutte"'. *Youtube*, 17 Sept. 2020, https://www.youtube.com/watch?v=mauSy2PPO2U.

63 Harm Kloosterhuis and Carel Smith, 'De strijd om het recht is de poëzie van het karakter', *Ars Aequi 69*, April (2020): n.p.

Biographies / Biographien

Gabriele Britz
Prof. Dr. Gabriele Britz ist Professorin für Öffentliches Recht und Europarecht an der Justus-Liebig-Universität Gießen. Zusätzlich ist sie Richterin am Bundesverfassungsgericht. Zu den jüngsten Veröffentlichungen gehören ‚Kooperativer Grundrechtsschutz in der EU. Aktuelle Entwicklungen im Lichte neuerer Rechtsprechung des BVerfG' (NJW 2021, S. 1489 – 1495) und ‚Gleichberechtigungsgebote in der Weimarer Reichsverfassung: frühe Ausgriffe in die Moderne, in: H. Dreier/C. Waldhoff (Hg.), Weimars Verfassung. Eine Bilanz nach 100 Jahren (Göttingen 2020, S. 249 –269).

Jeanne Gaakeer
Jeanne Gaakeer is Professor of Jurisprudence: Hermeneutical and Narrative Foundations at Erasmus School of Law, Rotterdam, the Netherlands. She also serves as a senior justice in the criminal law section of the Court of Appeal in The Hague. The focus of her academic research is on the relevance of theoretical notions developed within Law and Literature and/or Law and the Humanities to legal practice. Currently she is working on topics pertaining to legal narratology. With Greta Olson (University of Giessen), she co-founded the European Network for Law and Literature (www.eurnll.org). Her recent publications in English include Judging from Experience. Law, Praxis, Humanities (Edinburgh, Edinburgh University Press, 2019); 'Interdisciplinarity 3.0: The Hub of the Universe or Fantasy Island?,' Pólemos, vol. 14, issue 2, 2020, pp. 319-336; 'Judicial Narration as Explanation of Facts and Circumstances,' in: Frode Helmich Pedersen, Espen Ingebrigtsen and Werner Gephart (eds), Narratives in the Criminal Process (Frankfurt am Main, Vittorio Klostermann, 2021), pp. 29-61; 'Law and Literature,' in: Mortimer Sellers and Stephan Kirste (eds), Encyclopedia of the Philosophy of Law and Social Philosophy, Living Edition, Meteor.Springer.com, DOI link: https://doi.org/10.1007/978-94-007-6730-0_989-1.

Thorsten Keiser
Prof. Dr. Thorsten Keiser ist Professor für Bürgerliches Recht und Rechtsgeschichte an der Justus-Liebig-Universität Gießen und geschäftsführender Direktor des Rudolf-von-Jhering-Instituts für rechtswissenschaftliche Grundlagenforschung sowie Fellow zur „Geschichte des Arbeitsrechts

der Europäischen Union" am Max-Planck-Institut für Rechtsgeschichte und Rechtstheorie in Frankfurt am Main. Seine Forschungsschwerpunkte liegen in den Bereichen Privatrecht und Rechtsgeschichte seit der Frühen Neuzeit, insbesondere europäische und vergleichende Privatrechtsgeschichte. Er hat zahlreiche Beiträge insbesondere zur Rechtsgeschichte veröffentlicht, zu den jüngsten Publikationen zählen neben Aufsätzen auch Lexikonartikel. Voraussichtlich im August 2022 erscheint Wege zur Rechtsgeschichte: Die rechtshistorische Exegese. Quelleninterpretation in Hausarbeiten und Klausuren, welches er zusammen mit Peter Oestmann und Thomas Pierson herausgeben wird.

Sylvia Kesper-Biermann
Prof. Dr. Sylvia Kesper-Biermann ist Professorin für Historische Bildungsforschung an der Universität Hamburg. Zu ihren Forschungsschwerpunkten zählen unter anderem Schulgeschichte, Geschichte von Folter und Menschenrechten sowie Strafrechts- und Kriminalitätsgeschichte. Zurzeit arbeitet sie unter anderem an dem DFG-Projekt „Comics als Bildungsmedien in der Bundesrepublik Deutschland, 1960er-1980er Jahre". Zu ihren Publikationen zählen beispielsweise die Monographie Einheit und Recht. Strafgesetzgebung und Kriminalrechtsexperten in Deutschland vom Beginn des 19. Jahrhunderts bis zum Reichsstrafgesetzbuch von 1871 (Frankfurt a. M. 2009) sowie zahlreiche Herausgaben sowie Aufsätze wie ‚Transnational Education in Historical Perspective. The Deutsche Kolonialschule (1898-1944)', in: Diskurs Kindheits- und Jugendforschung / Discourse. Journal of Childhood and Adolescence Research 2019 (Heft 4, S. 417-430 (18.12.2019), URL: https://doi.org/10.3224/diskurs. v14i4.04)

Frans-Willem Korsten
Frans-Willem Korsten is Professor of 'Literature, Culture, and Law' at Leiden University and holds the chair by special appointment 'Literature and Society' at the Erasmus School of Philosophy. He has published monographs and an edited volume on the baroque, theatricality and sovereignty, including A Dutch Republican Baroque (Amsterdam: Amsterdam University Press, 2017). He was responsible for the NWO internationalization program 'Precarity and Post-Autonomia: The Global Heritage' and participated in ITEMP: 'Imagineering Techniques in the Early Modern Period' – a research program funded by the NWO/FWO that focused on representations of violence. With Sybille Lammes, Sara Polak, Bram Ieven, Alex Gekker and Frank Chouraqui, he is part of the NWO funded program entitled 'Playing Politics: Media Platforms, Making Worlds.' He has pub-

lished extensively on the relation between literature, art, politics, justice and law, including Art as an Interface of Law and Justice: Affirmation, Disturbance, Disruption (Hart, 2021). His latest textbook for International Studies is Cultural Interactions: Conflict and Cooperation has just been published (Amsterdam: Amsterdam University Press, 2022).

Greta Olson
Greta Olson is Professor of English and American Literary and Cultural Studies at the University of Giessen, Germany. She is General Editor of the *European Journal of English Studies* (EJES), and, with Jeanne Gaakeer, co-founder of the European Network for Law and Literature. Greta aims to facilitate work on the nexus between political and artistic practice and academic analysis. She is involved in a project called "Beyond the Gaze: Media Awareness for Media Inclusivity" with filmmaker Lisa Friederich, and in one on the impact of images of migration. Recent publications include From Law and Literature to Legality and Affect (Oxford University Press, 2022); "Legal Facts, Affective Truths, and Changing Narratives in Trials Involving Sexual Assault: Harvey Weinstein and #MeToo," Routledge Companion to Narrative Theory (2022); with Laura Borchert, "Narrative Authority, Affective Unreliability, and Transing Law," Research Handbook in Law and Literature (Elgar 2022); and the co-edited Beyond Gender: Futures of Feminist and Sexuality Studies (Routledge 2018).

Franz Reimer
Prof. Dr. Franz Reimer ist Professor für Öffentliches Recht und Rechtstheorie an der Justus-Liebig-Universität Gießen und Mitglied des Direktoriums des Rudolf-von-Jhering-Instituts für rechtswissenschaftliche Grundlagenforschung. Zu seinen Forschungsschwerpunkten gehören Verfassungsrecht, allgemeines Verwaltungsrecht, Umweltrecht, Bildungsrecht und Rechtstheorie. Zu seinen aktuellen Publikationen zählen unter anderem das Lehrbuch ‚Juristische Methodenlehre' (2. Aufl., Baden-Baden 2020), das Werk ‚Gerechtigkeit als Methodenfrage' (Tübingen 2020), verschiedene Mitherausgeberschaften und Beiträge wie ‚Schulpflicht für alle – Zweck oder Mittel? Der verfassungsrechtliche Rahmen für schulische Bildung und Chancen(un)gleichheit vor und nach der Pandemie', in: DDS – Die Deutsche Schule (113. Jahrgang 2021, Heft 4, S. 409-421, https://www. waxmann.com/index.php?eID=download&id_artikel=ART104634&uid= frei) und ‚Das Recht auf Bildung in Zeiten der Pandemie. Vom Präsenz- zum Distanzlernen und zurück?' In: RdJB 2021 (S. 363-381; DOI: 10.5771/0034-1312-2021-4-363).